SHARING MORE THAN A PASTOR

by Joan C. McKeown

Copyright 1993 by Joan C. McKeown.

All rights reserved. No part of this book may be reproduced or transmitted in any form or by any means, electronic or mechanical, including photocopying, recording, or by any information storage and retrieval system, without permission in writing from the Publisher.

For information address:
  Arc Research Co.
  11595 State Rd 70
  Grantsburg WI 54840

Library of Congress Catalog Card Number: 93-071072

ISBN 0-9636183-0-X

To Fr. John,
who opened my eyes
and my heart
to the wonders of God

TABLE OF CONTENTS

PREFACE 7

CHAPTERS
- I. Introduction 9
- II. Definitions 11
- III. Current Levels of Cooperation 15
- IV. Advantages in Cluster-wide Cooperation 31
- V. Disadvantages in Cluster-wide Cooperation .. 41
- VI. Obstacles to Cluster-wide Cooperation 47
- VII. Developing Cooperation 59
- VIII. Lest You Think it Can't Be Done...
  A Case Study 73
- IX. A Closing Thought 108

APPENDIX A. Tally of pastors' questionnaires ... 109
APPENDIX B. Cluster Commissioning of Liturgical Ministers 122

BIBLIOGRAPHY 126

INDEX 127

PREFACE

... It began as a simple curiosity over the unusual sense of community that had developed among a group of parishes. It evolved into a detailed study of parishes that share a pastor. The result of that study is this book.

The parishes of the Diocese of Superior were the focus of the study. Covering most of northern Wisconsin, this diocese has the largest area but smallest population of any of the Wisconsin dioceses. Currently, there are 69 priests serving as pastors in the 131 parishes. The travel time between the parishes that share a pastor ranges from 10 to 40 minutes.

These statistics are not unique to this diocese. Of the 172 Roman Catholic dioceses in the U.S.A., only two report that all their pastors are serving single parishes. In the other 170 dioceses, whether Boston or Austin, San Diego or Spokane, there are pastors serving either a parish with a mission and/or two or more parishes [Kenedy, pp. 1-1169].

Traveling the U.S.A., living and talking with people from large cities and small towns, from east to west and places in-between, I've discovered two things: People are very different, and people are very much the same. We may express ourselves differently, we may have different priorities, but life, love, family, and faith in a God are common bonds that unite us all. There is a universality in what this book has to say about people, parishes, and cooperation.

— — —

I am grateful to the pastors who responded to a lengthy questionnaire on their clustered parishes. The information from these questionnaires provided a good assessment of what is actually happening in clustered parishes. A number of pastors also consented to interviews, providing me with a great deal of information on the step-by-step process of developing cooperation and the possible pitfalls. I am indebted to all of them for the hours they spent discussing this topic.

Staff members also took time out of their schedules to discuss cooperation in clustered parishes. Their perspectives added a great deal of worthwhile information for this project and I thank them for their efforts.

My appreciation also extends to the number of parishioners who responded to questionnaires. Many of these parishioners not only wrote lengthy responses to the specific questions, but they added other important comments on parish life that were very pertinent to this topic. A special thanks to Joe, Dick, Ed, Pat, Gene, Ruth, and John in this area.

A number of people proofread the manuscript. Their critiques were very important in the final stages of editing this book, so I thank Jim McKeown, Betty Solomonson, Fr. John Drummy, Mary Modjeski, and Deacon Bud Heiser for their hours of time.

Numerous others provided me with information and support. Whether at a meeting, workshop, or social gathering, whenever I mentioned this study, people asked insightful questions and related their own experiences concerning cooperation in various settings.

I also am grateful to Terry Fisk, a local cartoonist who took my illegible pencil marks and created the drawings on the following pages.

Finally, this book would not exist if I had not crossed paths with Fr. John Drummy a few years ago. Seeing the bond that had developed in the parishes under his guidance and encouragement and seeing the positive results of that bond in the parishes, themselves, and the communities in which they are located, convinced me that cooperation is a very worthwhile goal. From the initial development of the questionnaire, to the final proofreading of the manuscript, and in every step in-between, Fr. John was just a phone call away, adding insights, criticism, and encouragement. Thanks, Fr. John!

CHAPTER I:

INTRODUCTION

There are numerous books, magazines, seminars, and workshops, on parish life and the development of programs within a parish. Unfortunately, the primary, and many times only, focus for this information is the urban church. Very little attention has been paid to the differences in the lives of urban and rural parishes.

This book focuses on the rural church, specifically, rural parishes that share a pastor. Many of these parishes function as independently as possible, sharing the pastor's time, but nothing else. Other parishes have started to cooperate with their neighboring parishes. These parishes are now seeing a number of benefits in this cooperative approach to parish life.

By sharing their time, talent, and treasure, the parishes are able to enrich the lives of their parishioners and their communities in ways that were not possible when they operated in a strictly parochial manner. These parishes also seem to model Christian values in a way that surpasses other parishes. For these reasons, many pastors of clustered parishes are now attempting to build a spirit of cooperation among their parishes.

Numerous examples of shared programs and activities highlight the first half of this book. These examples are based on actual events in the parish clusters that were studied. A detailed description is also given of a very cooperative cluster of three parishes. This case study details the blending of parochial and cluster activities in the parishes' everyday lives.

It is often difficult to know where and how to begin when implementing a new idea, so a step-by-step process for developing cooperation among parishes is provided. Pastors and parishioners who have lived and worked in cooperative parish clusters agree that the initial struggles to

develop cooperation are well worth the efforts.
   We already share a common faith. It is time that our parishes recognize this and start
   Sharing More Than a Pastor.

CHAPTER II:

DEFINITIONS

Cluster.
For many parishes in this sparsely populated Diocese of Superior, Wisconsin, sharing a pastor with a neighboring parish has always been a way of life. The term "cluster" has become the popular term to describe this relationship. The Catholic Encyclopedia says, "Because of the shortage of priests, there has developed what is called 'clustering' which means that several church communities may be served by one priest" [Broderick, p. 451]. A cluster, then, is a group of two or more parishes that function under the leadership of the same pastor.

Mother Parish / Mission Parish.
The terms "mother parish" and "mission parish" predate the use of the term "cluster". The terminology is used to distinguish between the parishes that are being served by the same pastor (the grouping that is now called a cluster). The parish in which the pastor resides is the "mother" parish. The Official Catholic Directory gives the following definition of mission: "A mission, or quasi-parish [N.B. see Canon Law 5.16], is a parish which has not been established because it lacks one or more qualifications, i.e., resident pastor, necessary financial resources; ..." [Kenedy, p. A-47]. Though this is the formal definition, many areas informally use the term "mission" to refer to any parish (whether canonically established or not) without a resident pastor. Thus, each "cluster" consists of a "mother" parish in which the pastor resides, and one or more "mission" parishes, which might or might not be fully established, canonical parishes.

The use of this terminology can create some problems. If a cluster is reorganized and its mother parish is incorporated into a neighboring cluster, the status of that parish will change from mother to mission. In some areas, the pastor's residence has shifted from one town to another because of a shift in the population. This relocation of the pastor changes the status of the two parishes from mother to mission and mission to mother.

Because a mission parish is often looked upon as being of lesser importance than the mother parish, this change in status can strongly affect the interaction between the parishes. For this reason, many pastors are no longer using the mother/mission terminology. Instead, they simply refer to the parishes as "clustered" parishes, i.e., instead of saying, "St. Joe is the mission parish of St. John," they say, "St. Joe is clustered with St. John."

Cooperation.

As I discussed the issue of cooperation with various pastors, staff members, and parishioners, I found that there were many different understandings of what the term "cooperation" means. The understandings ranged from a mere toleration of the fact that the parishes must share the pastor's time, to a view that the parishes would become mirror images of each other. Needless to say, how a person defined cooperation greatly influenced his or her feelings about the benefits or detriments of a cooperative approach to dealing with clustered parishes.

According to Webster, cooperate means "To act or operate jointly with another or others, to the same end. To act together; to unite in producing an effect."

Simply stated, cooperation is working together. It implies more than a cold toleration of the other parish, but it does not imply that each parish must give up its identity, its history, its individuality to become "just like" the other parish(es). Cooperation does not mean creating one formula for parish life and making all parishes follow that formula.

It is also important that the term "cooperation" not be confused with the term "collaboration". Collaborative ministry necessitates a change in the structure of the parish's leadership team. While that may be a worthwhile idea to explore, it is not the topic being addressed in this book. Here, we are looking only at cooperation among the parishioners in two or more parishes. Though this cooperation could and should be developed in collaborative parishes, this book assumes that the parishes are operating under the more traditional model where one pastor (not a leadership team) has the authority.

• • •

> **Example:** Parishes Alpha and Omega share a cemetery. They decide to cooperate on the spring cleanup. Because of various community events, they cannot find a day when both parishes are free to work at the cemetery. Instead, they agree on the date when all cleanup should be finished. Alpha agrees to make the necessary repairs to the fences, pathways, and roads; Omega takes responsibility for the lawn, bushes, and trees. The pastor, driving past the cemetery a few weeks later, notes how nice the cemetery looks and is glad to see that the parishes "cooperated" so well on this project.

• • •

> **Example:** St. Lucille and St. Andrew parishes have decided to cooperate in their youth Religious Education programs. Since many of the families are busy with community functions, school events, differing work schedules, and other family activities, the class schedule has to be flexible. St. Lucille holds classes on Wednesday and Sunday afternoons. St. Andrew holds classes on Sunday morning. Each family in the two parishes is allowed to choose the class time and location that works best for them. Consequently, many children from St. Andrew attend the Wednesday afternoon classes in St. Lucille. Some children from St. Lucille attend the Sunday morning classes at St. Andrew. The

only requirement is that the child is asked to stay in the same class for the entire school year. In this situation, "cooperation" resulted in a blending of the two youth religious education programs.

• • •

CHAPTER III:

CURRENT LEVELS OF COOPERATION

The Questionnaire.
A questionnaire was mailed to the 37 pastors of parish clusters in the Diocese of Superior. Twenty-one pastors responded to the questionnaire. Seven pastors returned blank questionnaires because their experience in clusters was too limited for them to respond. Nine pastors did not respond.

The questionnaire sent to the pastors focused on two aspects of cooperation in parish clusters: 1) The level of cooperation that currently exists among clustered parishes; 2) The level of cooperation that is considered to be the most desirable by pastors of clustered parishes. Other questions dealt with the advantages and disadvantages of cluster cooperation.

Of the twenty-one pastors who responded, two saw only minimal value in cooperation. The others felt there were numerous benefits in cooperation, some of these benefits being very concrete, others, more abstract. A tabulation of the answers to the questionnaire appears in Appendix A.

To supplement the information on the pastors' questionnaires, interviews were conducted with some of the pastors and staff members in clustered parishes. Short questionnaires were also sent to a number of parishioners who are active members of clustered parishes. The opinions expressed by these three groups (pastors, parishioners, staff) on the advantages and disadvantages of cooperation were surprisingly similar. The parishioners' notations on obstacles to cooperation were similar to, but more expansive than, the information from the pastors and staff.

These questionnaires and interviews are the sources of the quotes in this book, unless another source is indicated in the text.

Adult Christian Formation.

Most pastors are using a cluster-wide approach to adult formation. The planning for these programs is usually done centrally for the entire cluster. Because of the small number of people involved, RCIA (Rite of Christian Initiation for Adults) formation meetings are usually held in one location and attended by all the parishes in the cluster.

Most clusters hold parental preparation classes for infant baptism centrally for the cluster. The baptisms, though, usually take place in the family's parish, enabling the parishioners' immediate community to join in the celebration. (Most pastors encourage the families to celebrate the baptism during the weekend liturgy.)

Parental preparation classes for First Reconciliation are held centrally in most clusters. Because of the time involved in administering First Reconciliation, most pastors prefer that this sacrament be celebrated in the individual parishes, instead of bringing the groups together.

Other Adult Education classes, including parental preparation for First Eucharist, are held on a centralized basis in about half the clusters and in the individual parishes in the other half. Some clusters have both individual and centralized classes, depending on the program.

• • •

Examples of the RCIA:

Example 1: The cluster of St. Rose, St. Anne, and St. Leo has a large number of RCIA candidates each year. Biweekly RCIA information meetings are held in the mother parish for the candidates and sponsors. The meetings are conducted by one or more of the following: the pastor, deacon, DRE (Director of Religious Education), catechists. During the other weeks, the candidates and their sponsors meet with the catechists in their own parishes in smaller, more personal groups for prayer, faith-sharing, and further discussion of issues that were raised in the larger meeting.

Example 2: When the number of RCIA candidates is small, the cluster holds weekly RCIA meetings in the mother parish for the candidates and sponsors. The meetings are a blend of prayer, faith-sharing, information, and discussion, with the pastor, deacon, DRE and catechists sharing the leadership roles.

• • •

Examples of Parental Preparation for Infant/Child Baptism:

Example 1: The Four Lakes Cluster has a large number of new parents. It holds weekly baptism preparation classes in the mother parish. Each family is also visited at least once in its home by the program's director (usually the deacon, but sometimes the DRE or pastor).

Example 2: When the number of parents is small, the program director meets privately with each set of parents, usually in their homes.

• • •

Examples of Parental Preparation for First Reconciliation: When the number of parents is small, the cluster holds centralized meetings that all parishes attend. When the number of parents is too large to comfortably bring them all together, several approaches are used. Sometimes, each parish holds its own parental preparation classes. Other times, two of the smaller parishes combine their meetings, while the larger parish(es) hold separate meetings. Some clusters schedule 2 or 3 sessions at different times and locations and give the parents the options to choose the sessions that fit their schedules.

• • •

Examples of Parental Preparation for First Eucharist: When the classes are large, they are usually held in the individual parishes to enable the pastor to get to know each family. When the classes are small, the pastors prefer to bring the families together in a cluster-wide meeting so they experience a sense of community as they prepare for this sacrament. The sacrament is usually celebrated in the individual parishes.

• • •

Examples of other Adult Formation:

Example 1: Since Bible Study usually draws the largest attendance, it is most common for each parish to hold its own meetings. Where the distances between the parishes is not a problem, the meetings are held in each parish on different days of the week. Parishioners ignore parish boundaries and attend whichever meeting fits their schedules.

Example 2: When the number of participants in a program is small, one cluster-wide meeting is held each week. The meetings are held in the parish that is the most central for the participants.

Example 3: St. Jerome wants to begin a class in church history, but the other parishes in the cluster do not see the need for it. So, St. Jerome plans the program for its parishioners, keeping the other parishes informed of the class schedule to avoid conflicts in activities. Members of all the parishes are invited to attend these classes at St. Jerome.

• • •

Youth Education.

There is a great deal of diversity in the way that clusters plan and implement their youth education programs. Some clusters use centralized planning and hold joint classes. A greater number have each parish plan and implement its own program. A few use a combination of those two approaches, with some of the parishes in the cluster working together on the planning and the classes and other parishes acting more independently. The locations of the public schools and the distances from the schools to the church facilities are the major influences in determining how the youth education programs are designed. An example was given earlier of a religious education program that had an enormous amount of cluster cooperation and flexibility.

When the parishes run separate programs it is still advantageous for them to maintain the same general class schedule, starting and ending on the same weeks. This gives them the option of bringing in guest speakers, or planning other joint activities without making major modifications to anyone's program. The pastor also finds his preparation is easier if the parishes celebrate First Reconciliation or First Eucharist at approximately the same time.

• • •

Examples of Confirmation preparation: In most cases, centralized Confirmation preparation classes are held in the cluster. Some clusters, though, are using a combined approach, with the pastor conducting one cluster-wide class each month and catechists leading classes in the individual parishes during the other weeks. Both these approaches are preferable to holding all the classes in the individual parishes because the students are able to develop relationships with each other instead of meeting for the first time at Confirmation. At the bishop's request, the parishes in a cluster jointly celebrate the Sacrament of Confirmation.

• • •

Parish Councils.

The level of cooperation among parish councils is quite variable. In half the clusters, the Pastoral Councils hold joint meetings to discuss topics of mutual concern. The same is true of the parishes' Finance Councils. In the other clusters, the Pastoral Councils never meet together; nor do the Finance Councils. Nearly all of the pastors prefer that the Pastoral Councils hold some joint meetings. The same is true of their preferences for Finance Council meetings.

Some pastors think it would be better if the cluster had one cluster-wide Pastoral Council, drawing its members from all the parishes in the cluster. They have found that there is less divisiveness in cluster-based organizations than parish organizations that come together for joint discussions. Currently, the diocese requires that each parish have its own Pastoral Council.

One reason that pastors aren't stressing joint Pastoral Council meetings, even when that is their preference, is that many council members don't understand their roles. Some think that the councils are simply information dissemination bodies — the pastor tells them what is happening and they pass the word on to the parishioners. Others think that the councils are decision-making bodies — that the final decision should be theirs on all matters. In one parish, the council voiced strong objections when the pastor changed the size of the bulletin, saying that he had "no right" to make that decision without their consent! Other members have no notion of what the council's role is. It is difficult to bring together the parishes' Pastoral Councils when the individual members have such poor understandings of their roles.

Most pastors agree that, ideally, efforts at cooperation should start with the Pastoral Councils, for those groups are the visionaries and the coordinators of the programs and activities of the parish. The Pastoral Council should view every activity, including efforts at cooperation, within the context of the parish mission statement. This is the ideal.

In reality, many parishes never developed a mission statement. Of the ones that did, many considered it a one-time task; something that was written, signed, and forgotten. The various organizations within the parish plan and run activities with little or no communication with the Pastoral Council. No one ever steps back to see if the activities are in keeping with the parish's mission, or if the activities are taking place so randomly that the parish has lost its focus. In a setting where the various organizations within the parish are not communicating and cooperating with each other, it can be extremely difficult to move them towards communication and cooperation with the other parishes.

Without a solid understanding of what the Pastoral Council should be doing, elections can become mere popularity contests. The people who are the visionaries and the ones with the talents to develop a cohesive approach to the parish programs aren't necessarily the ones elected. Consequently, many Pastoral Council members have no future-focus and without a future-focus, all that they hope to accomplish is to maintain the status quo during their time in office. Hence, the last thing that they want to do is to consider a new approach, a new way of looking at the parish, a new way of interacting with the other parishes. For these reasons, many pastors have found that bringing the Pastoral Councils together in joint meetings works better as a mid-step in the process of developing cooperation, rather than the first step.

• • •

Examples of the Pastoral Councils:

Example 1: The Pastoral Councils of the two parishes meet monthly. On the even months, they meet in one of the parishes; on the odd months, they meet in the other parish. From 7:00-8:00 pm, the councils meet in separate rooms to discuss matters that pertain to their parish only. At 8:00 pm, they move into a joint meeting to discuss matters of concern to both parishes. The meeting always ends with a social hour, a time to informally gather and get better acquainted in a casual setting.

Example 2: The Pastoral Councils meet monthly. On the even months, each council meets in its own parish; no joint meeting is held unless an urgent matter has surfaced. On the odd months, the councils hold a joint meeting, the site of which is rotated among the parishes that have adequate facilities. Matters of mutual concern are discussed first, but time is also spent discussing each parish's issues. Because the parishioners from one parish usually have no biases concerning the issues of another parish, they can provide helpful insights into those issues.

• • •

Example from the Finance Councils: Holy Week is one of the busiest weeks of the year for the pastor of a cluster. One pastor decided that having one Holy Thursday Mass and one Easter Vigil for the cluster made more sense than trying to schedule separate liturgies in each parish on those days.

Most parishioners were agreeable to this, but there were a few people who were very outspoken in their disagreement. No matter how much the pastor explained that these Masses were being held for the entire cluster and the Liturgical Ministers from all the parishes would take part in them, these few parishioners kept insisting that it "wasn't fair."

Finally, the pastor caught on to the underlying issue: financially, it wasn't fair because one parish would receive all the collection money on those two days. The pastor called a joint meeting of the Finance Councils. After discussing the alternatives, they decided that each parish would receive a portion of the loose collections. The pastor readily agreed that this was a "fair" way to handle the situation and the Holy Week Liturgies proceeded as scheduled.

• • •

Committees.

Since almost all parishes have Liturgy, Education, and Social Concerns Committees, the questionnaire addressed these areas. One cluster has cluster-wide committees in all three areas; five clusters have cluster-wide committees in two of these three areas.

In the clusters that have separate committees in each parish, it is common for the Education Committees to hold joint planning meetings. In only one-third of the clusters, do the Social Concerns Committees meet together. All but one pastor preferred that these separate committees meet together at least some of the time.

Most pastors prefer that the Liturgy Committees meet together to plan at least some of the parishes' liturgies. In most clusters, this is not happening yet. The pastors' comments show that they do not view this as a problem in cooperation; instead, they attribute it to the fact that many Liturgy Committees do not fully understand how to perform their tasks. Once the committees have acquired more experience, it will be easier to bring them together for joint liturgy planning.

• • •

Examples of the Education Committees:

Example 1: Each spring, the Education Committees in both of the parishes review the textbooks being used and compare them with other books on the market. The process occupies a number of meetings and a great deal of time. One year, it was suggested that members from the two Education Committees meet together for this review process.

Some of the committee members were concerned about this approach since "our" parish and "their" parish might not have the same priorities. Nevertheless, they agreed to try it.

During the discussions, the committee members realized that the input from the other parish was invaluable precisely because they had different priorities and different perspectives. In the end, both parishes switched to the same textbook series, but the members stated that even if they had chosen different books, they would continue the two-parish review process because the insights had benefited everyone.

Example 2: The Education Committee of one parish decided to start a tape library. Someone mentioned that another parish in the cluster already had a number of tapes, so maybe it could recommend the best ones to buy. Others felt that they didn't need "the other parish's advice." The committee decided that it wouldn't hurt to at least talk to someone from the other parish, so members from the two Education Committees scheduled some joint meetings. The result: the parishes decided not to make duplicate purchases of any tapes. Instead, each parish purchases tapes that the other parish does not own and they then share the tapes between the two parishes. The pastor has agreed to shuttle the tapes between the parishes every week, as long as someone in each parish takes the responsibility of getting the tapes to him.

A joint sub-committee now meets twice a year to discuss the weak areas of their libraries, how much each parish wants to spend in the coming months, and what tapes they would like to purchase.

• • •

Example from the Social Concerns Committees: Each Thanksgiving, the Social Concerns Committee from one parish put together food baskets for the poor of the area. The other parish in the cluster thought this was a good idea, so one year they decided to do the same. Since parish boundaries become rather loosely defined in the rural areas, some families received two food baskets because both parishes considered them to be living within their territory and other families received nothing because each parish thought the other one was giving them a basket. The following year, the two Social Concerns Committees met together to compare their lists of names to eliminate this problem. The year after that, the two committees pooled their resources and met together to prepare the food baskets. The Thanksgiving food baskets are now a joint activity of the cluster.

• • •

Examples from the Liturgy Committees:

Example 1: One parish has had an active Liturgy Committee for a number of years. The continuity in the focus of each liturgy is very apparent. The parishioners from the other parishes in the cluster realized that they were lacking that continuity in their liturgical celebrations, but no one felt knowledgeable enough to become involved in liturgy planning. At the suggestion of the pastor, they began to imitate what the one parish was doing. As they did this week after week, they began to understand the process the parish went through in developing the liturgy plans. They still rely on the ideas generated by the one parish, but they are becoming very skillful at modifying the ideas to fit their parish settings.

Example 2: The cluster Liturgy Committee decided that a focus on families was appropriate for the following weekend's liturgies. They thought that one way to express this focus would be to use families as the Liturgical Ministers. The first parish chose a mother and son as lectors, wives and husbands as Eucharistic Ministers, etc. The second parish followed suit. The third parish chose only widows and widowers for Liturgical Ministers that weekend, saying that these people are very special "families" in their parish because one of the members of those families is already sitting at God's side.

• • •

Knights of Columbus (KC) and Council of Catholic Women (CCW).

In twelve of the twenty-one clusters, the KCs is a cluster-wide organization. This is in sharp contrast to the CCWs which, in most clusters, never meet with the other parishes' CCWs. The pastors would like to see more cooperation in this area.

• • •

Examples of the CCW:

Example 1: One parish decided to honor the women who have given 25 or more years of service to the CCW. The pastor agreed to the idea and they chose a weekend when the readings focused on the theme of service. At the end of Mass the pastor gave a special blessing to these women. The other parish in the cluster heard what the first parish had done and, a month later, they decided that they wanted to do the same thing. Had the CCWs been in communication with each other, they could have both chosen the same weekend where the theme of service was a natural focus.

Example 2: Each year the CCW of one parish would design a parish Christmas card and send it to all their parishioners and the out-of-towners who had given money to the parish during the year. (They recorded the names and addresses from the checks in the weekend collection for this purpose.) The CCWs of the other two parishes bought Christmas cards and sent them only to the out-of-towners who had supported their parishes.

This created a great deal of confusion in two ways: 1) Most tourists viewed the three parishes as a unit, so the wasting of money and time to send three separate cards bothered them. 2) Some parishioners, not realizing what criteria the CCWs used in sending the cards, couldn't understand why they received a card from the neighboring parish, but not from their own parish.

The CCWs spent a few years trying various alternatives. Now, the first parish designs the Christmas card, the lists of recipients are compared to eliminate duplicates, and all the Christmas cards are sent on behalf of all three parishes.

• • •

Example of the KCs: The clustered KCs were looking for an area of ministry in which they could become involved. The Youth Groups and CCWs already held numerous dinners, bake sales, and other social and fund-raising activities and they didn't want to compete with them. When one KC told another that he would "pick him up" for the next meeting, someone else exclaimed, "That's it!"

The KCs have now become the official "carpoolers" for the cluster. They bring the elderly and other non-drivers to the weekend liturgies and other parish and cluster activities. They have started branching out, driving people to doctors' appointments and other weekly errands. They ignore the parish boundaries and treat this as a cluster-ministry, helping wherever they can.

• • •

Social activities.

Half of the parishes <u>always</u> invite the other parishes in the cluster to their social activities. The other half of the parishes <u>sometimes</u> invite the other parishes in the cluster to their social activities. Most clusters hold three or more cluster-wide social activities each year.

• • •

Example 1: Nativity parish had a reputation for putting on marvelous dinners that created a nice sense of camaraderie and were good fund-raisers as well. Rather than compete with them, Holy Spirit parish decided to lend its full support. Not only do they help to advertise Nativity's dinners, they also offer car-pooling from their parish to the dinner and back. The elderly, who can't drive, or don't like to drive a distance, love the idea.

Wanting to return the favor, some of the women from Nativity now help Holy Spirit cook and serve all their funeral luncheons. Since Holy Spirit has few parishioners who are able to become involved in daytime activities, they are very appreciative of the help.

Example 2: Many parishes have yearly celebrations on the parish's feast day, but one cluster started a new tradition. On each parish's feast day, the other parishes in the cluster plan a special liturgy and reception to honor that parish. They thank the parish for the many good things that it does during the year for its parishioners, the cluster, and the community. It is an uplifting day for all.

• • •

Deacons and Staff.

Two-thirds of the clusters have at least one deacon or deacon candidate. Most of these deacons serve (will serve) all the parishes in the cluster.

In the majority of the clusters, some or all of the office staff members work for the entire cluster. Only two clusters had office staffs in each parish. The staff members that are most commonly hired for the cluster are a secretary, bookkeeper, and DRE. Other clusters have also hired liturgists and Pastoral Assistants.

The maintenance staffs work for one parish only.

CHAPTER IV:

ADVANTAGES

IN CLUSTER-WIDE COOPERATION

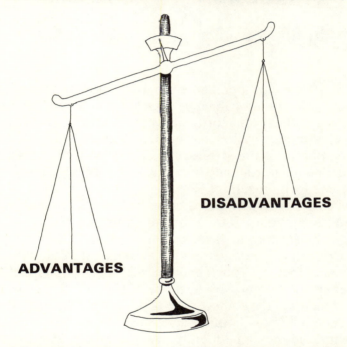

Most of the pastors see definite pastoral advantages in using a cooperative approach to parish activities. The pastors expressed these advantages in a variety of ways, many of which are summed up by one pastor's statement that it "makes for a better appreciation and use of (1) time, (2) talents, and (3) treasure". The remaining comments can be grouped into a fourth category expressed by another pastor as "fosters Christian values".

Time.

A pastor can spend an enormous amount of time each month just attending the meetings of the councils, committees, and other parish organizations. Multiply this by two, three, or more parishes and it becomes an impossible task. By combining some of these into cluster-wide meetings, the "pastor can participate more fully without being overburdened with meetings."

An area in which this is especially helpful to the pastor is liturgy planning. If the liturgy committees meet together (with the pastor) to discuss the weekend liturgies, then each parish will be developing that weekend's liturgies with the same focus. Though each parish might implement the ideas in a different way because of the differences in the buildings or in the composition of the parish, the pastor will be developing his homily, selecting the optional prayers, etc. around the same focal points for all the Masses that weekend.

Cooperation also makes better use of the parishioner's time, as two pastors stated, "there's no sense in reinventing the wheel." Though clustered parishes are not always involved in the same activities, when they are, joint planning eliminates a duplication of efforts. A good example of this comes from the just-completed RENEW process in which almost every parish in the diocese participated.

• • •

Example: As clustered parishes set up their RENEW Teams, many of them combined some of the committees. For example, instead of having a Publicity Committee in each parish duplicating the same basic work, one group was formed that planned the publicity for all the parishes in the cluster. Another cluster-wide committee designed the small group sign-up form which was used in all the parishes. A combined Take-Home Materials Committee prepared the bulletin inserts for all the parishes.

• • •

Even when parishes are running many of their programs independently, if a spirit of cooperation prevails, the parishes are less likely to schedule their programs in a manner that conflicts with the programs of another parish. Keeping a cluster-wide calendar of events avoids the frustrations of having to reschedule activities. It also makes it easier for everyone to keep track of the programs and events that are taking place.

Talent.

The larger the population base, the greater the range of skills and abilities that can be tapped. The benefits of one person's expertise will not be limited to just one parish, but will be experienced by the entire cluster. Looking at the long-term effects shows the magnitude of this benefit. People with little skill in an area, but a great deal of interest, will be able to develop their skills by working with a knowledgeable person. This expands the base of talent for the next project. One person with expertise can become the catalyst for growth for numerous others across the entire cluster.

The cluster-wide population base also gives the parishes access to a larger number of volunteers for the routine work that is a part of any undertaking. Many people hesitate to volunteer for projects because all too often they've seen others become trapped in open-ended, almost lifetime commitments. Knowing there's a larger population base to draw from and that others will be approached the next time around, people are more likely to volunteer when asked for a finite commitment of their time. Not only does this prevent burnout among the people who are usually involved, but by activating a larger group of parishioners more people will feel ownership in the projects making it more likely that the projects will succeed.

Having this larger pool of workers is especially helpful to very small parishes which often do not have enough people to plan and run all the parish programs that they want to make available to their parishioners. When the small parishes try to function independently from the other parishes, the results in most cases are either a large number of poorly run programs, or a very limited number of satisfactory programs. By joining with the other parishes in the cluster, assisting in the planning but not bearing the full burden by themselves, the small parishes are able to offer to their parishioners all the programs and services that are available in the larger parishes.

It is only natural for parishes to compare themselves with each other. In the process, they may discover weaknesses in their parishes that previously had not been identified. A parish reacts to this discovery either by trying to strengthen the area from within, or by establishing a firmer bond to the other parishes in that area, strengthening the parish from the outside. Either way, the parish benefits.

• • •

> **Example:** Trinity parish thought its numbers of lectors and Eucharistic Ministers were "just fine," until they heard members of St. Gregory parish discussing which week of the month they were scheduled to serve. "Which week? What do you mean, which week?" It had never occurred to them

that having 3 lectors and 5 Eucharistic Ministers in a parish with 100 families was a less than adequate response to their call to minister to each other through the liturgy.

• • •

A pooling of people's talents promotes creativity. It can be difficult for one or two people to continually generate new ideas, but a brainstorming session with a small group of people can be very productive.

• • •

Example: The parishes wanted to do something special to kick off the RENEW process. They wanted something that would draw attention to RENEW and would tie the parishes together because RENEW was being implemented on a cluster-wide basis. Midway through a planning session, one person jokingly suggested that as a symbol of unity, the pastor could jog from one church to the next; another added that as he jogged, he could unwind a long (very long!) ribbon, which would then be cut in a grand-opening ceremony; a third person said the entire ribbon could be cut up and each person who jogged with the pastor could be given a piece of ribbon. The result of this fluid conversation was a decision to give every family in the parishes green bows to tie onto their front doors, mailboxes, fence posts, etc. to show that they were RENEW families — an idea that had not occurred to anyone before the meeting.

• • •

Treasure.

The increased financial strength that comes from sharing some of the financial responsibilities was a benefit that almost everyone noted. Working from a greater financial base enables the parishes to jointly hire a more competent, specialized staff. Instead of each parish hiring a person to do multiple tasks, a cluster can afford to hire a secretary, skilled bookkeeper, experienced D.R.E., etc.

These qualified staff members perform their jobs in a more efficient and effective manner than people with little or no training, making the dollars spent more cost-effective and the programs more substantial. One pastor noted that this is a crucial concern in the area of bookkeeping, since the number of regulations in this area is always increasing and errors can be disastrous.

Hiring competent staff members also frees the pastor's time, allowing him to focus more on his pastoral and sacramental duties. Although some parishes have been successful in using volunteers as secretaries, bookkeepers, or C.R.E.s (Coordinators of Religious Education), most pastors found that the amount of time that they spent monitoring and assisting the constantly changing group of volunteers greatly diminished the value of that approach.

One pastor commented that even when the parishes see little or no value in running any joint programs, they realize that they must cooperate financially with the other parishes in the cluster because by themselves, they cannot even "afford a priest."

Christian values.

Our society places a great deal of emphasis on individuality. This is reflected in the strong sense of parochialism in many parish communities. Pastors who have been successful in promoting cooperation have "incorporated members' natural tendencies toward parochialism into a feeling of being a part of something greater than a single group" [Johnson, p. 115]. Narrow parochialism diminishes and people develop a sense of the larger church. They begin to realize that there can be unity in their diversity, that everyone can "win" <u>if they put aside competition in favor of cooperation</u>. The people learn to work together, to trust each other, to develop tolerance and patience toward each other, to support each other. When parishes hire a centralized staff for the cluster, that staff can model these values for the parish communities. [N.B. Does your staff realize that non-Christian attitudes toward each other can be a very negative model for the parish communities?]

As a result of the RENEW process, many parishioners are more aware of the effects of prayer at parish meetings. When prayer "penetrates the organizational life of the parish, becoming part of everything it does as a group" [Quinn, p. 45], the changes are amazing. Disagreements are put into the proper perspective. The spiritual values that should be the basis for all decisions come into sharper focus. The tone of an entire evening can change because of those minutes spent in prayer.

When parishioners from different parishes gather to discuss cluster issues, this time of prayer is even more important. To experience these effects, "prayer must be an integral part of the decision-making process, not a token observance crammed into five minutes at the beginning or end of the meeting" [Quinn, p. 45].

The positive effects of having a cluster-wide team

working together, "pulling in the same direction", to accomplish a common goal have to be experienced to really be understood. Every time this occurs, the ripple effects lead to a more open, more Christian attitude among everyone. Many of the clusters that have joined together for outreach programs have found that their combined efforts far exceed what the parishes were able to accomplish individually.

As the pastor works with the parishioners in cluster-wide planning, the parishioners become more aware of the concern that the pastor has for their welfare. His obvious desire to bring to them the best possible programs and activities for their spiritual growth and personal enrichment leads them to develop the same concern for themselves and each other.

Combining some aspects of the Youth Education program is very important, especially when the parishes are in different school districts. Young people can be even more territorial than adults, especially when the primary contact they have with the other group is in a competitive setting (predominately through sports programs). Working, playing, and learning together in cluster-wide youth activities teaches them the value of communication and cooperation at a young age.

Many people view diversity as an obstacle to cooperation, but the diversity of the parishes can be a great asset to them. It is very common for parishioners in small parishes to develop a common focus. When another parish in the cluster has a different focus, the diversity of their viewpoints can lead everyone to rethink their positions. This can be a time of growth for the individuals and for the parish, as they explore new ways to deal with parish life.

• • •

Example: The parishioners of Immaculate Heart parish were mainly Senior Citizens who had moved to the area after retirement. Their children and grandchildren lived in other areas, often in other states, so the few children who lived in the parish were very precious to all of them.

Holy Redeemer parish had numerous young families among its parishioners and was very focused on the responsibilities and the enormous amounts of time and energy that are expended in raising a family. Being able to step back now and then from their daily responsibilities to view the families from the grandmotherly and grandfatherly eyes of Immaculate Heart, gave them a different and much needed perspective on family life.

• • •

In some clusters, cooperation has lead to a uniformity of development and formation among the parishes. If this happens, the staff will be able to make more effective use of its time, since its attentions won't be divided among various levels of formation. This uniformity cannot be forced. If it is to occur, it must occur in a natural process. To try to force parishes into a common mold under the guise of "cooperation" will be detrimental to everyone. Pope Paul VI stated:

> In the mind of the Lord, the Church is universal by vocation and mission, but when she puts down her roots in a variety of cultural, social and human terrains, she takes on different external expressions and appearances. Only continual attention to these two poles of the Church will enable us to perceive the richness of this relationship between the universal Church and the individual Churches. [On Evangelization in the Modern World, no. 62.]

This statement is true within the setting of the local parish, as well.

CHAPTER V:

DISADVANTAGES IN CLUSTER-WIDE COOPERATION

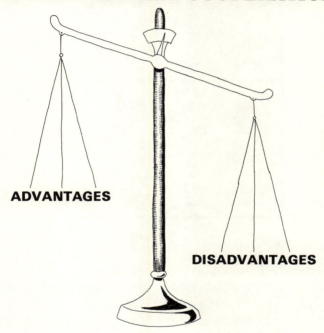

Most of the disadvantages that were cited are not inherent to cooperation, itself. Rather, they occur because there is a poor understanding of what cooperation entails.

Loss of local traditions.
A parish's history, traditions, and local identity should be considered important assets of the parish. The pride and self-esteem that are fostered by the parish's local traditions

are important for the health and well-being of the parish and parishioners. Sometimes, as parishes work towards greater cooperation, the unique qualities of the parish can be threatened. Pastors and others in leadership positions must keep in mind that "cooperation" does not mean

"Finally! Cooperation!"

"sameness". The local traditions of a parish should not be stifled. Instead, they should be encouraged and supported as an enhancement to the entire cluster. As one parishioner stated, "The cluster's greatest strength is the sum total of the strengths found in the individual parishes. When the strengths of the individual parishes are not fostered, the cluster is only a tool for efficient administration and not for shepherding the people."

Preferential treatment.
The cluster's office is usually located in the mother parish. This often gives rise to a complaint from the mission parishes that they are forgotten entities. Because the pastor

and staff spend more of their time in the mother parish, it appears that the pastor and staff are giving that parish preferential treatment. While these complaints are sometimes valid, many times parishioners are blind to the fact that the pastor and staff are looking out for the interests of the mission parishes as well, even though they're doing it from an office in the mother parish. An enormous amount of friction and jealousy can develop between the parishes over this issue.

It is important that the pastor take a step back every so often and try to review his and the staff's attitudes and actions from the parishioners' point of view. Knowing why they are feeling ignored can help the pastor deal with their feelings. Some pastors have found that scheduling a "Listening" meeting in each parish once a year improves the situation. At the meeting, the pastor listens to their opinions and addresses their concerns.

Having at least one weekday Mass in each parish also helps to reduce the ill feelings between the parishes. Not only do the parishioners appreciate the weekday sacrament, they also know that the pastor will be there in the parish to listen to any problems or concerns that they have. Some parishes have developed this time into an informal social event by having coffee with the pastor after the Mass. This provides the parishioners with the opportunity to talk with the pastor in a relaxed atmosphere.

One pastor offered the following tip: Never say to a group of parishioners, "your" parish. Instead, speak to them about "our" parish. Refer to the other parishes as "their" parishes. It's a subtle, yet effective, way of identifying yourself with the parish, instead of distancing yourself from it.

If the pastor's or a staff member's name is being mentioned in an article, make sure that the parishes are given equal billing. Too often the priest is identified as the pastor of the mother parish and the mission parishes are ignored. The effect on the self-image of the parish when it sees its name in print is subtle, yet important.

Training the parishioners to minister to each other is another good way of providing them with needed services. A network of lay ministers can be established to visit the elderly, the sick, and the grieving on a regular basis.

Programs designed for the larger parish.
Sometimes the smaller parishes in a cluster feel that programs are designed by the larger parishes without the interests and needs of the smaller parishes receiving due consideration. Any time an issue is put to a vote, the smaller parishes are outnumbered. This can lead to a loss of ownership and involvement by the smaller parishes.

Educational and formational programs "are the principal means for bringing people into contact with the great Catholic ideas and traditions that form part of a world-wide expression of religious faith" [Quinn, p. 57]. The pastor must ensure that the voice of the small parish is heard throughout the planning stages of a program so that no segment of parishioners is excluded. All should be "exposed to the teaching of the Church as past generations have lived it, and as it is now expressed in unity and diversity within many nations and cultures... helping them integrate their religious knowledge with their experience" [Quinn, p. 58].

This is not just the pastor's responsibility. It is an obligation of all leaders in the larger parishes, as well. The Decree on the Apostolate of Lay People states:

> The laity will continuously cultivate the "feeling for the diocese," of which the parish is a kind of cell. They will not confine their cooperation within the limits of the parish,... but will endeavor, in response to the needs of the towns and rural districts, to extend it to interparochial, interdiocesan... spheres [No. 10].

The larger parishes should work to develop the programs in a way that includes the smaller parishes and will be meaningful to them. In some situations, this involves making modifications to the program so that it will work in the smaller setting. In other situations, it means making deliberate efforts to include members of the smaller parish in all phases of the larger parish's program, or putting the smaller parish in charge of the development of one aspect of the program.

• • •

Example: All the meetings of a week-long cluster-wide retreat were going to be held in the larger parish of the cluster. To help the smaller parish feel a sense of ownership in the retreat, it was given the responsibility for the morning sessions, i.e. providing hosts and hostesses, assisting at the morning prayer services, serving the brunches, etc.

• • •

When the small parishes become as enthused about new programs as the large parishes, they want to implement all of them. Only after they have committed to do so, do they realize that in their smaller setting, saying "Yes, we'll do it" too often means "Yes, I'll do it." The larger parishes must help the smaller parishes come up with workable alternatives, such as, running some programs in the large parish and inviting the smaller parishes to attend, helping the small parishes with modifications of the program, and jointly planning the cluster program but holding the meetings in each of the parishes.

Small vs. large community.

Some people join a small parish because they prefer the smaller setting. They don't want to be drawn into the larger gatherings and bigger programs of the large parishes. A clarification that cooperation does not mean allowing the smaller parish to be swallowed up by the larger parish usually resolves any problems that arise on this area. Supporters of cooperation are not saying that bigger is always better. No one is being asked to give up the strong community spirit and more intimate gatherings that are possible in a small parish. As "a basic building block of the universal Church," the parish is "designed, above all, to make religion an integral part of people's lives" [Quinn, p. 8]. There are many small parishes that do this very effectively. If people are using their preference for a small parish as an excuse not to develop any programs at all, preferring to just be "Sunday" Catholics, then it is time for them to reevaluate their understanding of the Gospel message.

Drop in volunteerism.
A parish depends a great deal on volunteers. Sometimes the number of volunteers drops when parishes start to cooperate because everyone decides its someone else's turn to do the work. This happens most often when the parishes are being forced to cooperate and are looking for a way to make the activities fail. The parishioners may have agreed to an activity "in principle but vetoed it by not working" [Johnson, p. 42]. Getting the parishioners to step back from the issue and view the desirability of the activity versus the motivations for their actions can be very useful at this point.

CHAPTER VI:

OBSTACLES

TO CLUSTER-WIDE COOPERATION

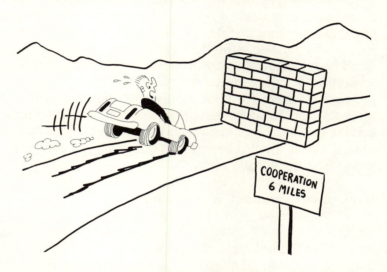

No one is looking at this subject through rose-colored glasses. Some of the pastors who had the longest lists of advantages in cluster-wide cooperation also had long lists of obstacles to accomplishing their goals. Most pastors, though, are finding ways of dealing with these obstacles.

Distance.
By far, the most commonly expressed problem is that created by the distances between the parishes and the amount of time required to travel those distances, especially at night in regions that are so heavily populated with deer. The problem is compounded when the pastor's attitude is

that his time is far more valuable than the combined time of any number of parishioners. People do not arrive at a meeting or event in a cooperative frame of mind if they always have to drive to where the pastor is and he is never willing to drive to meet them.

Some pastors are rotating the joint meetings and activities among the parishes so the same people are not always required to drive the longest distances. If some meetings can be held during the day, that will lessen the problems inherent in night driving. Holding the meeting or event before or after a weekend liturgy also draws a better attendance, since many people do attend the liturgy at another parish when it better fits their schedules.

The real root of this problem comes into sharper focus when the following question is posed: Why is it that some people will drive for two hours for a shopping trip or to attend a baseball game, but they refuse to spend 20 minutes driving to a meeting in a neighboring parish? When we are honest about the answer to that question, the problem of travel time may solve itself.

Lack of parishioners' understanding.

Most parishioners have never been involved in any cluster-wide cooperative programs, so they consider it an impossible undertaking. No amount of explaining helps them to understand that it is a workable and beneficial approach to parish life. Parishioners will have to personally experience the benefits before they can understand them.

It must be repeatedly stressed that cooperation doesn't mean that all the parishes must be running the same programs at the same time.

• • •

Example: During Lent, Annunciation parish decided to have soup suppers before the weekly Stations of the Cross. In a spirit of hospitality, they informed St. George parish of their plans and invited those parishioners to join them. St. George liked the idea of gathering the parish together, and some of its parishioners accepted the invitation and attended the soup suppers. As a Lenten activity for its parish, though, St. George decided to hold a morning prayer-brunch after the Sunday Mass each week. Both parishes were made aware of what the other parish was doing, but neither felt obligated to change its decision to match that of the other parish.

• • •

Lack of pastors' understanding.
What was just said about some parishioners must be repeated concerning some pastors. Most pastors were trained to handle the affairs of one parish. They have little or no training in how to deal with a cluster of parishes. Consequently, many pastors either exhaust themselves trying to duplicate the single-parish plan in each parish, or, realizing that this is an impossible task, they divide their time between the parishes as best they can, shortchanging each parish by an equal amount of time. Neither of these choices is healthy for either the pastor or the parishes.

Some pastors said that cooperation might work in some clusters, but not in their setting because of "unique" circumstances. Other pastors responded to this by saying that every cluster is unique, just as every parish and every human being is unique. The unique characteristics of the cluster affect the degrees of cooperation in the different areas of parish life, but it doesn't affect the underlying benefits or desirability of cooperation.

Even when pastors are convinced of the benefits of a cluster-wide approach to parish life, many of them don't know where to begin in implementing intra-parish cooperation because their worldview has always been parochial. They make the mistake of assuming that cooperation means combining all the programs and activities and doing everything in exactly the same way and at exactly the same time in all the parishes. Again, it must be stressed that cooperation doesn't mean making the parishes into clones of each other.

• • •

Example: St. Mark parish has a coffee hour each weekend after its only Mass. This gathering time is especially important for this parish because the church is in a remote area, with no town nearby to provide a sense of community. Assumption parish is located in town, has more than one weekend Mass, and is not interested in starting coffee hours each weekend.

The pastor insists that since one parish has coffee hours, both should be doing it, since the parishes have agreed to cooperate in their programs and activities.

• • •

Little support from diocesan and national levels.
Most programs are designed for one, large parish in one location. Little thought is apparently given to the program modifications that are necessary for a rural setting; even less thought seems to be given to implementing the programs in a cluster setting. This may not seem to be a matter of crucial importance until one looks at the U.S.A. statistics and realizes that there are thousands of parishes in this country that share a pastor with one or more parishes [Kenedy, pp. 1-1169].

With very little help forthcoming from the national or diocesan level, each pastor and each cluster finds itself struggling to make the modifications that are necessary to successfully run these single-parish programs in multi-parish settings. With the ever-growing number of clustered parishes, more thought must be given to clusters and their special needs.

Use of parish facilities.

Each parish in the cluster would like to be the center of the cluster activities. For some parishes this is impossible because they have no facilities other than the church. For other parishes, their facilities might be adequate for some groups, but not large enough to handle the entire cluster. In both of these situations, parishioners often respond by not supporting the cluster-wide activities that are held at the largest parish.

One solution to this problem is to hold the larger activities at the parish with the largest facilities, and hold the smaller events at the parish with the smaller facilities. If a parish has no facilities, it can still take its turn sponsoring the activities, no matter where they are held.

• • •

> **Example:** The location of the yearly Confirmation Service is determined by the size of the class of confirmands. When the class is small enough, the celebration is held at the smaller parish, which has adequate, but smaller facilities. For the larger classes, the celebration takes place in the larger parish. The sense of pride that the parishioners of the small parish feel on the years that the bishop arrives at their church door is immeasurable.

• • •

Don't let the small parishes that have limited facilities develop a "poor me" attitude — one which says they can't hold or sponsor activities or help with programs because they have less money, fewer people, etc. This attitude is self-defeating. Treat them like co-partners in the cluster. Have them do their fair share, providing some financial support for cluster activities and some workers for the cluster events. Help them to identify the strengths of their parish and the talents of their parishioners and encourage them to share those.

Develop in all the parishes a sense of ownership in the cluster office and other facilities that are located in the mother parish. Let each parish use the mother parish's church and hall for its activities, especially its funerals, funeral luncheons, weddings, and wedding receptions if its facilities aren't adequate.

• • •

Example: It was not uncommon for the 40-family St. Thomas parish to have 500 people attend its outdoor summer Masses. Rain was threatening one weekend and the church was far too small to accommodate the entire congregation, so the decision was made to move the Mass to the mother parish, 10 miles away. In many clusters, the small parish would have strongly resisted and resented this change. St. Thomas' feelings about the situation were more than obvious when the reader began the greeting before Mass with the words, "Welcome to the Southern Campus of St. Thomas church." There couldn't be a stronger statement of ownership from a small parish than that!

• • •

Fear of closure.
Parishioners in the small parishes are sometimes afraid that their cooperation with the large parishes will be taken as a sign that they are not capable of functioning on their own and this will lead to the closure of their parish. One of the factors that is considered during discussions on closure is whether or not the parish is a "full-service" parish, i.e. whether the parish "contains all the basic elements that Catholic life requires – the Sacraments, teaching authority, the pastoral office, and the baptismal ministries of comfort, challenge, evangelization, witness and service" [Quinn, p. 4]. If the parishioners from the small parish are actively participating in the planning and implementation of the

programs in the cluster, then all the services of a "full-service" parish are available to them. In many places, this is the only way that a parish can fully provide for itself. While no one can guarantee that cooperation prevents closure, an active parish is less likely to close than a Sunday-only parish.

Financial responsibilities.
Each parish feels an obligation to its parishioners to remain financially sound, so conflicts can develop concerning the amount that each parish must contribute to the expenses for cluster programs, cluster staff members, etc. Before deciding on the fair share for each parish, it helps if all parishes are made aware of the financial obligations of the other parishes, such as building debts, loans, etc. While this might not resolve the conflict, it usually lessens it.

Parish size.
The relative size of a parish with respect to the other parishes in the cluster doesn't seem to have much affect on how quickly they accept the cooperative approach. Some of the smallest parishes want to prove they can provide for themselves, so they oppose cooperation. Others quickly realize that if they are to remain viable, they must do some things in conjunction with the other parishes.

Mission parishes with 100 to 150 families, seem the most determined to remain independent. Their population is large enough that they can provide for themselves, albeit in a limited way, in most areas of parish life, so they view cooperation as a lessening of their control over their own parish. In time, though, many of them realize that they can have the best of both worlds. Their parish is large enough to hold its own programs in its own facilities if it so desires, but if they work cooperatively with the cluster, the facilities and staff in the mother parish will be available whenever they need them.

Most mother parishes have a neutral attitude towards cooperation. If the other parishes want to work with them, that's fine, if they don't, that's fine, too. To suggest to the mother parish that cooperation also means the mother parish working with the other parishes meets with a little more opposition, but nothing of critical proportions.

"See how nicely we're cooperating!"

A few mother parishes have a snobbish, "better than thou" attitude towards the other parishes, an attitude that they can sometimes hide from the pastor. Be aware: if the mission parish balks at every suggestion of cooperation, it might be less of a sign of stubbornness on its part and more of a reaction to the attitude of the mother parish.

Autocratic leadership style.

"How important is the pastor? I will answer that with another question. How important is oxygen to your body?" [Johnson, p. 109].

An autocratic pastor does not allow the parishioners to be involved in the planning or decision-making in the parish. He wants everyone to simply follow his directives and implement his plans. This approach is not conducive to cooperation. External actions can be mandated; internal attitudes cannot.

Involving the parishioners in the planning process has two benefits. It gives them an ownership in the program and it builds a rapport among the parishioners from the different parishes. This ownership and rapport are major factors in building cooperation, but they will rarely develop if the parishioners are simply doing what they were told to do.

One pastor explained that as the parishioners in the two parishes worked together with him in accessing the needs of the parishes and developing cooperative programs and activities to meet those needs, the question on their lips changed from "What should we do next, Father?" to "Is that okay, Father?" Through their work with the pastor they had developed a sound perspective of the parishes, so their ideas were usually "okay". An autocratic pastor, who is never open to the ideas of others and never relinquishes any of his control, will stifle this process.

• • •

Example: The location of the weekly meetings of EAO, "Everyone's Afternoon Out", alternated between the two parishes in the cluster. At the EAO, some people played cards, others worked together on needlepoint, sewing, and quilting projects, others brought in plants that needed doctoring, etc. They took turns looking after their preschoolers in the playroom. One group always baked some treats which were eaten hot-from-the-oven at the end of the afternoon. In the course of the afternoon's conversations, ideas developed for new parish and/or cluster activities. Sometimes, questions and suggestions on current programs were also raised.

The EAO lasted for only a few months after the new pastor arrived. He didn't actually say they couldn't meet, but he said that he didn't think playing cards at the church was proper; he said it was too dangerous to be baking when there were young children around; he said the group was too exclusive, since anyone who worked during the day couldn't attend; he said it cost too much to heat the building for the afternoon, etc. With the EAO gone, the pastor no longer has to deal with the parishioners' new ideas, questions, or suggestions.

• • •

Parochialism.

The issue of parochialism has already been mentioned, but it is worth repeating because it can be one of the major obstacles to developing cooperation. One parishioner expressed it this way: "Many parishioners, though, use the distance and other 'priorities' as excuses not to support cluster functions. They seem to feel that if the function is taking place at a different parish from their own, it is extraneous to their Christian faith and not important for their faith development."

Parishioners also noted that parochialism can be especially strong in the families that have lived in the area for generations and know that their parish has "always" done things a certain way. Even the newcomers, in their desire to be accepted, can quickly develop very protective instincts towards the parish. If an isolated, rural parish never looks beyond its boundaries, the inbreeding of ideas can turn the parish into a spiritual ghetto. The parishioners refuse to look at other perspectives, new insights, and fresh approaches to the Gospel message. They let "long-standing jealousies, ingrained ignorance, and personal interests" determine their actions, rationalizing these factors to convince themselves that they are actually thinking of the good of the parish. Their views are so parochial, they have so little interest in increasing their faith or in spiritual growth, that they won't even listen when fellow parishioners talk about the positive faith experiences that they had when they worked with the other parishes. They are afraid to admit to any commonality among the parishes for that would open the door to communication and possible change.

Other issues, such as town rivalries, or differences in the demographics, economic conditions, or nationalities of the areas can increase the chasms between the parishes. The terminology of "mother" versus "mission" parish can also be problematic. Thus, even when some parishioners decide it's worthwhile to consider developing cooperative activities, they have trouble making their voices heard.

The issue of parochialism can also be one of power and control. Many times the long-standing leaders in the parish are fearful of supporting any activity that might lessen their power. It may seem that they are putting their own self-interests above the good of the parish, but "quite frequently the control is unconscious, with no intent to hinder the work of the church" [Johnson, p. 41]. One way to work with this situation is to allow the current leaders to be in charge of the initial cooperative programs. Once they realize that the service they have given to their parishes for so many years is still valued, they may be more open to the new approach. In a few situations, pastors have found that the current parish leaders continually oppose them in every area, creating as much dissension in the parish as they can, and working hard to undermine everyone else's efforts. At times like this, it might be necessary to remove these very parochial power-holders from their leadership positions before anything can be accomplished.

Parochialism, at its worst, can become schismatic. The attitude that their parish "is unique" and therefore no one else could possibly understand what is important in their lives leads to a rejection of any outside authority. Some parishioners have openly stated that the pastor, who came into their community from the outside, and the bishop, who lives in another part of the state, and the Council of Bishops, and most of all the Pope, couldn't possibly understand their parish and therefore these people have no right establishing regulations for them to follow.

Pope John Paul II said:
> The cry of Saint Paul continues to resound as a reproach to those who are "wounding the Body

of Christ". "What I mean is that each one of you says, 'I belong to Paul', or 'I belong to Cephas', or 'I belong to Christ!' Is Christ divided?" (1 Cor 1:12-13). No, rather let these words of the apostle sound a persuasive call: "I appeal to you, brethren, by the name of our Lord Jesus Christ, that all of you agree and that there be no dissensions among you, but that you be united in the same mind and the same judgment." [Christifideles Laici, no. 31]

Yes, each community, each parish, is unique, but the basic gospel values are the same whether a parish has 60 members or 2000. "The structures of local community should in no way set up barriers to the unity in Christ which should transcend every human culture and style of life" [Quinn, p. 34].

Solutions?

There are a number of approaches that can be used to deal with these issues. No one way will always be successful, but over time the barriers can be broken down. Some of the pastors said that when they arrived in the cluster they did not experience any major difficulties in developing joint programs because cooperation was already "a way of life" for the parishes. This means that through the efforts of a previous pastor, the parishes had realized the advantages of working together and now consider it the normal way to approach issues.

If the obstacles center around the pastor, the situation is a much more difficult one. Since the pastor has the ultimate authority in the parish, anything that he is not supporting will not happen. The pastor is the key player when it comes to developing and continuing cooperation.

CHAPTER VII:

DEVELOPING COOPERATION

Should cooperation be promoted among clustered parishes? For pastors who have assessed the situation, the answer is a definite "Yes". Though there can be a number of obstacles to overcome and some disadvantages that must be considered, the quantity and quality of the advantages far outweigh the problems.

As cooperation develops, the parishioners come to realize that their faith goes beyond the church building; it goes beyond the people who gather in that building for Sunday Mass. They realize that their faith makes them a part of a faith community, and that faith community is expressed not only in their little parish, but in their cluster of parish communities, and in the diocesan community, as well.

Parish cliques slowly dissolve. The true meaning of the word "Catholic" begins to open up for everyone. People become more aware of their faith in their everyday lives. Lay ministry, social justice, catechesis, etc., become more than just activities to be involved in; they become a way of life. The parishes and parishioners encourage and support each other, as they all search for the best ways to touch the world around them through their faith.

The Secular World.
Looking beyond the parish boundaries to cooperate with nearby parishes is a foreign idea to most people. It is a concept that is foreign to most of the organizations which they deal with in their secular lives. Neighboring towns and cities compete with each other in many aspects of life.

Businesses are focused on outdoing the competition. Civic organizations try to draw members away from other organizations. Neighboring schools compete throughout the year. Is it any wonder that forming an alliance among parishes seems like a strange idea?

The Pastor's Approach.

Because people have little or no experience of large-scale cooperation, it is difficult for them to understand the enormous advantages to it. During the initial stages of developing cooperation, it falls on the pastor to be the initiator. Parishioners repeatedly said that the pastor is the key player. He must be willing to work at developing a spirit of cooperation in the parishes. He can't just suggest (or mandate) that they start cooperating and expect it to happen. He must work to bring the parishioners to an "acceptance of the situation that clustering is an unchanging factor of their existence" and then lead them to a willingness to work together.

This doesn't mean that the pastor should be doing all the work himself. Numerous parishioners stated that the pastor should keep the parishioners involved in the process, encouraging them in the various ministries that support the parish and the cluster and giving them the training to apply the talents they have developed in their everyday lives to the numerous tasks in the life and spiritual growth of the parish.

It is important for the pastor to maintain a balanced perspective of all the parishes in the cluster. This does not mean treating each one exactly like the others: it would be foolish to suggest one should try to treat a parish with 40 families "exactly like" a parish with 200 families. What it does mean is that the pastor's actions should show that he is there to nourish each congregation, that he is aware of the needs of the parishioners in each parish and is working towards meeting those needs (personally, through the staff, and by empowering the parishioners to meet the needs). A strong pastoral sense is far more important than administrative skills.

For liturgies and other activities which require the pastor's presence, the parishioners realize that the pastor can't be in two places at once. Though the parishioners may not like the cooperation that is required of them for these activities, they usually feel they have to go along with the schedule. In some cases this is a first, small step leading to cooperation. In other cases, though, if one parish feels that the others always have priority in the pastor's schedule, this can lead to a defensiveness that hinders cooperation.

When parishioners were asked to describe the pastor's approach when he initially raised the subject of cooperation, they used phrases such as "pleasantly insistent" and "diplomatically authoritative". These perceptions of the parishioners seem to agree with the pastors' descriptions of their approach.

Most pastors have found that taking a pleasant, but firm, stance is the best approach. The pastor pleasantly, but firmly, insists that the parishes must meet together to deal with areas that are affecting all of them. When the parish representatives (usually the Pastoral Council members) meet, the pastor explains the problem, suggests alternatives, and then discusses the issues with them. It is important that the pastor maintain an open attitude at the meeting, listening to their objections and answering their questions. Pastors have found that when the parishioners sense that the pastor is open to their suggestions, many times the parishioners will come up with other workable alternatives. If, however, the pastor seems to be merely going through the motions of listening, the parishioners will often fight any attempts that the pastor makes to bring them together.

Not all people will express their opinions in a group setting, so the pastor can expect to hear them expressing their opinions in subtle (and not-so-subtle) ways in other conversations. If the pastor takes advantage of these times, he will have the opportunity to "pleasantly" reinforce the need to take action in a certain area. Some pastors try to have these "spontaneous" one-to-one conversations with a number of people before the group meets, so that he knows in advance what objections they might raise, and they have a chance to ponder his ideas before the meeting.

Sometimes the parishioners will reach an agreement on the cooperative approach that can be taken. More often than not, at least in the beginning, the parishes will not be in favor of any cooperative approach. They will not want to seriously discuss the possibilities. They view the situation as "them against us." One pastor said that he is constantly striving to make the parishes realize that we're all on the same side; we're all working towards the same ends; we're all trying to improve the spiritual and pastoral life of our parishes. If we are the Christians that we profess to be, we should be able to improve our parishes while working with, not against, the other parishes. This pastor asked: "What kind of witness of our Christian and Catholic values are we giving to the surrounding community, if there is constant strife between us?"

Most pastors said that, as a last resort, they will tell the parishes that this is "just the way it's going to be." This type of statement could be counterproductive and should be made with a great deal of caution. The church is more likely to lose them as parishioners, than to force them into compliance. A better way to make the statement is to ask them to just try it, to just go along with it for now and see what happens.

One parishioner, after agreeing to the pastor's request to "try it" for awhile, told the pastor a week later that he had tried it and didn't like it. The pastor asked him to try it for a little while longer. The parishioner did, but came back again with the statement that he was still trying it and he still didn't like it. It has been three years now, and every so often the parishioner again reminds the pastor that he's "still trying it," implying that he still doesn't like it. The important thing is that the parishioner is still there, still active, still trying it. What could have become a situation of alienation has become an inside joke between the pastor and parishioner.

One pastor made the following observation: "Every parish has its own 'teddy bears', objects or actions that are symbolic of deeper issues. Many times, the real issues are so buried or hidden by rhetoric, that even the parish no longer realizes why it considers those items to be of supreme importance." The pastor must help the parish to discover the underlying issues. Only after this has been done, will the parish be able to honestly weigh the importance of those items and to ask itself if it is willing to modify or give up any of them for the overall good of the parish and cluster.

The pastors were all in agreement that it is best to work on cooperation in one area at a time. Let the parishes get used to functioning in a cooperative way in one area. Give them some time to start to see some of the advantages of working together. Gauge how much they have accepted the cooperation in one area before moving on to the next. Don't let the process stall, but it can be self-defeating to act too quickly. People need time to adjust to any change, no matter how beneficial it is.

After the parishes have worked together on a project, have them step back and take a look at what they've accomplished. Point out one or two specific items that are better now than they were before. Cooperation in each new area builds on the positive responses to the last ones, so help them recognize all the positive results of their cooperative efforts. If the pastor insistently moves ahead without trying to bring the parishioners along with him, there will ultimately be too much opposition for anything to work. The pastor must stay aware of the parishioners' perspectives, meeting the parishioners where they are and then stretching them into new growth and deeper understandings of the universality of their Christian values.

Pastors have found that in settings where there are a great number of similarities between the parishes, this "diplomatically authoritative" approach only has to be used a couple of times. The parishioners quickly begin to see that the benefits to cooperation outweigh any problems and they begin to make the adjustment from a purely parochial worldview to one that includes the possibility of cluster activities. One pastor said that he was amazed that within a matter of a few months, the parishioners were already thinking in terms of both parishes as they proposed and developed new projects.

This early acceptance of cooperation, though, seems to be the exception rather than the rule. In most clusters, the pastors are faced with the same opposition, the same parochial worldview, every time they try to establish cooperation in a new area. Each time, the pastor must be calmly persuasive that the new approach should be tried. One parishioner was very frank in stating that when he moved into a clustered parish eight years ago, the idea of cooperating with the other parishes "took some getting used to." He went on to say, "Originally, my view was parochial, but after getting involved in the Finance Council, lectoring, meeting many people from the other two parishes, I began to see the cluster approach as a very positive means for the church to respond to a very serious, almost unsolvable situation." He is now a very strong supporter of his parish AND the cluster, and he believes that "parish leaders doing cluster planning must be willing to work together for the betterment of all, not just their parish."

As parishioners begin to accept the idea of doing joint planning, it still falls on the pastor's shoulders to move things along, to continually bring the parishioners together, to continually present new ideas that promote cooperation. Even when the parishioners have reached the stage where they seem to understand the benefits of working together, for awhile they will still make no attempt to initiate the joint efforts. Consequently, the process of developing cooperation can take a great deal of the pastor's energy. If a pastor stays with the process, eventually it does become very natural to the parishioners to think in terms of the cluster. Pastors of clusters that have reached that stage say the benefits for the parishes make the personal expenditure of time and energy well worth the effort.

STEPS TO DEVELOPING COOPERATION.

STEP 1: Invite all the parishes to one parish's social activity.

People are, by nature, territorial. Cooperation can be interpreted by some as having to "give up" something. A good place to start the joint efforts is in a setting where no one has to give anything up. The group of people who have "always" planned and run an event can still plan and run it. The only thing they are being asked to do that is different from their past routine is to invite the other parish(es) in the cluster.

This invitation has to be more than a notice in the bulletin that the event is taking place. Efforts must be made to make the parishioners of the other parishes feel welcome. Have a parish representative extend a personal invitation to the other parishes before or after the weekend liturgies in the weeks preceding the event. Have the presider add his words of invitation, encouraging the parishioners to support the other parish by taking part in the activity. The pastor, on a one-to-one basis, should encourage some of the members of the councils, CCW, etc. to attend the event. Focus on people who are prominent in the parish and have outgoing, positive personalities when extending these personal invitations. After the event, these people will, by nature, spread a positive word about the activity and how much they enjoyed it.

During the activity, some parishioners from the host parish should have the task of watching for parishioners from the other parishes. When they spot these other parishioners, they should greet them, introduce themselves, answer any questions the parishioners have, and talk with them for awhile to help them feel comfortable. They should ensure that the parishioners from the other parishes don't feel like outsiders who have stumbled into a private affair, otherwise the experience will stifle further cooperation instead of encouraging it.

STEP 2: Hold some non-threatening cluster-wide social activities.

Steps 2 and 3 will overlap. Here, the focus is still on social activities for, as one pastor said, "Profoundly religious or profoundly social activities are the most effective in binding people together, because those two types of experiences really meet their needs."

It's important that the activity be something that is new to all the parishes. Trying to modify one parish's activity to make it into a cluster-wide activity does not work well because the one parish will want to hang on to "the way we've always done it." At this stage, you don't want people focusing on things they have to change or give up when they cooperate.

"But, we ARE cooperating!"

Keep the social activity non-threatening and non-competitive. You want them to have a positive experience of a cluster-wide activity. A softball game which pits one parish against the other is not the best place to start when trying to develop cooperation. A Christmas Song Fest would be a much better idea. Invite each parish to provide an equal portion of the entertainment — musicians, soloists, or choral groups — and end the program with a group sing-along. Parental pride is a common bond for people, so make sure that a lot of children perform. A social hour should follow with coffee, punch, and cookies, giving everyone time to mingle and congratulate each other on the fine performances (which they'll do even if the performances don't quite merit Oscars).

The group that plans the event should include an equal number of parishioners from all the parishes in the cluster. The pastor or a staff member who understands the cooperation that the event is promoting should also be a part of the group to make sure the event is designed to foster an open, friendly environment.

In deciding where to hold the event, defuse the territorial reactions by suggesting that it be held in the parish with the largest facilities, so that there is room for everyone to attend. Divide up the responsibilities for bringing the cookies and punch between the parishes. Most importantly, schedule the kitchen workers so that members from each of the parishes are working together at all times. Don't schedule one parish for set-up, another to serve, and a different parish for cleanup. That defeats the plans to bring them together.

A short welcome address should be given by the pastor and a prominent parishioner of the hosting parish. The program would then be turned over to the emcee who should be a parishioner of a non-hosting parish. If there are more than two parishes in the cluster, the concluding sing-along should be led by members of the other parishes, reinforcing the equal status of all the parishes for that event.

Activities like this one bring the parishioners together in an event that benefits everyone. Through it, they learn to work together in a non-competitive way. They also learn to have fun together and to recognize some of the talents of the other parishioners. Since good music and good food are things that everyone appreciates, there's no better way to bring them together in this early stage.

If a Christmas Song Fest doesn't fit the parishes' schedules, try having a similar event in the fall or spring. A summer picnic with games and activities for the children, or a winter sledding or skating party with supper afterwards could all be organized following this same basic plan. If any of the activities are competitive, use criteria other than parish boundaries when choosing the teams, e.g., have the lectors from all the parishes play volleyball with the Eucharistic Ministers. Hopefully, the people will find the experiences so much fun, that they will want to repeat them. It is very beneficial to the parishes to develop two or three annual cluster-wide social activities.

STEP 3: Hold one-time adult and youth formation events.

The focus here is still on one-time events, but in the area of formation. Bring the catechists from all the parishes together for their fall in-service. If more than one parish has adequate facilities, use a different parish as the site of their winter in-service. Using the facilities in the different parishes for these one day events shows the parishioners that no parish is receiving preferential treatment. If some parishes don't have adequate facilities, ask those parishioners to "co-sponsor" the event by helping with the opening prayer, serving at the coffee break, etc.

A retreat at the beginning of the Confirmation program, a day of reflection for the Liturgical Ministers, a guest speaker for the CCWs are the types of activities that should be planned during this step. Each of these activities should conclude with a social hour, allowing the participants to continue to build on the communal faith experience of the day.

STEP 4: Initiate a short-term activity.

Only a very limited commitment was required of the parishioners in Steps 2 and 3. In this step, we are looking for a commitment that is longer in duration. It is still very useful at this step to choose an activity which is new to all the parishes. An area of adult formation, such as Bible Study, Prayer Groups, Support Groups, etc., is a worthwhile focus because activities of this nature bond the participants.

It is important that you choose something that addresses the parishioners' needs, otherwise their support will be very limited. This is not always easy to do, because your perception and their perceptions of their needs might not be the same. For some parishes, RENEW was the perfect choice for an activity to bring the parishes together. The organizational structure required a large number of people, so it worked well for the cluster to jointly develop the process. It was something new to all the parishes and many saw RENEW as a wonderful opportunity to enliven their parishes on many levels. Other parishes had a more difficult time with RENEW because they didn't see the need for it in their parishes. Consequently, they were just going through the motions with very limited overall benefits.

Whatever activity you choose, promote it as a cluster-wide program. Give the starting and ending dates for it so people know what commitment is expected of them. If there is enough interest, the meetings could be held on different days in the different parishes, but stress that everyone from the cluster is welcome to attend the meeting that best fits his or her schedule, even if that meeting is being held in another parish. Hopefully, there will be enough interest to start a second session after the first one ends, but most people will not initially sign-up for a program that is open-ended.

It is not a good idea to alternate these weekly meetings between two parishes that both have adequate facilities. Not only will the schedule be confusing, but people will have a tendency to attend every other meeting — the meeting that is held in their parish. This is a bad habit to let them fall into at this early stage.

STEP 5: Establish cooperation in the current programs.

Where you begin will partially depend on the environment in the parishes. Consider the people who are involved in the various programs and focus on the areas where the people are the most open-minded and least parochial. Look for the areas where the need is the greatest and acceptance will be the easiest to obtain. Adult and Youth Formation or Liturgy are common areas to focus on first.

—— If all the parishes are weak in a certain area, bringing them together to share ideas and jointly develop a program will be beneficial to all — a benefit that will become obvious to them as they work.

—— If one parish has a fully developed program in some area and the other parishes have no program at all, you have a good opportunity here to help those parishes develop a new area of involvement as they learn cooperation. The benefits to the parishes should be obvious to them as they proceed. (It is important that the lead parish does not have a condescending attitude when the groups meet together.)

—— If all the parishes have strong programs in an area, bring them together to share what has and hasn't worked for them. They can then explore ways to improve the programs that currently exist.

In some areas, the parishes may decide to combine their efforts into one cluster-wide program. In others areas, it might work best to stay in communication with each other, but to run the programs separately. Exactly what form cooperation takes in each area will vary from cluster to cluster, and will also vary at different times within a cluster. Chapter III, Current Levels of Cooperation, details the types of cooperative programs that are currently in place in clusters.

Pastors say that the more the parishioners work together on creating and running joint programs, the more confident they become in their abilities to deal with these large-scale endeavors. These feelings of confidence and empowerment lead to an increased initiative on the part of the parishioners. No longer do they sit and wait for Father to tell them what to do. Instead, they begin to explore new possibilities on their own, taking the pressure off the pastor as the sole initiator of activities which enhance the lives of the parishes.

STEP 6: A cluster outlook.

The movement from Step 5 to Step 6 should be encouraged and supported by the pastor and staff, but it will occur only when the parishes are ready for it. Step 6 involves a fundamental change in the parishioners' identity. This change will be reflected in a change in their attitude and approach to parish life. They will no longer think of issues only in terms of their own parish, but will reflect on them simultaneously in terms of the cluster. They will have reached the point where they not only say with great pride, "I am a member of St. Theresa's Parish," but they also proudly say, "I am a member of the Northwoods Cluster." If this doesn't seem possible, consider for a moment the pride that a teenager feels in his High School AND in the specific grade that he belongs too; or the pride a person feels as a resident of a particular town or city and as a resident of a particular state. Taking pride in one of the two units does not preclude taking pride in the other.

The members of one cluster explained: "We're like the Holy Trinity — three parts of one whole. Each of the three parts (parishes) has its own identity — special, unique, and distinct from the others — but we are also united, joined together in a way that strengthens all of us."

Parishes with a cluster outlook view each new activity in terms of the cluster. They weigh the advantages and disadvantages of functioning on an individual basis or as a unit. They are equally comfortable in both approaches. They know that sometimes it is better to work independently, while other times it is better to combine their efforts with the other parishes.

One parishioner used the phrase "independent cooperation" to summarize this worldview. He explained: "I tend to deal with each function separately (i.e. finances, Religious Ed, social, etc.) rather than having a standard answer of either 'for all' or 'against all'. I believe some functions should be joint and others individual. This mix probably changes from time to time depending on size, time and people involved."

The change to a cluster outlook will not happen overnight. Most clusters said it was a long process, but one that was well worth the effort. Eventually, this "independent cooperation" does become a natural way of doing things. Even at that stage, it is important for the pastor to continue to visibly support cooperation. Parishioners noted that the pastor must understand that to maintain the cooperative efforts of the parishes and to promote further growth in building solid relationships and understandings between the parishes, more is required than having an occasional social get-together. Common faith experiences and on-going communication must be promoted among the parishes, or all the gains can be lost.

CHAPTER VIII:

LEST YOU THINK IT CAN'T BE DONE...

A CASE STUDY

Can it be done? Of course, it can! The following case study is based on a three-parish cluster in the Diocese of Superior Wisconsin.

By most standards, the size of this cluster is small, but their accomplishments are not. The cluster covers about 600 square miles and encompasses half a dozen incorporated and unincorporated towns. They call themselves "The Webster Area Catholic Churches" because the town of Webster is relatively central in the cluster's territory. The parishes are St. John the Baptist, Sacred Heart of Jesus and Immaculate Heart of Mary, and Our Lady of Perpetual Help. The travel time from St. John parish to Sacred Heart parish is about 25 minutes; from St. John parish to Our Lady parish, about 13 minutes; from Sacred Heart parish to Our Lady parish, about 35 minutes.

The parishes have been clustered with each other almost since they were founded, but, like many mother/mission parishes, for many years they did little to acknowledge each other.

St. John, the "Mother Parish".

St. John has 165 families. Its facilities consist of the church which seats 400, a parish center which can be used as overflow seating for the church, the cluster offices, and the rectory. As the largest of the three parishes and the one in which the pastor is resident, St. John knew from the beginning that it was the focal point of the cluster. It had a large enough population to manage the essential activities of a parish, so it didn't feel a need to reach out to either of the other parishes.

Its attitude towards the other parishes was "work with us", the implication being that the other parishes should come to St. John, do things St. John's way, always under the supervision of St. John. Their actions were similar to that of an older sister who knows the younger sisters aren't yet capable of handling matters on their own. There was no intended malice on St. John's part. They were merely being "helpful". The other two parishes, though, did not appreciate being treated like the not-quite-competent, lesser partners.

The first signs of a change in St. John's attitude appeared after the pastor started monthly "Core" meetings. At the Core meetings, the pastor met with the three Pastoral Council chairpersons to discuss both parochial matters and matters of mutual concern. Through these meetings, St. John began to realize that the other parishes had a lot going for them. Their parishioners were competent, caring people. It was only their numbers that were smaller, not their knowledge nor their skills.

Sacred Heart parish: a legacy.

Sacred Heart has 125 families, a church which seats 600 and a large parish center. The Catholic community traces its beginnings to the day, nearly a century ago, when two men rescued the Bishop from an intense snowstorm. The pioneer families have supported the parish for generation after generation. New families moving into the parish are quickly enveloped in this strong sense of parish pride.

Having this local pride and a parish size almost equal to St. John, it was natural for Sacred Heart to develop a sense of rivalry with St. John. They were determined not to be treated as a less-than-equal partner in the relationship and, for a while, they even had visions of becoming the "mother parish" of the cluster.

The Core meetings were beneficial to them, as well, helping them to focus on the positive qualities of the other parishes, particularily St. John. They slowly came to realize that by supporting the cluster in such things as hiring staff members and building up the facilities of the cluster offices, they were also reaping the benefits.

Our Lady parish: the little sister.
Our Lady has 45 families, a church which seats 150 and a new gathering space which can also be used for small meetings. The effects of cooperation on Our Lady parish are the most profound. Our Lady is, and always has been, a great deal smaller than the other two parishes. The parishioners became involved in the cooperative efforts almost as a defense so they wouldn't be cast aside as a weak and unimportant voice. Over the past twelve years, this small parish has made sure that it is well represented at planning meetings and cluster activities. Initially, the other parishes reacted with an "isn't that nice" attitude, but as the parishes saw Our Lady's parishioners constantly present, constantly involved, they began to give them equal consideration.

Our Lady's voices at the joint meetings of the Finance Councils are never ignored. They provide a number of teachers and teachers aids for the combined Youth Religious Education program, held at St. John. Their yearly parish celebration draws nearly a thousand people. The percentage of their women that are active in the CCW is larger than in the other two parishes.

A few years ago, Our Lady was building a small addition onto the church so that they would finally have indoor plumbing. Parishioners from the other two parishes decided to show their appreciation for the strong support that Our Lady has given the cluster for so many years. One-third of the money for the addition was anonymously donated by members of the other two parishes, allowing Our Lady to complete the project without needing a loan.

A YEAR IN THE LIFE OF A CLUSTER.

The best way to get a real flavor of parish life in this cluster is to walk through the year with them.

JANUARY

SUN	MON	TUE	WED	THU	FRI	SAT
					1 SJ - MASS	**2** SJ - MASS OL-MASS
3 SH - PARISH BRUNCH TRI - CHRISTMAS PARTY SJ - MASS SH - MASS	**4**	**5** OL - MASS	**6** SJ - MASS	**7** SH-MASS	**8** NURSING HOME-MASS SJ - MASS	**9** SJ - MASS OL-MASS
10 ALL-MARION HOUR OF PRAYER SJ - MASS SH - MASS	**11** TRI-BARCOL MTG	**12** OL-SCRIPTURE CLASS OL - MASS	**13** TRI-CATECHISTS' INSERVICE SJ - MASS	**14** SH-SCRIPTURE CLASS TRI PASTORAL COUNCILS SH-MASS	**15** SJ - MASS	**16** SJ - MASS OL-MASS
17 SH - CCD SJ - MASS SH - MASS	**18**	**19** OL-SCRIPTURE CLASS TRI - KC'S MTG OL - MASS	**20** SJ/OL - CCW MTG SJ/OL CCD SJ-SCRIPTURE CLASS SJ - MASS	**21** SH - CCW MTG SH-SCRIPTURE CLASS SH-MASS	**22** SJ - MASS	**23** SJ - MASS OL-MASS
24 SH - CCD ALL-COLLECTIONS FOR THE DOMESTIC ABUSE CENTER SJ - MASS SH - MASS	**25**	**26** OL-SCRIPTURE CLASS OL - MASS	**27** SJ/OL-CCD SJ-SCRIPTURE CLASS SJ - MASS	**28** SH-SCRIPTURE CLASS SH-MASS	**29** SJ - MASS	**30** SJ - MASS OL-MASS
31 SH - CCD SJ - MASS SH - MASS						

TRI = TRI-PARISH, CLUSTER ACTIVITY HELD IN ONE LOCATION
ALL = TRI-PARISH, CLUSTER ACTIVITY HELD IN ALL 3 PARISHES
SJ = ST. JOHN'S PARISH ACTIVITY
SH = SACRED HEART'S PARISH ACTIVITY
OL = OUR LADY'S PARISH ACTIVITY

JANUARY

Christmas-Epiphany Party.

For a number of years, the cluster has celebrated a Tri-Parish Christmas party. What started as a simple dinner has evolved into a full evening of activities, including entertainment presented by members of all three parishes and concluding with a sing-along. Since both St. John and Sacred Heart have adequate facilities, the party alternates between the two parishes. A committee with members from each of the three parishes plans the event.

Social Concerns.

Throughout the year, with the financial support of Our Lady, St. John runs a community food shelf. Sacred Heart also provides support to the food shelf at St. John and it runs another food shelf in cooperation with its neighboring Lutheran church. Monthly collections at the three parishes provide the needed funds. This is one project in which the three parishes have never hesitated to cooperate with each other.

The three parishes also strongly support the area's Domestic Abuse Center with quarterly collections of non-perishables and money.

The parishes are founding members of BARCAL, the Burnett (County) Association of Religious Communities And Leaders. This group meets quarterly to coordinate the efforts of the area churches.

The nursing home in St. John Parish holds an annual "Over 90's" party, honoring all its residents who are over 90 years of age. A number of St. John's and Our Lady's parishioners help with the activities.

Support for parishioners.

A few years ago a Tri-parish Pictorial Directory was published so that everyone would become better acquainted with their fellow parishioners and the parishioners in the other parishes. This has helped people tremendously as they gather for more and more cluster activities.

Through the efforts of the CCWs, each parish has its own prayer network. The weekly cluster bulletin has a Tri-parish listing of the names of the sick or injured and others who have requested prayers.

Each CCW sends plants to its parishioners who are hospitalized. The cluster sends congratulatory messages and condolences on behalf of the three parishes when appropriate occasions arise.

Each parish holds an after-Mass party for its parishioners who are celebrating 90th birthdays or 50th Wedding Anniversaries. Though these parties are sponsored by the individual parishes, the cluster's parishioners are always invited to attend.

Youth Religious Education.

St. John and Our Lady belong to the same school district with most of the school buildings within walking distance of St. John. Sacred Heart belongs to a different school district with the schools located 30 minutes from Sacred Heart and 45 minutes from St. John.

The three parishes cooperate in the Youth Religious Education program in the following way: One CRE runs the program for all three parishes. Students from St. John and Our Lady attend classes together at St. John on Wednesdays, immediately after school for the lower grades and in the evening for the older students. Parishioners from both St. John and Our Lady teach at St. John. Sacred Heart holds classes on Sunday morning following the only weekend Mass. The schedules of classes at both St. John and Sacred Heart begin in October and end in May, paralleling each other during those months. The same textbooks are used in both programs.

Cooperating in the Youth Religious Education program in this manner has allowed the parishes to jointly hire a staff member, to jointly share their knowledge, and to exercise the freedom they need to implement the program in the way that is most advantageous for each parish.

Catechists' Inservice.

Each semester, before the Religious Education programs begin, all catechists gather for a day of prayer, formation, information, and informal sharing. A luncheon or potluck supper is included in the day. Meetings such as these bring a continuity to the Youth Education programs.

Adult Formation.

Over 10 years ago, the cluster hired a DRE. In addition to her duties in youth religious education, she started a weekly Bible Study course that ran from September through May. Classes were held at both St. John and Sacred Heart; most people attended class in their own parish because it was closer. Over the years, the DRE added other sessions, such as a course in Spirituality for Women, and a support group for the divorced, widowed, and separated. All of these were cluster-wide programs with the meetings usually held at St. John.

Throughout the year, single-parish and cluster-wide meetings are held on various educational and formational topics. The single parish meetings are always promoted throughout the cluster. Tourists and parishioners from the non-sponsoring parishes often attend these parish events. The topics have included video tapes and talks on the Mass and other sacraments, the symbolism behind the Advent and Lenten traditions, and missionary presentations.

Most of these programs were set aside when RENEW began in the diocese, allowing the parishes to focus on that process. With the final Season of RENEW ending, the parishes are looking at other ways to continue Tri-parish Adult Formation. One of the activities that is planned is an Old Testament Scripture class.

The new Diocesan Evangelization and Small Christian Communities programs will be implemented on a cluster-wide basis.

RENEW

When the diocese started the RENEW process, about 40 parish representatives met to discuss how to implement this process in the three parishes. They were all in agreement that RENEW's organizational structure should be modified so they could work with RENEW as a cluster-wide activity.

For the normal RENEW process, the parish has one RENEW Coordinator and a Parish RENEW Team. Each team member has responsibility for one of the RENEW committees. This Tri-parish cluster appointed RENEW Tri-Coordinators (one from each parish) and a 9-member Parish RENEW Team made up of parishioners from the three parishes. Each RENEW committee was also formed with members from each parish. This ensured that all plans would be designed with the three parishes in mind. If some plans would be difficult to implement in one of the parishes, the committee always developed workable options for that parish's unique situation.

KCs.

The Tri-Parish KCs hold monthly meetings at St. John parish (cluster) center.

In honor of the January 1 Feast of Mary, the Mother of God, patron of two of the parishes, the Tri-Parish KCs hold a Marion Hour of Prayer on one of the Sundays during January. This Hour of Prayer is celebrated in each of the three churches. The prayer hours are scheduled in a way that allows parishioners to attend all three services, if they so desire.

CCWs.

The CCWs for St. John and Our Lady are combined. Because of Our Lady's small size and the relatively short distance between the parishes, this is a very workable arrangement. Sacred Heart has its own CCW. Both CCWs are very active, bringing in guest speakers for their monthly meetings and holding numerous fund-raisers throughout the year. If a CCW thinks that others might be interested in its presentations, it invites the other CCW (and sometimes the entire cluster) to its meeting. The meetings always conclude with Mass and a potluck lunch.

Pastoral Councils.

The first efforts at cooperation among the Pastoral Councils resulted in the Chairpersons meeting once a month with the pastor, DRE, and a Finance Council representative to discuss parochial issues and matters of concern to all three parishes. These meetings were held one week before the Pastoral Council meetings so the topics could be included in the Pastoral Councils' agendas.

As the parishes cooperated in more areas, it become necessary to further develop their communications. Instead of having just a joint meeting of the Chairpersons', the entire Pastoral Councils now hold a joint meeting every other month. Issues of common concern are discussed, as well as some parochial issues. On parochial issues, the council members appreciate the input from the other parishes, since the other parishes are able to view the issues more objectively. The other parishes can also draw on their past experiences to help one parish deal with a current parochial issue.

If a parish has lengthy issues to discuss, its Pastoral Council meets at a separate time from the joint meeting. Holding its council meeting immediately before or after the joint meeting, has been a productive way to address parochial concerns.

The location of the joint council meeting is rotated among the three parishes.

Tri-Parish Calendar.

In January, every organization in the parishes sets the dates for their yearly activities. Information on the dates is circulated among all the organizations so that problems with conflicting dates can be worked out well in advance of the scheduled events.

FEBRUARY

SUN	MON	TUE	WED	THU	FRI	SAT
	1	2 OL-SCRIPTURE CLASS OL - MASS	3 SJ/OL - CCD SJ-SCRIPTURE CLASS SJ - MASS	4 SH-SCRIPTURE CLASS SH-MASS	5 NURSING HOME-MASS SJ - MASS	6 SJ - MASS OL-MASS
7 SH - CCD SH - PARISH BRUNCH SJ - MASS SH - MASS	8	9 OL-SCRIPTURE CLASS OL - MASS/POTLUCK	10 SJ/OL - CCD SJ-SCRIPTURE CLASS TRI - EDUCATION COMMITTEE MTG SJ - MASS	11 SH-SCRIPTURE CLASS TRI - LITURGY COMMITTEE MTG SH-MASS	12 SJ - MASS	13 SJ - MASS OL-MASS
14 TRI - BREAKFAST BY THE KC'S ALL-FOOD SHELF COLLECTIONS SJ - MASS SH - MASS SH CCD	15	16 OL-SCRIPTURE CLASS TRI - KC MTG OL - MASS	17 SJ/OL-CCW MTG SJ/OL-FRUIT BASKETS FOR THE NEEDY SJ-SCRIPTURE CLASS SJ - MASS SJ/OL CCD	18 SH-CCW MTG SH-SCRIPTURE CLASS SH-MASS	19 SJ - MASS	20 SJ - MASS OL-MASS
21 SH CCD SJ - MASS SH - MASS	22	23 OL-SCRIPTURE CLASS OL - MASS	24 ALL-MASS/ASHES SJ/OL CCD AND PRAYER SERVICE/ASHES SJ-SCRIPTURE CLASS	25 SH-SCRIPTURE CLASS TRI - STATIONS/SOUP SUPPER SH-MASS	26 SJ - MASS	27 SJ - MASS OL-MASS
28 SH CCD SJ - MASS SH - MASS						

TRI = TRI-PARISH, CLUSTER ACTIVITY HELD IN ONE LOCATION
ALL = TRI-PARISH, CLUSTER ACTIVITY HELD IN ALL 3 PARISHES
SJ = ST. JOHN'S PARISH ACTIVITY
SH = SACRED HEART'S PARISH ACTIVITY
OL = OUR LADY'S PARISH ACTIVITY

FEBRUARY

Liturgy Committee.

A few years ago when the parish RENEW process was beginning, the Liturgy Committees from the three parishes united into a cluster Liturgy Committee. Because of the training received in RENEW, the cluster Liturgy Committee became more active in planning the weekend liturgies. After discussing how to connect each week's special RENEW focus with that week's readings, the committee developed suggestions on the decorations, processions, music, etc., that would express the week's focus. Each parish then made any adaptations that were the necessary to fit its setting.

Selecting the music for the liturgies is less complicated than it might have been, because all three parishes use the same hymnals and missalettes. After prayerful reflection on the readings for the week, the musicians on the committee decide on two alternatives for each piece of music needed. This allows the parishes and song leaders to adapt the music to fit their styles and capabilities. Though each parish has its own music ministry, the organists and guitarist will assist in any parish, if needed.

The Liturgy Committee meets on a seasonal basis. During the busier times of the year, like the Advent/Christmas and Lent/Easter seasons, additional meetings are usually necessary.

When planning Tri-parish Masses and prayer services, the Liturgy Committee chooses lay ministers from the full roster of Liturgical Ministers, insuring that all three parishes are represented.

Social Concerns.

During the week of Valentine's Day, the combined St. John / Our Lady CCW makes fruit baskets for the shut-ins of the local area, including the area around Sacred Heart parish.

KCs.

On the Sunday closest to Valentine's Day, the Tri-parish KCs serve a Pancake Breakfast at Sacred Heart. It begins after Sacred Heart's only weekend Mass and runs long enough to accommodate parishioners who arrive after St. John's morning Mass.

Ash Wednesday.

A Mass with the distribution of ashes is held in all three parishes. A special prayer service with the distribution of ashes is held in the afternoon for students in St. John's / Our Lady's religious education program. Catholics in the area often attend this service on their way home from work.

Lenten Soup Suppers.
Every Thursday during Lent, parishioners from the three parishes gather at St. John for the Stations of the Cross, Mass, and a soup supper. Various groups from the parishes, such as the KCs, the catechists, the CCWs, etc., take turns preparing and serving the suppers. These soup suppers are always held at St. John because it is the most convenient location for the greatest number of parishioners. Gathering on a weekly basis, especially during the Lenten season, strongly reinforces the common bond of faith of the parishes.

Weekday Masses.
Throughout the year, mid-week Masses are held in each parish: Tuesday afternoon at Our Lady, Thursday morning at Sacred Heart, Wednesday and Friday mornings at St. John. Lay ministers bring Communion to the local nursing home and the homebound after the daily Masses.

When the pastor has a meeting that takes him out of the area for the day, a Communion Service, led by the cluster's deacon or a lay presider, is held. Each parish has come to rely on its midweek liturgy as a time when it can gather its people for prayer, Eucharist, and sharing as a parish community.

For the Holy Days of the year, Mass is held in each parish on either the vigil or the Holy Day.

Our Lady's Potluck Suppers.
Because of its special devotion to Mary, about once a month near one of Mary's Feast Days, Our Lady has a potluck supper after the weekday Mass. This is a wonderful way for this small parish to keep in touch with its members. Since so much of their parish life is combined with one or both of the other parishes, this monthly parish gathering helps them to maintain their individual identity.

First Fridays.
On the First Friday of every month, Mass is celebrated at the local nursing home. The pastor also visits the homebound of all three parishes during the First Friday week, a much appreciated sign to the people that they are still valued parishioners of the parishes.

MARCH

SUN	MON	TUE	WED	THU	FRI	SAT
	1	2 OL-SCRIPTURE CLASS OL - MASS	3 SJ/OL CCD SJ-SCRIPTURE CLASS SJ - MASS	4 SH-SCRIPTURE CLASS TRI-STATIONS SOUP SUPPER SH-MASS	5 NURSING HOME-MASS SJ - MASS	6 SJ - MASS OL-MASS
7 SH CCD SH-PARISH BRUNCH SJ - MASS SH - MASS	8	9 OL-SCRIPTURE CLASS TRI-FINANCE COUNCILS OL - MASS	10 SJ/OL CCD SJ-SCRIPTURE CLASS SJ - MASS	11 SH-SCRIPTURE CLASS TRI-PASTORAL COUNCILS TRI-STATIONS/SOUP SUPPER SH-MASS	12 SJ - MASS	13 SJ - MASS OL-MASS
14 SH CCD ALL-FOOD SHELF COLLECTIONS SJ - MASS SH - MASS	15	16 OL-SCRIPTURE CLASS TRI-KC'S MTG OL - MASS	17 SJ/OL CCD SJ-SCRIPTURE CLASS SJ/OL-CCW MTG SJ - MASS	18 SH-CCW MTG SH-SCRIPTURE CLASS TRI-SOUP SUPPER SH-MASS	19 SJ - MASS	20 SJ - MASS OL-MASS
21 SH CCD SJ - MASS SH - MASS	22	23 OL-SCRIPTURE CLASS OL - MASS/POTLUCK	24 SJ/OL CCD SJ-SCRIPTURE CLASS SJ/OL-FIRST RECONCILIATION SJ - MASS	25 SH-SCRIPTURE CLASS TRI-STATIONS/SOUP SUPPER TRI-LITURGY COMMITTEE MTG SH-MASS	26 SJ - MASS	27 SH - FIRST RECONCILIATION SJ - MASS OL-MASS
28 SH CCD SJ - MASS SH - MASS	29	30 OL-SCRIPTURE CLASS OL-COMMUNAL PENANCE SERVICE OL - MASS	31 SJ/OL CCD SJ-SCRIPTURE CLASS SJ-COMMUNAL PENANCE SERVICE SH-COMMUNAL PENANCE SERVICE SJ - MASS			

TRI = TRI-PARISH, CLUSTER ACTIVITY HELD IN ONE LOCATION
ALL = TRI-PARISH, CLUSTER ACTIVITY HELD IN ALL 3 PARISHES
SJ = ST. JOHN'S PARISH ACTIVITY
SH = SACRED HEART'S PARISH ACTIVITY
OL = OUR LADY'S PARISH ACTIVITY

MARCH

First Reconciliation.
Towards the end of the Lenten Season, First Reconciliation is celebrated in St. John and Sacred Heart. (Because of their combined youth education program, St. John and

Our Lady prepare for and celebrate the sacrament together.) All parishioners are invited to participate in the sacrament with the children.

Communal Penance Service.

A communal penance service is held in each parish towards the end of Lent. The days and times of the services are varied to accommodate the largest possible number of people. A number of parishioners from the other two parishes attend the communal penance service at St. John on their way home from work.

Seder Meal.

As Easter approaches, the cluster holds a Seder meal. Because it is more central to the three parishes, the Seder meal is usually held at St. John, but members from all three parishes help prepare and serve the meal.

Holy Week / Easter.

One Holy Thursday Mass and one Holy Saturday Mass are celebrated at St. John by the cluster. Musicians and liturgical ministers from all three parishes assist at the liturgies.

Good Friday services are held in each of the parishes. The times for these services are chosen to accommodate the largest number of parishioners.

Easter Sunday starts with a dawn Mass at Our Lady which always fills the church. Sacred Heart and St. John follow their normal Sunday Mass schedules.

The services of this week are a nice blend of a parish/Tri-parish focus.

World Day of Prayer.

On the annual World Day of Prayer, the parishes gather with the other churches in the area for an ecumenical prayer service. The location of the prayer service rotates among the participating churches. The afternoon concludes with a social hour.

APRIL

SUN	MON	TUE	WED	THU	FRI	SAT
				1 SH-SCRIPTURE CLASS TRI-STATIONS/ SOUP SUPPER SH-MASS	2 NURSING HOME-MASS SJ - MASS	3 SJ - MASS OL-MASS
4 SH-PARISH BRUNCH SJ - MASS SH - MASS	5 TRI-SEDER MEAL	6 OL - MASS	7 SJ - MASS	8 TRI - HOLY THURSDAY MASS	9 ALL-GOOD FRIDAY SERVICES SJ - MASS	10 TRI-HOLY SATURDAY MASS SJ - MASS OL-MASS
11 ALL-EASTER MASSES	12 TRI-BARCOL MTG	13 OL - MASS	14 TRI-EDUCATION COMMITTEE MTG SJ - MASS	15 SH-MASS	16 SJ/OL - CCW RUMMAGE SALE SJ - MASS	17 SJ/OL - CCW RUMMAGE SALE SJ - MASS OL-MASS
18 SH CCD ALL-FOOD SHELF COLLECTIONS ALL-KC'S TOOTSIE ROLL DRIVE SH - MASS SJ - MASS	19	20 TRI-KC'S MTG OL - MASS	21 SJ/OL - CCW MTG SJ/OL CCD SJ - MASS	22 SH - CCW MTG SH-MASS	23 SJ - MASS	24 SJ - MASS OL-MASS
25 SH CCD ALL-COLLECTIONS FOR THE DOMESTIC ABUSE CENTER ALL-FIRST COMMUNIONS SH - MASS SJ - MASS	26	27 OL - MASS	28 SJ/OL CCD SJ - MASS	29 SH-MASS	30 SJ - MASS	

TRI = TRI-PARISH, CLUSTER ACTIVITY HELD IN ONE LOCATION
ALL = TRI-PARISH, CLUSTER ACTIVITY HELD IN ALL 3 PARISHES
SJ = ST. JOHN'S PARISH ACTIVITY
SH = SACRED HEART'S PARISH ACTIVITY
OL = OUR LADY'S PARISH ACTIVITY

APRIL

First Eucharist.

Each parish individually celebrates First Eucharist with its young parishioners. After the Mass, the parishes hold receptions to honor the first communicants on this special day.

KCs.

On a weekend in April, representatives of the Tri-parish KCs attend all the Masses in the three parishes, selling candy for the KCs annual Tootsie Roll drive. Because the proceeds from this sale benefit the handicapped, the sale is well-supported by the parishioners.

CCW.
St. John / Our Lady CCW holds a 2-day rummage and bake sale that recycles hundreds of pieces of clothing and other items to new owners. The proceeds support the CCW's numerous projects.

Confirmation.
The Tri-parishes have a two-year preparation program for Confirmation. Candidates from all three parishes meet together at St. John for their classes.

While it is a big event for any parish when the Bishop visits, it is even more special when his visit only occurs every two years. When time allows, a dinner with the Bishop, the Pastor, the Catechists, and the Tri-Parish Pastoral and Finance Councils' members and their spouses precedes the Confirmation. A reception honoring the confirmandi follows the ceremony.

MAY

SUN	MON	TUE	WED	THU	FRI	SAT
						1 OL - ROSARY SJ - MASS OL-MASS
2 SH CCD/PARTY /PARISH BRUNCH SJ - MASS SH - MASS	**3**	**4** OL - MASS	**5** SJ/OL CCD/PARTY SJ - MASS	**6** SH-MASS	**7** NURSING HOME-MASS SJ - MASS	**8** OL - ROSARY SJ - MASS OL-MASS
9 SJ - MASS SH - MASS	**10**	**11** OL - MASS/POTLUCK TRI-FINANCE COUNCILS OL - MASS	**12** TRI-CATECHISTS' INSERVICE SJ - MASS	**13** TRI-PASTORAL COUNCILS SH-MASS	**14** SJ - MASS	**15** OL - ROSARY SJ - MASS OL-MASS
16 ALL-FOOD SHELF COLLECTIONS TRI-CONFIRMATION SJ - MASS SH - MASS	**17**	**18** TRI - KC'S MTG OL - MASS	**19** SJ/OL - CCW MTG SJ - MASS	**20** SH - CCW MTG SH-MASS	**21** SJ - MASS	**22** OL-ROSARY SJ - MASS OL-MASS
23 SJ - MASS SH - MASS	**24**	**25** OL - MASS	**26** SJ - MASS	**27** SH-MASS	**28** SJ - MASS	**29** OL - ROSARY SH - MASS SJ - MASS OL-MASS
30 SJ - MASS SH - MASS	**31**					

TRI = TRI-PARISH, CLUSTER ACTIVITY HELD IN ONE LOCATION
ALL = TRI-PARISH, CLUSTER ACTIVITY HELD IN ALL 3 PARISHES
SJ = ST. JOHN'S PARISH ACTIVITY
SH = SACRED HEART'S PARISH ACTIVITY
OL = OUR LADY'S PARISH ACTIVITY

MAY

Baptisms.

Because of the limited number of births in the cluster, baptismal preparation is done privately with each family and not in a class. Each parish celebrates the sacrament in its own church, usually within the Mass, giving parish-wide support to the newest members of the parish family.

Marriage Preparation.
Marriage preparation meetings with the pastor and couple take place throughout the year as couples are preparing for the sacrament. The meetings are usually held at St. John, but can be scheduled in the other parishes, depending on the circumstances.

The Rosary.
Since Mary is patron saint of the month of May, and she is also the patron saint of Our Lady's parish, the Tri-parish KCs lead the rosary before the weekend Mass at Our Lady parish during this month. A Living Rosary is prayed at the May meeting of St. John / Our Lady CCW; Sacred Heart CCW and other cluster parishioners are invited to this time of prayer. Sacred Heart prays the rosary before their Thursday morning Mass throughout the entire year.

Youth Religious Education.
The youth religious education classes at St. John / Our Lady end the year with a short program, prayer, and potluck supper. Since Sacred Heart's classes meet on Sunday mornings after Mass, they end the year with a Sunday brunch.

The catechists gather for a final inservice for the school year followed by dinner.

Finance Councils.
Each parish has a 4-member Finance Council. The overriding atmosphere of cooperation in the parishes has led to the creation of many joint projects and programs. Because of this, many of the expenses are jointly incurred by the three parishes. Specifically, all the expenses for the rectory, religious education and adult formation programs, cluster office, and staff are shared by the three parishes. Consequently, most of the Finance Council meetings are held jointly.

Each May the Finance Councils sit down with the pastor to review the previous year's income and expenses. Together, they reflect on major changes that might be occurring in either of these areas. As a group, they discuss the percentage that each parish is paying of the cluster expenses and work out new percentages, if necessary.

Memorial Day Weekend.

From Memorial Day Weekend through Labor Day weekend, Our Lady's Saturday afternoon Mass moves outdoors to accommodate the influx of tourists. Many of the parishioners from St. John and Sacred Heart also enjoy attending this Mass.

JUNE

SUN	MON	TUE	WED	THU	FRI	SAT
		1 OL - MASS	**2** SJ - MASS	**3** SH-MASS	**4** NURSING HOME-MASS SJ - MASS	**5** SH - MASS SJ - MASS OL-MASS
6 SJ - MASS SH - MASS	**7**	**8** TRI-FINANCE COUNCILS OL - MASS	**9** TRI-EDUCATION COMMITTEE MTG SJ - MASS	**10** TRI-LITURGY COMMITTEE MTG SH-MASS	**11** SJ - MASS	**12** SH - MASS SJ - MASS OL-MASS
13 ALL-FOOD SHELF COLLECTIONS SJ - MASS SH - MASS	**14**	**15** TRI - KC'S MTG OL - MASS	**16** SJ/OL - CCW MTG SJ - MASS	**17** SH - CCW MTG SH-MASS	**18** SJ - MASS	**19** SH - MASS SJ - MASS OL-MASS
20 SH-FESTIVAL SJ - MASS SH - MASS	**21** SJ/OL-BIBLE SCHOOL	**22** OL - MASS/POTLUCK SJ/OL-BIBLE SCHOOL	**23** SJ - MASS SJ/OL-BIBLE SCHOOL	**24** SH-MASS SJ/OL-BIBLE SCHOOL	**25** SJ/OL-BIBLE SCHOOL SJ - MASS	**26** SH - MASS SJ - MASS OL-MASS
27 SJ - MASS SH - MASS	**28**	**29** OL - MASS	**30** SJ - MASS			

TRI = TRI-PARISH, CLUSTER ACTIVITY HELD IN ONE LOCATION
ALL = TRI-PARISH, CLUSTER ACTIVITY HELD IN ALL 3 PARISHES
SJ = ST. JOHN'S PARISH ACTIVITY
SH = SACRED HEART'S PARISH ACTIVITY
OL = OUR LADY'S PARISH ACTIVITY

JUNE

Sacred Heart's Feast Day.

On or near the feasts of the Sacred Heart of Jesus and the Immaculate Heart of Mary, the parish celebrates its summer festival. At the festival there is food, entertainment, and a bazaar which includes craft items, books, and plants for sale. It is an excellent fund-raiser and it attracts many people from the surrounding area.

Vacation Bible School.

A week of Bible School is held at St. John each summer

for the children of the area. Some Sacred Heart's children also attend, but most of them attend the Bible School sessions held at their neighboring Lutheran church.

JULY

SUN	MON	TUE	WED	THU	FRI	SAT
				1 SH-MASS	**2** NURSING HOME-MASS SJ - MASS	**3** SH - MASS SJ - MASS OL - MASS
4 SJ - MASS SH - MASS	**5**	**6** OL - MASS	**7** SJ - MASS	**8** TRI-PASTORAL COUNCILS SH-MASS	**9** SJ - MASS	**10** SH - MASS SJ - MASS OL - MASS
11 ALL-FOOD SHELF COLLECTIONS SJ - MASS SH - MASS	**12** TRI - BARCOL MTG	**13** OL - MASS	**14** SJ - MASS	**15** SH-MASS	**16** SJ - MASS	**17** OL - KATERI TEKAWITHA CELEBRATION SH - MASS SJ - MASS
18 SJ - MASS SH - MASS	**19**	**20** TRI-KC'S MTG OL - MASS	**21** SJ/OL - CCW MTG SJ - MASS	**22** SH - CCW MTG SH-MASS	**23** SJ - MASS	**24** SH - MASS SJ - MASS OL-MASS
25 ALL-COLLECTION FOR DOMESTIC ABUSE CENTER SJ-MASS SH-MASS	**26**	**27** OL - MASS	**28** SJ - MASS	**29** SH-MASS	**30** SJ - MASS	**31** SH - MASS SJ - MASS OL-MASS

TRI = TRI-PARISH, CLUSTER ACTIVITY HELD IN ONE LOCATION
ALL = TRI-PARISH, CLUSTER ACTIVITY HELD IN ALL 3 PARISHES
SJ = ST. JOHN'S PARISH ACTIVITY
SH = SACRED HEART'S PARISH ACTIVITY
OL = OUR LADY'S PARISH ACTIVITY

JULY

Our Lady's Blessed Kateri Tekakwitha Celebration.
   Long before Our Lady parish was officially formed, the area was the site of missionary activity to the Native American community. The strong tie to that community still exists. Each summer, near the July 14th Feast of

Blessed Kateri Tekakwitha (the first Native American candidate for canonization), a large celebration takes place. The Saturday evening outdoor Mass with the Bishop as the celebrant has drawn as many as 1000 people. The Masses at St. John and Sacred Heart are canceled on that evening so that everyone can participate in Our Lady's celebration. Neither parish has ever complained about the cancellation of their Masses (and the lost revenue). Instead, they, like everyone else, eagerly attend and support Our Lady's Kateri celebration.

Funerals.
The Trinity Choir was formed a few years ago to assist with the music at Funeral Masses. Members from all three parishes belong to this choir. Aware of the importance of this ministry, they never hesitate to drive to any of the three parishes for rehearsals and Funeral Masses.

The women of the parish serve a luncheon in the parish center after each funeral. Because the facilities at Our Lady are limited, its funeral luncheons are served at St. John. It is not unusual to see women from St. John helping Our Lady at large funerals, or to see Our Lady's women helping St. John when St. John's women would like to attend a funeral. There is no formal arrangement between them — just a "Do-unto-others" attitude.

AUGUST

SUN	MON	TUE	WED	THU	FRI	SAT
1 SJ - MASS SH - MASS	2	3 OL - MASS	4 SJ - MASS	5 SH-MASS	6 NURSING HOME-MASS SJ - MASS	7 SJ-POLKA FEST SH - MASS SJ - MASS OL-MASS
8 ALL-FOOD SHELF COLLECTIONS SJ - MASS SH - MASS	9	10 OL - MASS/POTLUCK	11 TRI-EDUCATION COMMITTEE MTG SJ - MASS	12 TRI-LITURGY COMMITTEE MTG SH-MASS	13 SJ - MASS	14 TRI-KC'S BOOTH AT COUNTY FAIR SH - MASS SJ - MASS OL-MASS
15 TRI-KC'S BOOTH AT COUNTY FAIR SJ - MASS SH - MASS	16	17 TRI-KC'S MTG OL - MASS	18 SJ/OL - CCW MTG SJ - MASS	19 SH - CCW MTG SH-MASS	20 SJ - MASS	21 SH - MASS SJ - MASS OL-MASS
22 SJ - MASS SH - MASS	23	24 OL - MASS	25 SJ - MASS	26 SH-MASS	27 SJ - MASS	28 SH - MASS SJ - MASS OL-MASS
29 SJ - MASS SH - MASS	30	31 OL - MASS				

TRI = TRI-PARISH, CLUSTER ACTIVITY HELD IN ONE LOCATION
ALL = TRI-PARISH, CLUSTER ACTIVITY HELD IN ALL 3 PARISHES
SJ = ST. JOHN'S PARISH ACTIVITY
SH = SACRED HEART'S PARISH ACTIVITY
OL = OUR LADY'S PARISH ACTIVITY

AUGUST

St. John's Polka Fest.
  St. John's big event of the summer is usually a Polka Fest. An afternoon of activities, including a bazaar and dinner, ends with a Mass and an evening Polka dance. Parishioners, tourists, and other local residents attend the events of the day.

KCs.
  The mid-summer fund-raiser for the Tri-parish KCs is a food booth at the County Fair.

SEPTEMBER

SUN	MON	TUE	WED	THU	FRI	SAT
			1 SJ - MASS	2 SH-MASS	3 NURSING HOME-MASS SJ - MASS	4 SH - MASS SJ - MASS OL-MASS
5 SJ - MASS SH - MASS	6	7 TRI-FINANCE COUNCILS OL - MASS	8 SJ - MASS	9 TRI-PASTORAL COUNCILS SH-MASS	10 SJ - MASS	11 SJ - MASS OL-MASS
12 ALL-FOOD SHELF COLLECTIONS SH-CCD PARENTS' MTG SJ - MASS SH - MASS	13	14 OL-SCRIPTURE CLASS OL - MASS/POT LUCK	15 SJ/OL-CCW MTG SJ-SCRIPTURE CLASS SJ/OL-CCD PARENTS' MTG SJ - MASS	16 SH-CCW MTS SH-SCRIPTURE CLASS SH-MASS	17 SJ - MASS	18 SJ - MASS OL-MASS
19 TRI-PIG ROAST SJ - MASS SH - MASS	20	21 OL-SCRIPTURE CLASS TRI-KC'S MTG OL - MASS	22 SJ-SCRIPTURE CLASS TRI-CATECHISTS' INSERVICE SJ - MASS	23 SH-SCRIPTURE CLASS SH-MASS	24 SJ - MASS	25 TRI-DAY OF RECOLLECTION SJ - MASS OL-MASS
26 SH CCD ALL-CATECHETICAL SUNDAY SJ - MASS SH - MASS	27	28 OL-SCRIPTURE CLASS OL - MASS	29 SJ/OL CCD SJ-SCRIPTURE CLASS SJ - MASS	30 SH-SCRIPTURE CLASS SH-MASS		

TRI = TRI-PARISH, CLUSTER ACTIVITY HELD IN ONE LOCATION
ALL = TRI-PARISH, CLUSTER ACTIVITY HELD IN ALL 3 PARISHES
SJ = ST. JOHN'S PARISH ACTIVITY
SH = SACRED HEART'S PARISH ACTIVITY
OL = OUR LADY'S PARISH ACTIVITY

SEPTEMBER

Pig Roast.

    The Tri-Parish Pig Roast is one of the biggest social activities for the cluster. The planning committee draws its membership from all three parishes. Everyone from the cluster, including the "summer residents" (tourists), is invited. The parishes pay for the pig and the beverages although, free will donations usually cover the cost. Everyone brings a salad or desert to round out the meal.

    Volleyball and other games are held for the children and the young at heart, with small prizes given to the winners. Somehow, every child manages to "win" at something, so they all leave with a prize. Dance music for the afternoon is provided by a parishioner's band. Adjacent to the dance hall, another room is set up for those who just want to relax and converse. Horseshoes and card games complete the rest of the activities.

Since none of the parishes has adequate facilities for all these activities, a private picnic area is rented for the day. The picnic area is located between St. John and Sacred Heart, so no one has a great distance to drive. The Pig Roast has been an annual event for a number of years now. Each year new activities are added to the day and the attendance increases, as well.

Days of Recollection.

Biannually, the tri-parishes hold a week-long retreat. Sessions are held in the mornings and evenings with the locations of the sessions rotated among the three parishes. A great number of people attend all the sessions, willingly driving to each parish to participate in these spiritually rewarding moments.

In the other years, a day of recollection is held in the fall at St. John for the cluster. The day includes guest speakers, private and communal prayer, Mass, and lunch. After the busy summer months, these autumn days of recollection help people to refocus their lives.

Parents' Meeting.

As the youth education program gets under way each year, meetings are held at St. John and Sacred Heart to discuss the program and activities, and to enlist the parents' support. A social hour is also a part of the evening, giving the parents the opportunity to become better acquainted with the catechists and with each other.

Catechists' Inservice.

Before the youth religious education programs begin in the fall, all catechists gather for a day of prayer, formation, information, and informal sharing. A luncheon or potluck supper is also a part of the day's activities.

Catechetical Sunday.
The liturgy for this weekend is planned jointly, but is implemented in each parish in the way that is most meaningful to the parishioners. The catechists for the year are commissioned during the liturgy. A parish potluck or brunch follows.

Preschool.
Because St. John has the largest population of young families, it offers preschool during the Sunday morning Mass from September through May. Many of Our Lady's families participate in the preschool. Sacred Heart has only a few families with preschool children. These families are also invited to participate in the preschool program but, because of the distance to St. John, most of them do not.

St. John's 75th Anniversary.
Though this was a one-time event, it is so typical of what takes place in these parishes, that it must be mentioned. Because this was a parish, not a cluster, celebration, the planning committee was from St. John.

"Parish" means more to these parishioners than arbitrary lines drawn across the map. They are well-aware that their parish's individual history is intertwined with the other two parishes, so when they decided to honor the oldest families and parishioners in the area, they automatically thought in terms of the entire area, regardless of the parish that the people had officially joined.

Parishioners from all three parishes were very touched when the strong presence of the Catholic faith in them and their families was acknowledged. It made perfect sense to everyone there that the oldest parishioners from Our Lady and Sacred Heart were introduced alongside the parishioners from St. John... the only people who were a little confused were some of the visiting priests, who didn't understand the bond that has developed among these parishes.

A presentation of plaques to the former pastors — made "on behalf of the Webster Area Catholic Churches" — was also a part of the ceremonies. The plaques were inscribed with the names and photos of all three parishes.

It was a day in which St. John celebrated its history and acknowledged the important roles that its fellow parishes have played in that history. The strong attendance by members from all three parishes surprised no one.

OCTOBER

SUN	MON	TUE	WED	THU	FRI	SAT
					1 NURSING HOME-MASS SJ - MASS	**2** OL - ROSARY SJ - MASS OL-MASS
3 SH CCD SH - PARISH BRUNCH SJ - MASS SH - MASS	**4**	**5** OL-SCRIPTURE CLASS OL - MASS/POTLUCK OL - MASS	**6** SJ/OL CCD/RESPECT FOR LIFE MASS SJ-SCRIPTURE CLASS SJ - MASS	**7** SH-SCRIPTURE CLASS SH-MASS	**8** SJ - MASS	**9** OL - ROSARY SJ - MASS OL-MASS
10 SH CCD ALL-FOOD SHELF COLLECTION SJ - MASS SH - MASS	**11** TRI-BARCOL MTG	**12** OL-SCRIPTURE CLASS OL - MASS	**13** SJ/OL CCD SJ-SCRIPTURE CLASS TRI-EDUCATION COMMITTEE MTG SJ - MASS	**14** SH SCRIPTURE CLASS TRI-LITURGY COMMITTEE MTG SH-MASS	**15** SJ/OL-CCW RUMMAGE SALE SJ - MASS	**16** SJ/OL-CCW RUMMAGE SALE OL-ROSARY SJ - MASS OL-MASS
17 SH CCD SJ - MASS SH - MASS	**18**	**19** OL-SCRIPTURE CLASS TRI-KC'S MTG OL - MASS	**20** SJ/OL-CCW MTG SJ/OL CCD SJ-SCRIPTURE CLASS SJ - MASS	**21** SH-CCW MTG. SH-SCRIPTURE CLASS SH-MASS	**22** SJ - MASS	**23** OL - ROSARY TRI-CONFIRMATION RETREAT SJ - MASS OL- MASS
24 SH CCD ALL-COLLECTION FOR THE DOMESTIC ABUSE CENTER SJ - MASS SH - MASS	**25**	**26** OL-SCRIPTURE CLASS OL - MASS	**27** SJ/OL CCD SJ-SCRIPTURE CLASS SJ - MASS	**28** SH-SCRIPTURE CLASS SH-MASS	**29** SJ - MASS	**30** OL - ROSARY SJ - MASS OL-MASS
31 SH CCD SJ - MASS SH - MASS						

TRI = TRI-PARISH, CLUSTER ACTIVITY HELD IN ONE LOCATION
ALL = TRI-PARISH, CLUSTER ACTIVITY HELD IN ALL 3 PARISHES
SJ = ST. JOHN'S PARISH ACTIVITY
SH = SACRED HEART'S PARISH ACTIVITY
OL = OUR LADY'S PARISH ACTIVITY

OCTOBER

Education Committee.

The cluster Education Committee meets bimonthly to lend its support to the education program and youth activities. One of their ongoing projects is keeping the book and tape libraries at St. John and Sacred Heart up-to-date. Our Lady recently started a library, also, to give its parishioners immediate access to materials. Each library has a slightly different focus because of the differences in the demographics of the parishes. Parishioners from all three parishes are welcome to use the materials in each library.

Rite of Christian Initiation of Adults (RCIA).
Because of the small population base of the area, the RCIA involves only a few people each year. The meetings are held at St. John for all candidates in the cluster and their sponsors. The candidates are encouraged to also participate in either Bible Study or the Small Group Faith-Sharing meetings in their parishes.

Sacred Heart's Finger Food Sunday.
Once a month, from October through May, Sacred Heart CCW sponsors a parish brunch called "Finger Food Sunday". The brunch follows their only weekend Mass. Parishioners take turns bringing the food and doing the cleanup. Everyone at Mass, parishioners and visitors alike, is invited to attend and to spend some time socializing.

Our Lady never started monthly parish brunches because it didn't have the facilities. St. John tried having a "Coffee and Donuts" Sunday, but found that it was not fully supported by the parish. Because there are two weekend liturgies at St. John, there isn't the same opportunity for a full-parish weekend gathering at St. John like there is at Sacred Heart.

Does this mean that Sacred Heart should end their Sunday brunches because the other two parishes aren't doing the same? Absolutely not! "Cooperation" doesn't mean becoming mirror images of each other.

Respect for Life.
A special Respect for Life Liturgy is celebrated with the children of St. John and Our Lady and their families on a Wednesday afternoon following the religious education classes. A potluck supper follows the Mass. Sacred Heart's families are also encouraged to attend.

The Rosary.

Mary is the patron saint of October. She is also the patron of Our Lady parish. So, the Tri-parish KCs lead the rosary before the weekend Mass at Our Lady during this month.

Confirmation Retreat.

A Saturday retreat is held for the confirmandi from the three parishes. Because St. John has the largest number of small meeting rooms for private prayer and discussions, the retreat is usually held there.

CCW.

St. John / Our Lady CCW holds a 2-day rummage and bake sale every October. Clothing that is not sold is donated to a local agency for the needy.

NOVEMBER

SUN	MON	TUE	WED	THU	FRI	SAT
	1	2 OL-SCRIPTURE CLASS OL - MASS	3 SJ/OL CCD SJ-SCRIPTURE CLASS SJ - MASS	4 SH-SCRIPTURE CLASS SH-MASS	5 NURSING HOME-MASS SJ - MASS	6 SJ - MASS OL-MASS
7 SH CCD SH-PARISH BRUNCH SJ - MASS SH - MASS	8	9 OL-SCRIPTURE CLASS OL - MASS	10 SJ/OL CCD SJ-SCRIPTURE CLASS SJ - MASS	11 SH-SCRIPTURE CLASS TRI-PASTORAL COUNCILS SH-MASS	12 SJ - MASS	13 SJ - MASS OL-MASS
14 SH CCD ALL-FOOD SHELF COLLECTIONS SJ - MASS SH - MASS	15 TRI-CCW'S FOOD BASKETS FOR THE NEEDY	16 OL-SCRIPTURE CLASS TRI-KC'S MTG OL - MASS	17 SJ/OL-CCW MTG SJ/OL CCD SJ-SCRIPTURE CLASS SJ - MASS	18 SH-CCW MTG SH-SCRIPTURE CLASS TRI-THANKSGIVING MASS/DINNER SH-MASS	19 SJ - MASS	20 SJ - MASS OL-MASS
21 SH-CHRISTMAS CRAFT SALE SJ - MASS SH - MASS	22	23 OL - MASS	24 SJ/OL-ECUMENICAL PRAYER SERVICE SH-ECUMENICAL PRAYER SERVICE SJ - MASS	25	26 SJ - MASS	27 SJ/OL - CCW ST. NICHOLAS FANTASY SJ - MASS OL-MASS
28 SH CCD SJ/OL-CCW ST. NICHOLAS FANTASY SJ - MASS SH - MASS	29	30 OL-SCRIPTURE CLASS OL - MASS				

TRI = TRI-PARISH, CLUSTER ACTIVITY HELD IN ONE LOCATION
ALL = TRI-PARISH, CLUSTER ACTIVITY HELD IN ALL 3 PARISHES
SJ = ST. JOHN'S PARISH ACTIVITY
SH = SACRED HEART'S PARISH ACTIVITY
OL = OUR LADY'S PARISH ACTIVITY

NOVEMBER

Thanksgiving Mass and Dinner.

Sacred Heart, with its large retired population, has always been concerned about the elderly of the community. A few years ago, Sacred Heart and St. John decided to sponsor a Mass and Thanksgiving Dinner for the elderly. The Mass and dinner were scheduled for the week before Thanksgiving. Since both parishes have adequate facilities, they decided to alternate the sponsorship and location of the dinner between the two parishes. Rides were provided for anyone who wanted to attend.

It only took a couple of years for this to become a popular event for everyone of retirement age. When the decision was made to open it up to people of all ages, it was also decided that it was Our Lady's turn to sponsor the event. Because Our Lady didn't have any facilities other than the church, it was decided that the Mass and dinner would be held at St. John, but Our Lady was in charge of the plans. After only a slight hesitation, they accepted the responsibility.

Our Lady parish only had 35 registered families and many of those adults had no free time during the day, so their biggest concern in planning the meal was getting enough workers to prepare and serve it. Rather than adopting a "we'll show them" attitude, letting their pride get in the way of common sense, they called the CCWs from the other two parishes and asked for their help. On the day before the dinner, something happened in those parishes that had never happened before: Women from all three parishes stood side by side in St. John's kitchen, peeling potatoes together, cleaning turkeys together, making stuffing together, cutting up vegetables together...

It might not sound like much, but it was a turning point in their relationships. Until that time, real cooperation between St. John and Sacred Heart was usually hindered by the undercurrent of rivalry between the two parishes. At social activities, the one parish was always treated like the "guest" of the other parish — a friendly, but distant relationship. Never would the parishioners of one parish have considered infringing on the other's territory by helping — or asking for help — in major matters.

Our Lady managed to wipe out the boundaries, in part because, as the smallest of the three parishes, it was not a threat to the other two. More importantly, though, the stage had been set by all the previous activities. The parishes were ready to take the step from external actions to an internal commitment. Our Lady's request for help, and the camaraderie that everyone experienced as they worked together that morning, made them understand for the first time that there was no need to view each other as adversaries and the remaining walls came tumbling down.

Thanksgiving Baskets.
Sacred Heart CCW and the neighboring Lutheran church prepare and deliver Thanksgiving food baskets for the needy of the entire cluster area.

Ecumenical Thanksgiving Services.
Two ecumenical prayer services are held on the day before Thanksgiving. One is sponsored by Sacred Heart and its neighboring Lutheran church, the other is sponsored by the churches around St. John and Our Lady. The sites of the prayer services rotate among the participating churches, with all the pastors and congregations sharing in the duties.

Advent Fair.
St. John / Our Lady CCW holds a St. Nicholas' Fantasy each year. This advent fair includes a bazaar with crafts, a bake sale, new and used gift items, the viewing of children's videos, lunch and dinner. The fair runs the entire weekend in the parish center at St. John.

Christmas Craft Sale.
On a different weekend from St. John's and Our Lady's St. Nicholas' Fantasy, Sacred Heart's Pastoral Council holds a craft and bake sale in its parish center. All proceeds go to missionary activities.

DECEMBER

SUN	MON	TUE	WED	THU	FRI	SAT
			1 SJ/OL CCD SJ-SCRIPTURE CLASS SJ - MASS	**2** SH-SCRIPTURE CLASS SH-MASS	**3** NURSING HOME-MASS SJ - MASS	**4** SJ - MASS OL-MASS
5 SH CCD SH-PARISH BRUNCH SJ - MASS SH - MASS	**6** ALL-MAIL CHRISTMAS CARDS	**7** OL-SCRIPTURE CLASS OL - MASS/POTLUCK	**8** SJ/OL CCD SJ-SCRIPTURE CLASS TRI-EDUCATION COMMITTEE MTG. SJ - MASS	**9** SH-SCRIPTURE CLASS TRI-LITURGY COMMITTEE MTG SH-MASS	**10** SJ - MASS	**11** SJ - MASS OL-MASS
12 SH CCD/PARTY ALL-FOOD SHELF COLLECTION SJ - MASS SH - MASS	**13**	**14** OL-COMMUNAL PENANCE SERVICE OL - MASS	**15** SJ/OL-CCW MTG SJ/OL CCD/PARTY SJ - MASS	**16** SH-CCW MTG SJ-COMMUNAL PENANCE SERVICE SH-COMMUNAL PENANCE SERVICE SH-MASS	**17** SJ - MASS	**18** SJ - MASS OL-MASS
19 SJ - MASS SH - MASS	**20**	**21** TRI-KC'S MTG OL - MASS	**22** SJ - MASS	**23** SH-MASS	**24** TRI-CHRISTMAS EVE MASS/PARTY SJ - MASS	**25** SH - MASS SJ - MASS OL - MASS
26 SJ - MASS SH - MASS	**27**	**28** OL - MASS	**29** SJ - MASS	**30** SH-MASS	**31** SJ - MASS	

TRI = TRI-PARISH, CLUSTER ACTIVITY HELD IN ONE LOCATION
ALL = TRI-PARISH, CLUSTER ACTIVITY HELD IN ALL 3 PARISHES
SJ = ST. JOHN'S PARISH ACTIVITY
SH = SACRED HEART'S PARISH ACTIVITY
OL = OUR LADY'S PARISH ACTIVITY

DECEMBER

Social Concerns.

During the holiday season, the parishes sponsor a number of area families providing food, clothing, and Christmas gifts for those in need. They also have Mitten Trees in each parish, collecting mittens, hats, and scarfs for the needy.

Christmas cards.

Artistic members of Sacred Heart parish design a Christmas card each year for three parishes. The cards are sent to all the "summer parishioners" of the three parishes — the tourists who so faithfully support the parishes while staying at their summer cabins or taking summer vacations in the area. The CCWs take charge of addressing and mailing the Christmas cards.

Communal Penance Services.

Communal Penances Services are held in all three parishes shortly before Christmas. The days and times of the services are varied — early afternoon, late afternoon, and evening — so at least one service will fit into everyone's schedule.

Youth Religious Education.

A short program followed by a chili supper is held at St. John for St. John's and Our Lady's religious education students in grades 1-6 and their families after the last class of the semester.

On the Sunday before Christmas, the students in grades 7-12 and their families gather at St. John to decorate the church. They then spend the afternoon caroling, and they end the day with a pizza supper. Students from Sacred Heart are encouraged to participate in these activities.

Christmas Masses.

Masses are held in all three parishes on either Christmas Eve or Christmas Day, but the big Tri-parish celebration is on Christmas Eve at St. John. Musicians from the high school and former parishioners who have returned for the holidays join the musicians from the three parishes to make this a celebration that is not to be missed.

After the Mass, everyone is invited to a social hour with coffee and Christmas cookies in the "cluster's" parish center at St. John. Besides sharing their Christmas joy, this gathering provides everyone with the opportunity to say good-bye to the "snowbirds" who will be escaping the cold Wisconsin winter for a few months.

CHAPTER IX:

A CLOSING THOUGHT

A few years ago at a diocesan meeting, parish representatives were asked to list all the activities that their parishes were involved in during the course of one year. When the lists were finished, one representative from each parish was asked to read their list outloud to everyone present.

Since the parishioners from the Webster Area Catholic Churches were sitting near the front, their representative was the first to speak. After their extensive list was read, no other parishioners would volunteer to read their lists.

During the next break, people approached the Webster group and asked them if it was true that their parish was involved in all of those parish and community activities. They just couldn't see how any parish could possibly be doing that much. A Webster parishioner responded, "You're right. No parish could, but a cluster can!"

APPENDIX A:

Tally of pastors' answers to the questionnaire

This questionnaire was sent to the pastors of clustered parishes in the Diocese of Superior. Next to each question, the tally of the answers is also listed.

A Survey of Clustered Parishes in the Diocese of Superior

Purposes:
A. To determine what level of cooperation currently exists among clustered parishes.
B. To determine what level of cooperation is considered to be the most desirable by the pastors of clustered parishes.
C. To determine which activities/attitudes/actions lead to the optimum level of cooperation.

Areas under study:
1. Religious Education
2. Sacramental Preparation
3. Pastoral and Finance Councils
4. Liturgy Committee
5. Other Committees
6. Lay Organizations
7. Social Activities
8. Staff

RELIGIOUS EDUCATION

Out of 21 clusters:
- __4__ Each parish plans its own Adult Ed program.
  - 2 pastors prefer that method.
  - 2 pastors prefer centralized planning.
- __9__ Centralized Adult Ed planning is done.
  - All 9 pastors prefer that method.
- __3__ A combination of individual and centralized planning is done.
  - All 3 pastors prefer centralized planning.
- __5__ No response.

- __8__ Each parish holds its own Adult Ed classes.
  - 4 pastors prefer that method.
  - 4 pastors prefer centralized classes.
- __8__ Centralized Adult Ed classes are held for the cluster.
  - All 8 pastors prefer that method.
- __1__ A combination of individual and centralized classes are held.
  - The pastor prefers that method.
- __4__ No response.

- __1__ Each parish plans its own RCIA program.
  - The pastor prefers that method.
- __17__ Centralized RCIA planning is done for the entire cluster.
  - All 17 pastors prefer that method.
- __3__ No response.

- __2__ Each parish holds its own RCIA formation meetings.
  - Both pastors prefer that method.
- __13__ Centralized RCIA formation meetings are held for the cluster.
  - All 13 pastors prefer that method.
- __6__ No response.

__9__ Each parish plans its own Youth Education program.
        6 pastors prefer that method.
        3 pastors prefer that centralized planning is done.

__9__ Centralized Youth Education planning is done for the cluster.
        All 9 pastors prefer that method.

__2__ A combination of individual and centralized planning is done.
        Both pastors prefer that centralized planning is done.

__1__ No response.

__12__ Each parish holds its own Youth Education classes.
        6 pastors prefer that method.
        6 pastors prefer that centralized classes are held.
        5 parishes hold their own teacher in-service.
        6 parishes hold centralized teacher in-service.
        All 11 pastors prefer centralized teacher in-service.

__6__ Centralized Youth Education classes are held for the cluster.
        All 6 pastors prefer that method.

__2__ A combination of individual and centralized classes are held.
        Both pastors prefer that method.

__1__ No response.

SACRAMENTAL PREPARATION
Out of 21 clusters:
- __5__ Each parish holds its own Baptism preparation classes.
    - 3 pastors prefer that method.
- __14__ Centralized Baptism preparation classes are held.
    - All 14 pastors prefer that method.
- __2__ No response.
    - Both pastors prefer centralized Baptism classes.

- __7__ Each parish holds its own First Reconciliation classes.
    - 5 pastors prefer that method.
    - 2 pastors prefer centralized classes.
- __14__ Centralized First Reconciliation preparation classes are held.
    - All 14 pastors prefer that method.

- __9__ Each parish holds its own First Eucharist preparation classes.
    - 6 pastors prefer that method.
    - 3 pastors prefer centralized classes.
- __12__ Centralized First Eucharist preparation classes are held.
    - All 12 pastors prefer that method.

- __5__ Each parish holds its own Confirmation preparation classes.
    - 3 pastors prefer that method.
- __14__ Centralized Confirmation preparation classes are held.
    - All 14 pastors prefer that method.
- __1__ A combination of individual and centralized classes are held.
    - The pastor prefers that method.
- __1__ No response.
    - The pastor prefers centralized classes.

_19_ Baptisms are celebrated in each parish.
   All 19 pastors prefer that method.
_1_ Individual and centralized Baptisms are celebrated.
   The pastor prefers that each parish celebrates its Baptisms.
_1_ No response.
   The pastor prefers that each parish celebrates its Baptisms.

_15_ First Reconciliation is celebrated in each parish.
   14 pastors prefer that method.
_6_ Centralized First Reconciliation is celebrated in the cluster.
   All 6 pastors prefer that method.

_18_ First Eucharist is celebrated in each parish.
   All 18 pastors prefer that method.
_2_ Centralized First Eucharist is celebrated for the cluster.
   Both pastors prefer that method.
_1_ Individual and centralized First Eucharist is celebrated.
   The pastor prefers that method.

_1_ Confirmations are celebrated in each parish.
   The pastor prefers that method.
_20_ Centralized Confirmations are celebrated for the cluster.
   17 pastors prefer that method.
   3 pastors prefer that each parish celebrates Confirmation.

PASTORAL and FINANCE COUNCILS

Out of 21 clusters:

__21__   Each parish has a Pastoral Council.

__11__   The Pastoral Councils never meet together.
   3 pastors prefer that they never meet together.
   5 pastors prefer that they sometimes meet together.
   2 pastors prefer that they always meet together.

__9__   The Pastoral Councils sometimes meet together.
   7 pastors prefer that they sometimes meet together.
   1 pastor prefers that they always meet together.

__1__   The Pastoral Councils always meet together.
   The pastor prefers that method.

__21__   Each parish has a Finance Council.

__13__   The Finance Councils never meet together.
   4 pastors prefer that they never meet together.
   5 pastors prefer that they sometimes meet together.
   1 pastor prefers that they always meet together.

__8__   The Finance Councils sometimes meet together.
   All 8 pastors prefer this method.

_21_ All parishes pay a portion of the priest's salary.

_1_ The Mother parish pays all the expenses for the rectory.
_19_ All parishes share in the expenses for the rectory.
_1_ No response.

_20_ All parishes pay a portion of the salaries of cluster staff.
_1_ No response.

_20_ All parishes share in the expenses for cluster programs.
_1_ No response.

Criteria for sharing the cluster expenses:
_1_ Size of parish and income.
_11_ Size of parish.
_2_ Income.
_1_ Expenses, including building debt.
_2_ Distance/time involved.
_4_ No response.

LITURGY COMMITTEE

Out of 21 clusters:
- __4__ There is one cluster-wide Liturgy Committee.
- _10_ Each parish has its own Liturgy Committee.
- __7__ Some of the parishes have a Liturgy Committee.

The committees meet together to plan weekend liturgies:
- __7__ never
- __9__ sometimes
- __1__ usually

  The pastor prefers that they meet together:
  - __8__ sometimes
  - __6__ usually
  - __3__ always

The committees meet together to plan Holyday liturgies:
- __7__ never
- __4__ sometimes
- __5__ usually
- __1__ always

  The pastor prefers that they meet together:
  - __6__ sometimes
  - __6__ usually
  - __5__ always

The committees meet together to plan Christmas / Advent:
- __7__ never
- __5__ usually
- __5__ always

  The pastor prefers that they meet together:
  - __1__ never
  - __4__ sometimes
  - __3__ usually
  - __9__ always

The committees meet together to plan Easter/ Holy Week:
___6___ always
___4___ usually
___7___ never
    The pastor prefers that they meet together:
    ___10___ always
    ___3___ usually
    ___3___ sometimes
    ___1___ never

The committees meet together to plan Communion Services:
___2___ usually
___3___ sometimes
___12___ never
    The pastor prefers that they meet together:
    ___2___ always
    ___4___ usually
    ___4___ sometimes
    ___7___ never

The committees meet together to plan Reconciliations:
___2___ usually
___5___ sometimes
___10___ never
    The pastor prefers that they meet together:
    ___4___ always
    ___5___ usually
    ___6___ sometimes
    ___2___ never

The committees meet together to plan Prayer Services:
___4___ usually
___4___ sometimes
___9___ never
    The pastor prefers that they meet together:
    ___2___ always
    ___7___ usually
    ___5___ sometimes
    ___3___ never

EDUCATION COMMITTEE

Out of 21 clusters:
- __6__ There is one cluster-wide Education Committee.
- __9__ Each parish has its own Education Committee.
- __5__ Some of the parishes have Education Committees.

- __6__ The Education Committees never meet together.
- __5__ They sometimes meet together.
- __2__ They usually meet together.
- __1__ They always meet together.

- __7__ The pastor prefers that they sometimes meet together.
- __7__ The pastor prefers that they usually meet together.
- __2__ The pastor prefers that they always meet together.

SOCIAL CONCERNS COMMITTEE

Out of 21 clusters:
- __4__ There is one cluster-wide Social Concerns Committee.
- __8__ Each parish has its own committee.
- __7__ Some of the parishes have Social Concerns Committees.

- __9__ The Social Concerns Committees never meet together.
- __4__ They sometimes meet together.
- __0__ They usually meet together.
- __2__ They always meet together.

- __1__ The pastor prefers that they never meet together.
- __10__ The pastor prefers that they sometimes meet together.
- __2__ The pastor prefers that they usually meet together.
- __2__ The pastor prefers that they always meet together.

LAY ORGANIZATIONS

Out of 21 clusters:

_12_ There is one cluster-wide KC organization.
_1_ Each parish has a KC organization.
_4_ Some of the parishes have a KC organization.

_1_ The KCs sometimes meet together.
_4_ The KCs never meet together.

_2_ The pastor prefers that they usually meet together.
_1_ The pastor prefers that they sometimes meet together.

_1_ There is one cluster-wide CCW.
_13_ Each parish has its own CCW.
_4_ Some of the parishes have a CCW.

_1_ The CCWs always meet together.
_1_ The CCWs usually meet together.
_6_ The CCWs sometimes meet together.
_9_ The CCWs never meet together.

_3_ The pastor prefers that they always meet together.
_2_ The pastor prefers that they usually meet together.
_9_ The pastor prefers that they sometimes meet together.
_1_ The pastor prefers that they never meet together.

SOCIAL ACTIVITIES

Out of 21 clusters:
When one parish has a social activity, how often are members from the other parishes in the cluster invited?
__11__ always
__4__ usually
__5__ sometimes
__1__ never

How often does the pastor prefer to see the other parishes invited?
__12__ always
__4__ usually
__5__ sometimes
__0__ never

Currently, there are:
__2__ No cluster social activities in a year.
__1__ 1 cluster social activity each year.
__8__ 2 or 3 cluster social activities each year.
__9__ 4 or 5 cluster social activities each year.
__1__ 10 or more cluster social activities each year.

The pastor prefers:
__1__ No cluster social activities in a year.
__4__ 2 or 3 cluster social activities each year.
__8__ 4 or 5 cluster social activities each year.
__4__ 6 cluster social activities each year.
__4__ 10 or more cluster social activities each year.

STAFF (Excluding the pastor)

Out of 21 clusters:
- __7__ There are no deacons in the cluster.
- __8__ One parish has a deacon / deacon candidate.
- __5__ More than one parish has a deacon / deacon candidate.
- __1__ All the parishes have a deacon.

- __11__ The deacon(s) serves the entire cluster.
- __12__ The pastor prefers that the deacon(s) serves the entire cluster.

- __2__ Each parish has its own office staff.
- __15__ One office staff serves the entire cluster.
- __5__ Some office staff members serve the entire cluster.

- __1__ The pastor prefers that each parish has its own office staff.
- __14__ The pastor prefers that one office staff serves the entire cluster.
- __5__ The pastor prefers that some office staff members serve the cluster.

- __21__ Each parish has its own maintenance staff (paid or volunteer).
- __20__ The pastor prefers that each parish has its own maintenance staff.
- __1__ The pastor prefers that some maintenance staff members serve the cluster.

APPENDIX B:

Cluster Commissioning of Liturgical Ministers

This recommissioning service for the liturgical ministers in a parish cluster demonstrates a blending of a cluster focus with an individual parish focus. It is written for a cluster of three parishes, but could be modified to include any number of parishes.

The church is dark except for reading lights by the ambo and lectern and a few aisle lights for safe movement around the church. One large, lighted candle is in the sanctuary. Seven other large candles are positioned nearby.

The pastor, a deacon, if possible, and one representative from each parish lead the prayer service. An organist and choir or cantor provide the music.

The liturgical ministers who are going to be recommissioned gather in the parish center. Everyone is given an unlit votive candle on which is painted a symbol of their ministry. These candles will be lit during the prayer service. The liturgical ministers quietly move into the darkened church as the choir begins the gathering song.

Gathering Music: "Holy Ground" by John Michael Talbot (organ and choir only, softly)

Parish #1 Leader: The Spirit enriches our lives by giving us his gifts and then calls them forth for the benefit of the whole community. As we respond to his gifts we begin to recognize that we must use them in the service of others.

All: There are different gifts, but the same Spirit; there are different ministries, but the same Lord.

[Deacon lights three candles as the parish names are read.]

Parish #2 Leader: Lord, our God, give us your grace and blessings as we prepare to take our gifts into your communities of faith at St. John the Baptist, Sacred Heart of Jesus and Mary, and Our Lady of Perpetual Help.

All: There are different gifts, but the same Spirit; there are different ministries, but the same Lord.

[Deacon lights four candles, symbolizing the four liturgical ministries, while 1 Cor 12:4-11 is read.]

Parish #3 Leader: There are different abilities to perform service, but the same God gives ability to everyone for their service. The Spirit's presence is shown in some way in each one, for the good of all. The Spirit gives one person a message of wisdom, while to another the same spirit gives a message of knowledge. One and the same Spirit gives faith to one person, while to another he gives the power to heal. The Spirit gives one person the power to work miracles; to another, the gift of speaking God's message; and to yet another, the ability to tell the difference between gifts that come from the Spirit and those that do not. To one person he gives the ability to speak in strange tongues, and to another he gives the ability to explain what is said. But it is one and the same Spirit who produces all these gifts, distributing them individually to each person as he wishes.

All: There are different gifts, but the same Spirit; there are different ministries, but the same Lord.

[As each group is called, the ministers come forward into the sanctuary. The parish leaders light their votive candles.]

Deacon: Would all the greeters and ushers please come forward?

Pastor: Lord of the Eternal Feast, help these greeters and ushers to welcome all with reverence and friendliness. May they perform their duties with hospitality and dignity for they represent not only these parish communities but Your Kingdom as well. We ask you this through Christ our Lord.

Ushers/greeters: Amen.

Deacon: Would all the lectors please come forward?

Pastor: Lord, invest these lectors with your power as they proclaim the marvel of your message. Free them of excessive concern over their performance, turning these apprehensions into an energy for proclaiming your Word with power and authority. We ask you this through Christ our Lord.

Lectors: Amen.

Deacon: Would all the sacristans and Eucharistic ministers please come forward?

Pastor: Lord, fill the hearts of these sacristans and Eucharistic ministers with awe and wonder for the Divine Mystery that takes place at your altar-table. Free them from any vanity or pride that might divorce them from their sacred duty as they share the Body and Blood of Christ with their brothers and sisters. We ask you this through Christ our Lord.

Sacristans / Eucharistic Ministers: Amen.

Deacon: Would all the musicians and singers please come forward?

Pastor: Lord, make these musicians and singers your sacred instruments. Free them of pride and of any desire to bring attention to themselves so the Divine Melody may be heard beneath each song and beneath every expression of their talents. We ask you this through Christ our Lord.
Musicians/Singers: Amen.

Deacon: On behalf of our parish communities, I thank each of you for generously sharing your gifts through these ministries. May God, in the fullness of the Divine Heart, bless, reward, and be ever present to each of you.
with Pastor: In the name of the Father, and of the Son, and of the Holy Spirit.

All: Amen.

Closing Song: "Here I Am, Lord" by Dan Schutte (all sing).

BIBLIOGRAPHY

Broderick, Robert C. The Catholic Encyclopedia. Nashville: Thomas Nelson Publishers, 1987.

Decree on the Apostolate of Lay People (Apostolicam Actuositatem). Vatican II, 18 November, 1965.

Johnson, Douglas W. Vitality Means Church Growth. Nashville: Abingdon Press, 1989.

Official Catholic Directory. New Providence NJ: P. J. Kenedy and Sons, 1992.

Quinn, Bernard. The Small Rural Parish. Washington: Glenmary Research Center, 1980.

Pope John Paul II. The Vocation and the Mission of the Lay Faithful in the Church and the World (Christifideles Laici). Washington: USCC, 1988.

Pope Paul VI. On Evangelization in the Modern World (Evangelii Nuntiandi). Washington: USCC, 1975.

INDEX

adult formation: 16, 18, 68-70, 79, 84, 86, 90, 97-98, 110, 112-113
advantages: 15, 31-39
baptism: 16-17, 89, 112-113
bookkeeper: 29, 36
calendar: 33, 76-107
catechists: 16-17, 19, 68, 78, 88, 90, 97
CCW (Council of Catholic Women): 26-27, 65, 68, 77, 80, 88, 90, 101-102, 105-106, 119
cemetery: 13
Christifideles Laici: 57-58
christian values: 37-39
Christmas: 27, 66-67, 76, 106-107
cluster (definition): 11
collaboration: 12-13
committees: 23-26, 77, 82-83, 100-101, 116-118
confirmation: 19, 51, 68, 88, 102, 112-113
cooperation (definition): 12
councils: see Pastoral or Finance Council
CRE (Coordinator of Religious Education): 36, 78
deacon: 16-17, 29, 121
Decree on the Apostolate of the Lay People: 44
developing cooperation: 59-72
diocesan support: 50
Diocese of Superior: 7, 11, 73
disadvantages in cooperation: 15, 41-46
distance: 7, 19, 47-48
DRE (Director of Religious Education): 16-17, 29, 36, 80
examples of cooperation: 13-14, 16-19, 21-28, 33-36, 38-39, 45, 48-52, 55
feast day celebrations: 28, 80, 84, 92-93
Finance Council: 20, 22-23, 80, 88, 90-91, 114
finances: 22, 36, 51, 53, 77, 115

First Eucharist: 16-18, 87, 112-113
First Reconciliation: 16, 17, 85, 112-113
food baskets: 25
interviews: 7, 15
KCs (Knights of Columbus): 26-28, 80, 83, 87-88, 95, 102, 119
liturgy: 23, 25-26, 29, 32, 34-35, 43, 68, 70, 82-86, 91, 94, 98, 101, 107, 116-117, 122-125
local traditions: 41-42
maintenance staff: 29, 62
mission parish (definition): 11-12
mother parish (definition): 11-12
national support: 50
obstacles to cooperation: 38, 47-58
On Evangelization in the Modern World: 39
parochial viewpoint: 9, 37, 49, 56-58, 64, 70
pastoral assistant: 29
Pastoral Council: 20-22, 61, 65, 80, 88, 105, 114
Pope John Paul II: 57-58
Pope Paul VI: 39
questionnaire: 7-8, 15, 109-123
RCIA: 16-17, 101
religious education: 13-14, 19, 23-24, 38, 68-70, 78, 83, 90, 101, 107, 110-111
RENEW: 32-33, 35, 37, 69, 79-80, 82-83
scheduling activities: 13, 17-18, 33
social activities: 28, 48, 50, 55, 65-68, 76, 78, 84, 92, 95-99, 101, 105, 120
social concerns: 23, 25, 77, 83, 85, 87-88, 105-106
staff: 29, 36-37, 39, 121
steps in developing cooperation: 65-72
tape library: 24
Thanksgiving: 25, 103-105
time, talent, treasure: 31-36
urban parishes: 9
World Day of Prayer: 86
youth education: see religious education

BROTHER'S KEEPER

R.W.K. CLARK

Copyright © 2016 R.W.K. Clark
All rights reserved, www.rwkclark.com
r@rwkclark.com

This is a work of fiction. All names, characters, locales, and incidents are the product of the author's imagination and any resemblance to actual people, places or events is coincidental or fictionalized.
Published in the United States by Clarkltd.
Po Box 45313 Rio Rancho, NM 87174

United States Copyright Office
TX8-286-924 June 2016
1-11057536966 Dec 2021

Library of Congress Control Number
2017907157

/220105

ACKNOWLEDGMENTS

I dedicate this novel to my wonderful readers and for all the amazing people I've met and those I haven't. To my family and loved ones, all your support will not be forgotten.

This book was made possible by reviews from readers like you.

Thank you

CHAPTER
ONE

Carly Reed squinted through the darkness at the road before her. She was leaning as close to the windshield of her Beetle as she could, her chin practically resting on her hands as they gripped the steering wheel. She hated driving at night, but she lost time visiting Aunt Belle earlier in the day, and she couldn't afford to lose more by pulling off the road until dawn. Her big job interview was at 10:30 a.m. the following morning, and if her calculations were correct, she was going to have to drive through the entire night just to get there on time. She realized she hadn't thought this through very well.

The road was deserted except for her. There were very few lights along the two-lane highway, allowing her to catch an extra glimpse here and there. She looked down at the gauges on her dashboard: a quarter tank of gas left. It should get her to the next town, whatever it's called. She would gas up there for the last time, she decided.

Carly's eyes felt like they were getting heavy. It was getting increasingly difficult to keep them from slamming shut. She cursed herself for being in this position. She had been driving all day, and it was just after one in the morning according to the clock on the dash. She probably shouldn't be pushing it, but she figured she could load up on coffee while she filled up the tank.

She reached for the knob on the radio without looking away from the road. Better! The car was filled with the sound of pop music, doing its job to wake her up just enough to get by. How far away was the next town, anyway? The road never seemed to end, and now there were cornfields on either side of the road. It made her feel boxed in.

Finally! Her headlights picked up the green and white highway sign just a short distance away. As she got closer, she read the sign out loud. "Burdensville 10 miles." Whew, Carly sighed. "It's about damn time."

She relaxed seeing that she had more than enough gas to make it ten more miles. But the feeling was very short-lived. A loud boom suddenly filled the air, startling her to the core. The Beetle began to fight against her control. She gripped the steering wheel as it jerked from left to right. Against her guidance, the tiny car began to careen sideways. It took every muscle she had in her small frame to maintain control of the vehicle.

Suddenly, the car came to a stop. It was partially in the road, with its back end on the shoulder in the gravel. Carly's heart was pounding, and her breath was erratic. She had no idea what just happened. Did she hit something?

Her hands and feet were shaking as she looked up and down the highway. She saw no headlights coming from either direction. The only light on this stretch was coming from the Beetle's headlights. It was unnerving, but she knew she had to get out and see what happened. She just prayed she didn't hit an animal, *or worse*.

Carly reached into the tiny back seat and grabbed her industrial-sized flashlight. As she opened the door, she turned the light on, thankful she recently replaced the batteries. Its brightness filled the car and illuminated the ground next to it. She slowly stepped out of the Beetle, looking cautiously up and down the highway for approaching vehicles.

She shined the light on the front driver's side tire, then the rear. Next, she walked to the passenger side. Thankful, and ticked at the same time, she could see the rear tire was blown. More like completely shredded. Damn, she hated dealing with things like this, especially in the middle of the night in a strange place.

She walked back to the driver's side and leaned into the car to turn off the engine and get the keys. Soon, she was staring into the hatch at her spare. "What the hell!" It was just as flat as the one that had blown.

"Damn it!" She stomped her foot on the ground and threw her head back. She felt the tears of frustration coming. It wasn't going to do any good to start crying now, but it was hard to hold back. She struggled to get her wits about her so she could deal with the problem before her.

Carly shut the hatch and fetched her duffle bag out of the Beetle's back seat. She was going to have to start walking. After locking the car doors, she pulled her smartphone out of her pocket. She would call roadside service and have it towed to Burdensville, where she could have the flat fixed and get back on the road as soon as possible.

But the cell wasn't getting a signal, none whatsoever. After shaking her head in disgust, she put the phone back in her pocket. She would have to deal with it when she got there. Carly began to walk up the highway, her duffle bag slung over her shoulder.

She shined the flashlight in front of her. Her mind was racing as she thought about the interview in the morning. It was her first since graduating college. The position was to teach second grade, and she was beyond excited about it. The thought of missing this interview over a flat tire made her furious with herself, so much so that she felt like throwing up. She peeled her ears and listened for sounds. But there weren't any. Not even a random coyote or anything. It felt quite... dead.

Carly walked for the next half-hour and even began to hum to herself to take her mind off her problems. She had given up the hope that anyone would drive by; after all, it was just after two now.

No sooner had she pushed that thought from her mind when she heard the rumbling of a car. It was loud, like it was missing its muffler. She looked over her shoulder with a glimmer of hope. Sure enough, a vehicle was coming. But it only had one headlight... either a motorcycle or a car with just one. In the darkness, she couldn't be sure.

She turned all the way around towards it, letting her flashlight shine in the direction the vehicle was coming from. Then Carly felt her hip pocket; yes, her pocketknife was there. She breathed a sigh of relief for carrying one.

The vehicle was closer now, and it was definitely a car. She began to wave her hands over her head as it neared, and soon the loud old beast slowed and pulled up beside her.

There was a man behind the wheel. He leaned over to roll the passenger side window down to talk to her after he turned on the dome light in his car. "Are you broke down?"

"Yes!" Carly replied eagerly. "You can't believe how happy I am to see you."

She silently took note of his appearance. He had thinning hair that could only be described as dishwater blonde, and he wore wire-rim glasses. Going with her gut instinct, he looked harmless enough.

"Well," the man said, "I'm going into Burdensville. I can take you there, but there ain't nothin' gonna be open this time of night." He coughed into his fist and cleared his throat. "There's a roadside inn just out of town, though. You could hole up there 'til mornin'."

Damn it! Carly thought. She was going to have to reschedule this interview, and she hated to have to do things like that. She shook her head in frustration. "Do you mind if I ride into Burdensville with you?"

"Don't mind at all!" The man's voice was slurring a bit, but she hardly noticed. She was just so relieved that anyone came to her rescue at all. She wasn't about to complain who.

He reached over and popped the lock on the passenger door. Carly hopped in the front seat without concern. She put the flashlight and duffle bag on the floor at her feet and then buckled her seatbelt. "Thanks again, mister. You are a real life saver."

"No problem," he said, smiling a friendly smile at her. With that, he turned off the dome light, and they were soon driving up the dark two-lane highway.

The man cleared his throat again. "So, what-cha doin' out here alone, ayuh?"

Carly let out a sigh. "I have a job interview in the morning. I was just trying to make good time."

They drove in silence for a while. Carly was busy mentally lining up her priorities and to-do list. She wouldn't have the luxury of time from here on out. She needed to be ready to take action first thing in the morning.

"If you want, you could stay on the sofa at my house," the man said.

She heard him but didn't hear what he said. She tuned back in to the present moment. "I'm sorry, I didn't mean to ignore you. What was that again?"

His voice took on a new tone, somewhere between agitation and frustration. "I said, you can stay on my sofa if you like." Yes, she thought, there's definitely an edge to his voice.

"Thank you, but I think I'll just get a room if it's all the same. I appreciate the offer though."

Silence again. Carly took notice of the next highway sign.

Burdensville 2 miles.

No sooner had they passed the sign when the man began to slow down the old vehicle. He took a right onto a narrow gravel road.

"Isn't the town straight ahead?" Carly asked as her heart began to pound.

He glanced at her out of the corner of his eye. "I'm just taking a shortcut to the motel."

Suddenly, the driver swung his right arm violently at Carly, his hand giving her throat a jab that could only be described as a karate chop. Carly grabbed at her throat and struggled to take in air, but all she could get was a gurgle. Fear set fully in, and she began to claw at the seat belt, still struggling to breathe. She grabbed the handle to the door and pulled it, causing the car door to swing open, then she flung herself from the vehicle. She wanted out, no matter what the price.

Carly hit the gravel hard, her body skidding for several feet. The rocks tore the flesh on her face and right arm, and she saw stars as she squawked for breath. She began to pull herself along the gravel.

She didn't hear anything at first, and the thought of the car coming back had not entered her mind. She was in shock, and all she could think about was getting to the road. Then she heard them. Footsteps in the gravel, and they were coming toward her. She tried to pick up the pace, but she was badly injured.

"Now, why didja have to go and do that?" She heard the man's voice clearly; he was right beside her. "Oh, well. It does make things easier on me, so I s'pose I owe you a thankee."

He reached down and grabbed her by her shirt, catching some of her hair behind her head. He violently threw her onto her back and began to unbutton his pants. "I s'pose this spot is good as any, girlie."

The man was on her then. Shock escalating deep

within her organs and bloodstream. She could barely breathe, let along fight him off. The knife was no longer an option, and she felt herself give in to the inevitable. She was barely aware that he was inside of her, his hand around her neck, squeezing the life out of her.

By the time he finished raping her, she was dead. He tossed her body in the ditch alongside the road, then made his way back to his car, singing as he went.

CHAPTER
TWO

The Goldline passenger train sped down the tracks noisily, drowning out the sound of the music they were pumping through the speakers. The sun was just beginning to rise in the sky, and some of its rays danced playfully through the windows of the train cars.

Scott Sharp was sleeping when the rays began to beat down on his face. His eyes fluttered open, and he looked out the window. The countryside flew by as the train made progress to its next destination. It was quiet on the train, and if the sun hadn't come, Scott might have slept right through the next stop. He was hungry and decided the night before that he would eat in the town of Burdensville.

Scott had been traveling for nearly a year on his own, ever since Kelly died. Kelly was his wife for two years but his girlfriend since high school. She was funny, smart, and breathtakingly beautiful. But cancer robbed him of her. When she finally passed, after everything they'd been through, he couldn't help but feel relief along with the grief. The guilt of that fact made looking in the mirror unbearable. He took off, giving up their cute little bungalow, and began to go wherever the road took him. He would know when the time was right to stop and go home.

As of today, the time still wasn't right. He rubbed his eyes as he tried to force the image of his Kelly out of his mind. His stomach growled loudly, giving him something else to think about for a split second. It didn't matter though; his mind was back on Kelly in no time at all.

"SCOTT, I WENT TO THE DOCTOR FOR MY YEARLY physical today," she told him over supper.

He scooped some mashed potatoes on his plate. "Yeah? How'd it go?"

Kelly had begun playing with her food. When she didn't respond right away, he looked up at her. She had a tear running down her face.

"Kelly, what is it?"

She cleared her throat and wiped her eyes. "He found a few lumps."

Scott absentmindedly put his fork down, his eyes not leaving her face. "What do you mean, he found a few lumps?"

Kelly sat back in her chair. "I have an appointment with the oncologist on Monday at Coos General for a biopsy."

"So, it could be nothing, right?" he asked.

Kelly shook her head. "I don't think so."

Kelly's mother, aunt on her mother's side, and one of her sisters had all suffered from breast cancer. Her sister had a mastectomy last year, but her mother and aunt were both gone, victims of the dread disease. Kelly knew the odds were stacked against her.

"I'm trying not to get all worked up, though. It could still be early enough to stop," she picked up her fork and continued to play with her food. Scott could tell by the sound of her voice that she wasn't convinced.

He stood up and walked over to her, where he knelt on the floor beside her. He stayed there, holding her while they both cried. He knew that no matter what happened he wouldn't leave her side.

Kelly was finally able to lift her head and look him in the eye. "Don't leave me, Scott."

"Oh, Kelly," he had replied. "I will never leave you, babe. Never."

THE PORTER APPEARED IN THE CAR'S DOORWAY. "We'll be stopping in Burdensville in approximately ten minutes, ladies and gentlemen. For those of you continuing on, you'll have a ninety-minute window to eat or shop before we re-board. Thank you for riding Goldline."

As quickly as he appeared, he disappeared, and Scott looked around the car. Ladies and gentlemen? There was only he and one other man in the car. The porter must have been as tired as Scott felt. He stood and went to the tiny restroom, where he relieved himself and splashed a bit of cold water on his face. He gave his armpits a whiff and satisfied that he didn't stink to high heaven, he went back to his seat. He grabbed his two bags from overhead and put them in the empty seat next to him. He could leave them on the car but the contents were all he had in the world, so he took them with him.

The train began to slow as it neared the station. Scott had his face pressed up against the glass window. The town looked pretty small to him. He was from Coos Bay, which had more than fifteen-thousand people. He guessed that Burdensville had only a small fraction of that. He hoped he could find a place to eat with halfway decent food.

He stayed seated after the train came to a complete stop and allowed the other passenger to get off first. Then he grabbed his two bags and followed. The sun hit him hard, but it felt amazing. He put his head back to feel the rays on his face, just soaking up the wonderful energy it provided.

After a moment, he looked around. Scott was standing on a wooden platform, just like the kind he'd seen at train stations in movies or on television. It made him smile; quaint, he thought.

Now he gave his surroundings a closer look. The small station was rectangular in shape and ran the length of the platform. A large navy blue sign with bright orange letters hung over the double doors that led inside. It read 'Burdensville Station.' From where Scott was standing, it seemed to be the only building in town. But certainly the rest was just out of view.

He walked up to the double doors. On the left door was a white hand-written sign which read 'No Firearms Past this Point: If you plan to shoot you'll get the boot.' He chuckled. *How original.*

The right door displayed the hours of operation, and he was surprised to see they only ran three days out of the week. It clearly wasn't a hub for commuters to reach jobs outside of town.

He grasped the door, swung it open, and stepped inside. There were two rows of four metal folding chairs which faced the large picture window that overlooked the platform. Soda and snack machines leaned against the left wall, along with a change machine. On the other side, several maps of the area were on display. He noticed a large cork board to the right with several missing person flyers tacked to it. He took a step closer, just enough to see all three of the victims were women and were stamped 'canceled.' This signified they were found or solved, so he wondered why they were still hanging. Very odd. This place is either full of slackers or they kept them up for remembrance. He raised his eyebrows and walked over for a closer look.

What a shame. All three were beautiful young women with their whole lives ahead of them. He shook his head in disbelief as he scanned them. Surely, these women weren't all from this small town. Burdensville couldn't possibly have lost so many. On further inspection, he discovered he was right. They had all been passing through. That's disturbing in of itself, he thought. He wondered if they were found dead or alive.

He shook his head again and turned to the right where he could see another door leading out to the town itself. He counted a few homes in the distance. Near the exit was a window with a frail old man behind it. He was reading a worn copy of a magazine through a pair of narrow reading glasses. Scott approached the window.

"Excuse me," he began. The man looked up at him over the top of his lenses. He didn't look too pleased to be interrupted. "Is there a café here where I can grab a bite?"

The old man sighed in frustration and jerked his head to the right. "Ayuh. Down the road two blocks. Dickie's

Café, it's called." He went back to his magazine as if Scott had already gone.

"Thanks for your time," Scott replied with a roll of his eyes, hoping the man heard the sarcasm in his voice. If he did, he gave no hint to such. Obviously, they didn't take too kindly to outsiders here.

He walked outside and down three steps. There, he stopped to take in the landscape. From where he stood, it appeared as though Burdensville was only about three or four blocks wide. He guessed a couple thousand people resided in the town permanently, at most. He could see the hand-painted sign on a brick building a couple blocks away: Dickie's Café. His stomach growled as though it were angry with him for neglecting it. It was so loud that he looked around to see if anyone had heard it, but he was alone. He laughed to himself.

The train station was situated at the dead end of a road which appeared to run right down the middle of Burdensville. The road was made of hard dirt and gravel. There was no sidewalk on the right side, so the property borders near the houses appeared to end at the road. The left side, however, did have a narrow sidewalk, and Scott could see that it ran right by Dickie's Café. He was on a mission. He moved quickly across the sparse train station lot and started up the pathway, which was crumbling in disrepair. Tufts of grass and weeds grew in the cracks, and in some spots, the concrete of the sidewalk had completely buckled. Scott watched his step, not wanting to fall victim to the hazardous path. That's the last thing he needed.

It was technically two blocks to Dickie's Café, but not exactly your usual suburban blocks. Scott had two streets to cross, and each block only had two houses facing the road. The houses were old and massive, some Victorian and others Craftsman-style. A few of them sported yard decorations, and plants hung from the porches. A few older ladies knelt in flower beds that reeked of perfection. A middle-aged man was using a manual push mower to manicure his sizable lawn, and a child played on a rusty old swing set in front of the house next to it.

As he walked, he took it all in. He couldn't help but notice that his presence sparked a bit of interest in the locals. As he passed, they stopped what they were doing to stare in his direction. The man with the mower managed a half-assed wave, but his eyes were filled with both curiosity and distrust. Scott waved back and uttered under his breath, "You'd think they weren't aware I got off the train..." but he was sure they were just nosy.

He finally found himself in front of the café. It had a single glass door with an 'open' sign hanging in it. A bell dangled next to the sign, inside the door. A large red and white striped awning hung in tatters over the door. Scott reached out and grasped the door handle and swung the door open.

The bell jingled to announce his presence, and as if

on cue, everyone in the restaurant went silent and turned their attention to him. He smiled and nodded, looking from one person to another. The place was packed, probably the only place these hicks had to hang out. Such a pity. Then again, perhaps it's the glue that keeps this community together. Not such a bad thing.

A long Formica counter with padded stools was on the opposite side of the room. A waitress stood behind it cutting a slice of pie. Another waitress, with ample hips and swollen ankles, stared at him as she warmed up a customer's coffee.

Scott nodded at the gawkers and made his way to one of the stools at the counter. He put his bags on the floor and took a seat, grabbing a single laminated card that served as the menu for the establishment. A quick glance told him they served the typical café fare. He would be able to fill his belly here, alright.

"Can I help you?" The waitress behind the counter asked as she placed the pie into a cooler. She was in her early twenties and had a very friendly face, free of makeup. She bordered on beautiful, but her tired eyes and unembellished countenance equated to your average girl-next-door.

Scott smiled at her. "So, what's good here..." he looked at the plastic name tag over her left breast. "Denise?"

She didn't return his smile. "If you're hungry enough, anything's good."

He searched her face, hoping she'd embellish a little, then said, "I guess, I'll need a few more minutes."

"Suit yourself." With that, she grabbed the plate with a fresh piece of pie on it and headed to one of the tables.

Scott was a creature of habit. No matter where he ate, he usually picked the same food. If it were breakfast, he ordered two eggs over medium, bacon, hash browns, and rye toast with cold milk. For lunch or supper, he always had a Reuben with fries and a salad, unless the establishment didn't serve them, in which case he would have roast beef or chicken.

Denise returned and set a glass of ice water in front of him on the countertop. Scott returned the menu to its spot between the napkin holder and salt and pepper shakers. "I'd like the Reuben with a soda on ice."

"You get two sides." Her voice was dull and had no enthusiasm. This should be a wonderful experience.

He cleared his throat. "Do you have salad?"

Denise shifted her weight from one foot to the other and looked like she may die of boredom. "Our salads are nothing but lettuce."

"How about fries?" The thought of plain lettuce with dressing threatened his appetite, and he was starving when he walked in.

"Yep," she replied. "Is that all then?"

He nodded and offered another smile. "Sure, thank you."

Denise began scribbling on her pad, then she tore

the sheet out and hung it on a carousel in the window that led to the kitchen. On to her next task, she grabbed a plastic pitcher of water and tended to her tables.

Scott's eyes scanned the room slowly. Most everyone in the place was still watching him out of the corner of their eyes, but they had all resumed whatever conversations they were having when he walked in. He reached into the inside pocket of his jacket and pulled out his smartphone.

No signal. *Seriously?*

He shook his head and put it back. Hearing the bell on the door jingle was music to his ears. Someone new for everyone to look at. The customers went silent once again. Must be the other passenger on the train, Scott thought. He turned to see.

At the door stood a man with sandy blonde hair and glasses. He was slight in build, standing only about 5'5" or 5'6", and he probably only weighed about a buck fifty soaking wet. His clothes and his face were smudged with dirt, and his eyes were glazed over.

"Whassup, Neece?" The man began to cackle as if he had just told the funniest joke ever. "Ima sittin' where I like, you see?"

The man began to stagger across the room toward Scott, mumbling to himself along the way. He was clearly drunk, and rather early in the day at that. Even a good five feet away the smell of him almost knocked Scott off his stool. He got closer to the stools and took his first real notice of the stranger seated at the counter.

He stopped in his tracks, but his body swayed back and forth as he tried to keep his balance. He smiled at Scott, his teeth stained brown with tell-tale chewing tobacco stains. He closed one eye and narrowed the other as he looked the stranger up and down.

"Hoo da hell you?"

Scott was amused, but he controlled his laughter in the name of diplomacy. "I'm just passing through by train; just here to get a bite to eat."

The man grunted and looked away. He took a seat two stools down from Scott and held tightly onto the counter to keep from falling off. Scott subtly shook his head and grabbed a menu to read. The last thing he wanted was to engage in conversation with this lush.

Denise appeared behind the counter and grabbed a plate from the window. She put it in front of Scott, along with an iced soda she had already poured. Then she turned and grabbed a small plate with fries and placed it in front of him.

"Thank you, Denise," he said with a smile.

She gave him a cold nod and turned to the drunk. "Ronnie, what will you have today?"

The man named Ronnie leered at her. "A little Denise with a side of... Denise." He began to laugh uncontrollably, spit flying from his mouth as he did. He almost fell from the stool but gained his composure just in time to avert disaster. Scott could smell the wave of alcohol emanating from him. It was mixed with the stink of sweat, BO, and grease. *Charming.*

"Look, Ronnie," Denise replied. "I just don't have time for this today, okay? You can see how busy we are."

Scott tried to keep his eyes on his own plate as the stinky man processed what Denise said to him. "I jus' don' care. All these people can kiss my ass."

She tensed by his ignorance, her shoulders squaring off and her eyes filling with dread. "You figure out what you want, and I'll be back in a minute, okay?"

She began to walk off, but the man was having none of it.

Ronnie spun around, turning a full circle before he adjusted and turned in her direction. "You know what I'll do, you lil' bitch. I can make you feel good or bad. What-cha want?"

Everyone in the place began to whisper and mutter amongst themselves as they pointed and stared. Scott turned away from his menu to focus his attention on the situation. Denise froze where she stood, and Ronnie tried to stand without falling.

"I'll take away your problems, lady," Ronnie slurred. "I'll throw you down and do you right. Then I'll cut you all the way from your neck to your crotch. I'll lay you open."

The customers were getting louder, some gasped. But, Scott couldn't help but notice that no one made an effort to intervene. They all seemed content to just watch to see how the scene played out. He noticed that Denise had begun to shake uncontrollably, and he felt the fury building up inside of him. He wasn't about to stand idle while a woman was being threatened and humiliated.

Scott stood up and put his hand on the drunk's shoulder. "Look, man, go easy on her. Maybe you need to sleep it off."

No sooner were the words out of his mouth when Ronnie swung a roundhouse at him, his fist connecting solidly with Scott's mouth and chin. Blood filled his mouth. He roared with anger and tackled Ronnie down to the floor. He put him in a tight headlock and punched him in the head hard a couple of times, hoping to teach him a good lesson.

"Denise, this annoyance is drunk," Scott shouted. "Call the police before someone gets hurt for real!"

CHAPTER
THREE

Ronnie struggled on the floor against Scott, who held him firmly in place. "Lemme go, you son-of-a..." Ronnie yelled every profanity in the book at Scott, as he squirmed and fought a likely losing battle in his condition. While the two men struggled, the customers closest to them stood up from their chairs to get out of the way. Luckily, they did, because the brawlers ended up flipping two of their chairs over.

"The more you fight me, the worse it's going to get, man. Just relax!" The room was loud with banter now among patrons and workers alike, and the entire café was consumed by the chaos. "Denise, did you call the police?"

"They're on the way," the waitress replied from behind the counter. Her voice was shaky, and it made

Scott look up to see if she was okay. She looked horrified, and tears were running down her face.

Relief washed over him as he heard the bell jingle. *About freaking time.* The dining room went silent yet again. Scott tightened his grip on Ronnie and looked toward the door. He saw the black patent leather shoes first. He raised his eyes to see a large, stout man with a badge and gun.

"What the heck is going on here, Ronnie?" The cop sounded frustrated, as if he'd dealt with this annoyance for far too long.

Ronnie went limp in Scott's arms as he tried to respond to the question, but the only thing that came out of his mouth was a loud whine. This guy was a real piece of work. He took another breath and yelled, "This guy's tryna beat the shit outta me!"

Now the cop, whose badge read 'Burdensville Sheriff,' kept his eyes glued on the two men. "Denise! What's going on?"

Denise remained silent. Scott shifted his eyes to her, but she was looking at the ground, appearing both afraid and embarrassed. *What's wrong with these people?*

"Sheriff, my name's Scott Sharp," he began, his voice grunting from the effort of controlling the drunken idiot he was wrestling with. "I'm just on a layover from the train. This guy is drunk, and he threatened to not only rape that waitress, but he also threatened to kill her as well." Ronnie began to struggle harder, spit flying from his mouth.

The sheriff didn't acknowledge Scott. He exhaled loudly and tried to form his own conclusion. He looked the two men over and said, "Is that right, Ronnie? Is this guy speaking the truth?"

Ronnie grunted and relaxed a bit. "I ain't done nuttin'."

Scott spoke up again. "He's putting up a heck of a fight. If you cuff him, I'll let you have him, but he's pretty damn violent."

Ronnie twisted his arms in a wasted effort to break free of Scott's hold. They began to struggle together once again.

The sheriff remained still, choosing only to observe instead of breaking it up. His arms were crossed over his chest, and he was shifting his weight from one foot to the other as he gathered his thoughts. He chewed thoughtfully on a toothpick which was poking out from the side of his mouth. His attention was focused only on Ronnie, and the frustrated looks and groans kept coming.

Finally, he spoke, but he still didn't make eye contact with Scott. "Let him go, son."

Ronnie immediately relaxed, as if on cue. Scott looked at the sheriff, confused. Wasn't he even gonna cuff this crazy guy? The sheriff made no motion for either the handcuffs on his belt or the gun in his holster. Scott was frustrated and internally fuming, but he concluded that the Sheriff must know this annoyance better than anyone. He must be a total town menace.

With that, he released his hold on Ronnie, who jumped up like someone lit a match under his ass. He ran his hand through his hair with a shaky hand and started chuckling. "You dumb," he said in broken English to Scott. "You done butt your nose in the wrong bidness, ayuh!"

No sooner was Ronnie free when the sheriff took his cuffs off his belt. He looked at Scott, making eye contact with him for the first time since he got to the café. "Put your hands in the air and turn around, stranger."

At first, Scott thought the sheriff was talking to Ronnie. He looked at the erratic man, who was still laughing, now even harder. Scott smirked at him with satisfaction.

"I'm talking' to you, boy," the sheriff said with a quiet but stern voice.

Scott looked back at the cop, utter confusion written all over his face. "Me? You're saying you want to arrest me?"

"Put your hands up and turn around now, or I'm gonna have to use force," the sheriff replied.

"What do you mean?" Scott asked incredulously. "Everyone in here witnessed it from beginning to end! The threats. The punch he threw at me." He began to look around the room which had gone completely quiet.

Each of them were either staring at the floor or pretending to be in conversation. Even Denise kept her eyes down as she anxiously fidgeted. "Waitress? I mean, Denise?" Scott begged her with his eyes, but she wouldn't look at him.

Defeated, Scott put his arms in the air and turned his back toward the cop as he'd been asked to. "This is just so wrong! I was trying to help the lady, and this guy assaulted me!"

The sheriff approached Scott and began to frisk him for contraband. "It's gonna go a lot better for you if you just don't talk, son." He put the cuffs on Scott and adjusted them with the key so they wouldn't tighten on him. "I'm gonna take you downtown and book you, and as soon as the judge is back in town, he'll set a bond, or he'll go ahead and sentence you, whatever His Honor sees fit to do."

Scott turned back to the sheriff with a shocked expression. "But my train is supposed to leave in a half-hour!"

Now it was the cop's turn to chuckle. "That wouldn't be my problem now, would it?"

Scott's head was spinning. What just happened here? He began to look around the room once again, looking for anyone to have his back. But everyone in the restaurant acted as though nothing had happened. They were ready to carry on with their days while Scott took one for the team, apparently. He finally shook his head and gave a resigned sigh. "The bags by the stool are mine. Please don't leave them here."

Ronnie began to laugh hysterically as he backed his way to the main door and reached behind him to open it. The bell gave a jingle as he backed out onto the step. "Yep, you done butt your nose in where it don't belong!" With that, he let the door swing shut and disappeared from sight.

Scott looked back at the sheriff, who had taken his arm in a firm grip. Denise was at the stool picking up his bags, which she brought to the cop. "Here you go, Sheriff Darby," she said shyly, still not looking the lawman in the eyes. "Do you want me to carry them to your car?"

"No, Denise," he replied. "I walked over here, so I expect you can bring them down to lockup after your shift if you kindly would."

"No problem, sir," she said.

Scott watched as she went around to the other side of the counter and put the bags there for safekeeping. Finally, she looked at Scott, her eyes full of remorse. "Don't worry, Mister. I won't let anything happen to them."

Scott just shook his head and, with a jerk to his arm by Sheriff Darby, was led out of the café and into the sunlight.

"I reckon you'll want to know how often the judge comes," the sheriff said as they started walking up the sidewalk.

Scott gave a sarcastic laugh. "Yeah, I suppose that would be helpful."

"Well," the cop replied, "He comes twice a month, once every two weeks. He was just here last Wednesday, so you'll have a week and a half to wait, son."

Scott stopped, his mouth agape. "A week and a half? Are you kidding me?"

"Now I'd be watching your mouth, boy," Sheriff Darby retorted, his eyes flashing. "You can't just go around from town to town assaulting citizens who live there. This is what happens." He gave Scott's arm another jerk, and they started walking once again.

"Sheriff, that Ronnie guy assaulted me! He hit me! Don't you see the blood all over me?" Scott said with exasperation. The sheriff just kept pulling him along.

About half a block away was a brick building that was about the same size as the café. A sloppy hand-painted sign hung over the door:

City Hall
Sheriff
Jail

Scott was relieved. The handcuffs were cutting into his wrists. He couldn't wait to get them off. He stood next to Sheriff Darby, who had a firm hold on his upper arm as he shuffled through one of several keys on a ring.

He soon found the right one and unlocked the door, after which he shoved Scott inside first.

"You have a seat right there, son," Darby said. "I'm gonna grab some booking paperwork so we can get you signed in."

Scott did as he was told, sitting forward in the chair so his hands, which were behind his back, didn't get more banged up. He looked around the room, taking in his surroundings. It reminded him of the jail on "The Andy Griffith Show." Along the back were two cells separated by a cinderblock wall. Each cell had a toilet, sink, and flat metal bed with a mattress folded in half at the foot of each. There were two desks in the room: the one before him, which had a nameplate reading "Sheriff Robert Darby." It was piled high with paperwork and dust. Another desk was situated directly across from the first, and Scott had to partially turn around to see it. It was much neater than the sheriff's, with only a telephone and two stackable boxes marked 'In' and 'Out.' Both were empty. There was another nameplate on the desk marked "Honorable Rupert Allen." The desk had a thick coat of dust on it that hadn't been disturbed in some time. Scott groaned and rolled his eyes before hanging his head in frustration.

Sheriff Darby sat down hard in the chair at his desk, grunting as he did. In his hand were a few sheets of paper, and he laid them on his desk before taking the first one.

He wound it into a cast iron typewriter that had to be older than both of the men sitting there.

"So, Mr ..." The sheriff began.

"Sharp," Scott replied. "Scott Sharp"

The sheriff began pecking at the keys. "Middle initial?"

"W," Scott said.

Peck, peck, peck.

"Birthdate and social security number?" The sheriff glanced at Scott and then turned back to the typewriter, fingers poised impatiently over the keys.

Scott gave the information, and as they went through the process of filling out the paperwork, he decided that he would be as cooperative as possible, no matter how angry he was. He had to face the fact that this was a very small town, with its own ways. If no one came to his rescue at Dickie's Café, odds are, he was going to have to completely fend for himself. It would be like shooting himself in the foot to be rude, sarcastic, or combative.

The third piece of paper was for his fingerprints, which he gave eagerly because the handcuffs were finally removed. He allowed Darby to take his mug shot, after which he was given a navy blue jumpsuit, two sizes too big. Then he handed Scott some bedding and a pillow. Sheriff Darby locked him securely in the first cell.

"I suppose, you'll be wantin' a toothbrush?"

Scott looked at the cop in disbelief, but he didn't voice his thoughts.

"I'd appreciate that, sir."

Darby went into a closet and brought back a towel, a washcloth, a small bar of soap, and a toothbrush. "Don't have paste, so you're gonna hafta make due."

Scott took the items and put them on his bed and turned back to Darby. "I just want to clarify, sir. I will be here for the next week and a half?"

"Yep," Darby replied as he pulled a toothpick from his chest pocket and tucked it into the corner of his mouth.

"At least. Maybe longer, though. It depends on whether or not Judge Allen has more important cases on his docket. You'll just have to cool your jets and be patient. Now, I'll bring you some supper from the café around five or five thirty. I don't take orders. What you get is what you get. Got it?" Scott nodded. "You'll be here alone most of the time, so you'd best get used to the silence around here."

Darby plucked his hat off the lamp on his desk and put it on. Then he grabbed the paperwork on Scott and placed it in a manila envelope, which he placed on the blotter on his desk.

"Well, I'm outta here then," he said in a gruff voice. "I'll see you at dinnertime."

"Wait!" Scott went up to the bars and put his face as close to them as he could. "Don't I get a phone call, or get to talk to a lawyer?"

Darby turned around, his eyes flashing. "This here

ain't like the big city, boy. We don't have the manpower to let you have all kinds of 'big city' privileges. You'll get a call when I have time, and then only one, so you'd better use it wisely." With that, he walked out the door. Scott could hear him lock it from the other side.

He plopped down on the thin plastic mattress and put his head in his hands. "What the heck am I gonna do?"

He knew he had to think of something, but he was at a loss. This was like a bad dream. All he could do was wait for Sheriff Darby to return and hope he would get to make a call. He wanted to bail himself out; he had plenty of money. But he wasn't even going to see a judge for two weeks.

He stood and made his bed, then lay down. He was going to stay calm. Causing a ruckus was only going to hurt him at this point.

CHAPTER
FOUR

Denise Jensen stacked the last of the clean drinking glasses on the shelf beneath the counter. Then she gave the countertop one last wipe down before turning to Dickie, who was sitting in one of the booths tallying the day's earnings.

"If you got nothin' else for me, Dickie, I'm gonna head on home."

Dickie looked up from his paperwork and smiled at the girl. She had worked for him since her parents died when she was only sixteen. Now she was twenty-five and just as pretty as a picture. Dickie loved her like his own daughter.

"I'd like you to wait for me, if you don't mind Denise," he replied, setting his pen down on top of his notebook. He turned closer so he could look at her head on. "Ronnie went completely overboard earlier, and I don't feel comfortable letting you walk home alone."

Denise hated to look weak or dependent, but she was relieved by his offer. "That would be fine," she said as she put her jacket on. "Actually, I couldn't be more thankful."

Dickie nodded and went back to his paperwork. Denise walked up to the big window on the side of the room and looked out into the night. Ronnie had really freaked her out today. She saw him behave badly on numerous occasions, and Sheriff Darby always seemed to catch him when he fell. He was considered, by most everyone, to be the town idiot. He was always getting drunk and threatening people, but this was the first time she ever saw him get violent. And the things he said to her were terrifying.

It was also the first time she watched the sheriff arrest someone who didn't deserve it just to take the focus off Ronnie. She couldn't understand why. But after saving Ronnie's hide time and again maybe he just didn't know what else to do, given the situation with the stranger and all. She hoped he had a plan to straighten Ronnie out.

"Dickie, why do you suppose Sheriff Darby arrested that man from the train?" Denise continued to look out the window, but she was also watching Dickie's reflection in the glass. His pen froze over his paper, and he looked at her in silence.

She turned around to face him. "I mean, everybody

here knows that the stranger didn't do anything wrong," she continued. "We all saw Ronnie punch him! None of it makes any sense."

Dickie laid his pen down and sat back, crossing his arms over his chest. He cleared his throat. "You know, I've lived here in Burdensville my whole life, just like you. Bobby Darby has always had a weak spot for Ronnie, almost like he feels obligated. I don't have an answer for you. The only one who knows is Sheriff Darby himself. Maybe he feels sorry for him because he's so off. I mean, Ronnie Smith is as crazy as a jaybird, and he can't be trusted. I suppose, someone has to look out for him."

Denise nodded and turned back to the window. She thought about Ronnie and the things he said to her. A chill ran up her spine as she considered his threats and harassment. Then, she thought about the murders.

In the last two months, Burdensville had a few unsolved murders. Each was a young woman, all of them strangers to the town. They had passed through, each one, and then their bodies were found shortly after that. The latest body was that of a young college graduate. She hadn't technically been in Burdensville at all. Her parents said she was traveling for a job interview. They gathered that she was close, perhaps making her way to Burdensville in need of gas. Her body was found in a ditch on a gravel road outside of town.

Whoever killed those girls hasn't been caught. Denise toyed with the idea that it was Ronnie. She never suspected him before, at least, not until now. She found herself wondering why she wasn't suspicious before.

But Ronnie was harmless, wasn't he? The threats he made were all just smoke. He was a raging alcoholic with issues, that's all. No one in town was afraid of him. But they were certainly sick of his drunken behavior.

But today, suddenly, made her wonder. She shook her head hard, as if to rid it of its thoughts. Couldn't be. She walked away from the window and sat in a booth to wait for Dickie. She closed her eyes and leaned her head back against the window. She could feel a headache coming on.

Suddenly, the stranger reemerged in her mind. He sure had no idea what he was getting himself into when he came to her defense, did he? She recalled the way Ronnie punched him and how furious the man had gotten when he realized he was bleeding. She felt terrible that the sheriff put the poor guy in jail for basically nothing at all. She also felt guilty for not standing up for him in the moment. After all, he was defending her, plus he was kinda cute, to say the least.

"Are you ready, Neece?" She opened her eyes to see Dickie standing there putting his jacket on. He had always been there for her when she needed him, and even he knew that what had taken place that afternoon had been wrong. Regardless, Dickie hadn't come out front from the kitchen to protect her. Nobody in Burdensville liked to cross Sheriff Darby when it came to Ronnie Smith. Nobody.

She smiled at Dickie and pulled her tired body out of the booth. "Thanks for walking me home. We'll have to drop that man's bags off down at the jail. I hope you don't mind. I could've walked myself, but I have to admit that having you with me makes me feel better."

"Well, Ronnie's an unpredictable so-and-so, girl," Dickie said, shaking his head. "You know as well as I do that not a one person in this rinky-dink town trusts him behind their back."

Denise zipped up her jacket and followed Dickie out the front door, letting him shut off the lights and lock the place up. "I know, but none of us have ever seen him hurt anyone. He's never hurt anyone that I know of, anyway."

"No, but we all know he's unstable, and you know what that means." Dickie finished locking up and offered Denise his elbow. "Shall we depart, Madam?"

"Oh, thank you, kind sir," she replied, offering him a curtsy. Together they began walking to their homes with only the streetlights guiding them in the darkness.

Dickie talked during the entire five-minute walk. He told her he was going to take her home first, then he would drop the stranger's bags off to Sheriff Darby. After that, he talked about his oldest daughter who lived and worked in Sacramento. He talked about how he hated her 'holier than thou' attitude and how she alienated him and her younger sister. He talked about how the younger sibling was such a mess, taking drugs and hitchhiking all over the United States. It worried him sick.

"Well, here we are, Neece," Dickie said, walking the girl to her front door. He stood by as she unlocked the door. "I'm not leaving until you are secured inside there, got it?"

Denise smiled at her boss and stood on her tiptoes to kiss his whiskered cheek. "Thank you, Dickie. I don't know what I'd do without you."

"Well, now. You better figure it out. I won't be around forever, you know."

She patted his cheek after kissing him and then went inside, closing the door and locking it behind her. As soon as it was locked, she leaned against it and took a deep breath. What a relief to feel safe. She had been a nervous wreck since the incident with Ronnie and the stranger at the café.

She hung her jacket on a hook by the door and dropped her purse on a small table next to the front door. Denise made her way down the short hallway where the bedrooms and bathroom were. She opened the door at the end of the hall and held it open just enough for the hall light to shine in. Her sister, Diane, was curled up under her blanket sleeping peacefully. Denise smiled in spite of herself; her kid sister was the light of her life. She could only hope to do right by the teenager because she really had no idea what she was doing.

She went back out to the living room and kicked her shoes off before going into the kitchen for a bite to eat. She chose a piece of cold chicken and pulled it apart to make a sandwich. She was hungry and exhausted. What a day it had been! Ronnie was trouble, but he had never spoken to her like that, or anyone that she could think of. And she had known him a long time. She put a handful of chips on her plate with the sandwich, poured a cold glass of milk, then plopped on the couch. She turned the television on, and the news greeted her loudly. She quickly turned it down a couple of notches so the noise wouldn't disturb her sister's sleep.

"The latest news concerning a young woman's body found outside of Burdensville has nearby communities feeling unsettled, to say the least. According to the victim's family and friends, Carly Reed was heading to an interview for a teaching position," the anchor was saying. "When she didn't arrive, and no one heard from her, she was reported missing. Her car, a 2001 Beetle, was discovered abandoned ten miles from Burdensville. Her body was discovered only two miles outside of the town. The state medical examiner claims that the injuries discovered on her body were consistent with at least five other rape and murder victims in the area over the last couple of years. Miss Reed had a crushed larynx and was sexually assaulted. Burdensville police are investigating the murder. We'll keep you posted on updates as we get them."

Denise shut the television off and tossed the remote onto the coffee table. Her mind was reeling. Everyone in Burdensville was on edge because of the murders, and Sheriff Darby was none too eager to share information with the locals. He claimed the murderer had to be someone either living in Burdensville or nearby. It made her stomach ache just thinking about it. For all she knew, it could be Dickie himself. How well do you really know anyone?

Denise stood up and made her way to her bedroom. She wasn't scheduled to work tomorrow, but Donna had an important doctor's appointment in the city, so she agreed to fill in for her. She didn't mind. She could always use the money, but she was getting terribly behind on house and yard work. She asked Dickie numerous times if he was ever going to hire a third girl, but he always dodged the topic. He said that she and Donna were all he needed, and so far, he had been right, but it was rare that either of them got a legitimate day off.

The murders made her nervous. What would she do if something ever happened to Diane? The thought was petrifying. Doing her best not to make a noise, she turned the knob and opened the door just a crack. There was just enough light to shine on the figure sleeping peacefully. From where she stood, she could see her sister's chest moving up and down as she breathed. She smiled, satisfied, and closed the door.

Diane was all she had left, and it was her purpose in

life to keep the girl safe and sound. She was seventeen, and would graduate from high school this year. She planned to become a nurse and had already been accepted on a full scholarship to Central Medical Center School of Nursing. She was at the top of her class, and she was highly gifted as well as beautiful.

Denise had taken responsibility for Diane when their parents were killed. Diane was only eight at the time, and Denise had to quit school and start working, but it was worth it. The girl was going to go places. She was going to get out of Burdensville and be somebody. Denise was going to make sure of it even if it took the life out of her trying.

She went to the bathroom, brushed her teeth, and washed her face, then went to her room and climbed back into bed eagerly. It felt like sheer heaven to be off her feet, and she smiled and moaned out loud, in spite of herself. She tossed and turned for a couple of minutes before falling sound asleep. Soon, she was dreaming. She dreamt of a faceless man chasing, raping, and murdering a young woman that looked a lot like herself.

SHERIFF ROBERT DARBY, KNOWN AS BOBBY TO local folk, locked the door of the jail securely after looking in on the prisoner. With the guy being a stranger in town, he felt he had to take special precautions, but not because the guy was a hardened criminal. Heck, he hadn't even broken any laws.

No, he just needed to make sure that the guy was more than ready to leave when the time came. In a tiny community like Burdensville, the people had their set ways, and Sheriff Darby was no exception. The last thing he or any of the locals needed was to have their lives disrupted, especially by some strange guy that Ronnie pissed off. It was just the scenario that could upset everything.

Darby would make sure that the trumped-up charges didn't stick. He would just play dumb until Judge Allen came to hold his hearing, then he would say he had re-evaluated the evidence and decided to drop the charges. By then, this guy would leave town running, and that's what Darby wanted.

"Hey, Bobby," a voice said in the darkness. Darby turned around to find Dickie. He was carrying the prisoner's personal effects. He had forgotten all about the bags and was relieved Dickie remembered to bring them by.

"Thanks, good buddy," he replied. He unlocked the jail door and placed the bags on a chair just inside. He relocked and turned to the café owner. "Sorry about Ronnie this afternoon," he continued. "Hope it didn't shake people up too much."

"Well, it didn't hurt business if that's what you

mean," Dickie replied with a grin. "But it helps that I'm the only eatery for miles."

Darby laughed. "Ayuh, I suppose it does now."

Dickie cleared his throat. "I was wondering if I could ask you a question?"

The sheriff stopped and gave the man his full attention. "You can ask me anything, so shoot."

"Why'd you arrest this poor bastard, anyway?"

Darby paused before responding, weighing his words carefully. Finally, he said, "You know as well as I do that Ronnie ain't really got no one. I mean, Doc Smith don't really have time for his own brother, so I feel an obligation to protect him. I mean, the guy's a damned idiot. If he can't depend on townsfolk, who can he depend on? If I arrest him and let the charges drop, he's much more likely to go quietly, you see?"

Dickie heard the words, but to him, it sounded like a bunch of bull. Who was he to argue? Burdensville was Darby's town, and it had been for years. In general, Darby had always been a good cop, so Dickie figured he shouldn't second-guess his motives or instincts.

He gave the sheriff a pat on the shoulder. "You know what you're doing, Darby. What the heck do I know? I just sling hash for a living."

The two men parted ways. Dickie headed home, and Darby forced his fat frame into his police cruiser. He got winded struggling to put his seatbelt on. Once it clicked, he put the car in gear. He needed to talk to Ronnie and fast. He wanted to hear that moron's side of things. His entire version would be a lousy explanation full of outright lies. Ronnie didn't know any other way.

He drove down the main street heading away from the train station. Ronnie lived in a breezy shack, a mile out of town on the first gravel road. The shack was once owned by Darby's parents, and when they died, they left it to him. He let Ronnie live there rent free. Lord, if he didn't look out for that retard, no one would.

He took a right on the gravel road. The shack was about a half-mile down. Darby felt an obligation to keep an eye on Ronnie, and he had his reasons. Sure, it was wrong to keep letting the guy screw up over and over and then shift the blame. But Darby couldn't live with the alternative. He couldn't live with the guilt of blowing off what he felt was his responsibility.

Darby pulled the cruiser into Ronnie's overgrown gravel drive and parked it behind Ronnie's beat up jalopy. The car used to be Darby's. He wanted to restore it, but Ronnie didn't have transportation, so he gave it to him for Christmas one year.

He shut the cruiser off and heaved his large frame out of the car. Darby took off his hat and wiped the sweat from his forehead with his shirt sleeve. Getting in and out of the cruiser was getting harder every day. Maybe he should cut back on Dickie's pies from the café. But, Damn, they were good.

"Ronnie! It's Bobby! You come out here now, boy!"

He looked around and peeled his ears, but the place was dead quiet. Darby shook his head. The poor miserable pain in the neck was likely passed out cold. Well, it was time to wake him up. They needed to get a few things straight... *again*.

Darby put his hat back on his head and hiked his pants up before heading to the old beat up house. He hadn't been here in a few weeks, and the place looked abandoned. The grass was starting to catch up to the weeds. He knew Ronnie wasn't capable of being responsible. He'd have to take care of this for him, too, and clean it up for him.

The front door had been out of use for years, so Darby automatically headed for the back. He grabbed the knob and tried it. The door opened easily with a loud creak. He poked his head inside and was hit with the smell of rotten food and garbage.

"Ronnie! It's Bobby! Wake your butt up, now. We need to talk!"

Suddenly, Darby spotted him. He was peeking around the corner from the living room, quietly watching Darby to see if he was angry. Darby smiled at him and relaxed his shoulders.

"Now, don't you be hidin'. I'm just here to talk to you, Ronnie." He opened the door all the way and stepped inside the filthy kitchen. Flies were everywhere, their buzzing terribly loud. How did he live like this?

He removed his hat and looked around. "Jeez,

Ronnie, we're gonna have to get someone out here to help you clean this place up, aren't we?"

Ronnie slowly nodded and came around the corner, his hands trembling and his eyes full of trepidation. Darby could tell the man was no longer drunk. He had a look of fear and regret so thick Darby could've cut it with a knife.

"Look, Ronnie," Darby began. "I didn't come out to hassle you, but the two of us gotta have a heart-to-heart, understand?"

"I... I didn't mean to scare Pretty Denise. I was just havin' me some fun for a bit," he said, stuttering slightly. He did this only when he was scared.

Darby smiled at him. "I know that. Don't you think I know that?"

Ronnie smiled and began to nod enthusiastically.

Darby continued. "The problem wasn't Denise. She knows you. But now you done picked a fight with a stranger, a man that doesn't know you, and now I gotta clean up the mess."

Ronnie continued to nod, his smile fading slightly.

"You know, if you ever lose control around the wrong person, they're liable to lock you up but good," Darby continued, "And there wouldn't be nothing I could do about it."

Ronnie started to snivel, which tugged at Darby's heart. "Listen, now. Just listen. It's all gonna be all right." He held out his arms to Ronnie to show him acceptance, and Ronnie all but ran into them.

"I didn't mean to make trouble," the man bawled. "I only wanted to have a little fun with the pretty girl."

Now, Darby held the man by the shoulders at arm's length. "Now, we both know that ain't altogether true, don't we?"

Ronnie's lower lip began to tremble, and snot began to leak out of his nose. He shrugged in response and tried to look away, but Darby took him by the chin and made him look him in the eye.

"You threatened her, Ronnie. You threatened her with sex and physical harm, didn't you?"

Ronnie shrugged again and began to kick at the cap from a milk jug that was on the floor.

"Now I have done told you time and again that you can't be talking that way to the townsfolk, haven't I?"

Ronnie's toe connected with the cap and it went flying. This made him smile, which frustrated Darby. "Haven't I, Ronnie?"

He nodded vigorously in response.

"Now I'm gonna do what I can to make this go away, but you need to keep your butt at home until the stranger leaves, do you got it?'

He nodded again.

"This weekend, I'm gonna come over and help you get this yard cleaned up," Darby continued. "Now, in the meantime, I want you to clear all this damn garbage out of this house and burn it in the barrel out back. Understand? You don't have to clean, just get the trash out and burn it. Can you handle that?"

More nodding.

"Well, it better be done, because I don't want you leaving this house till this guy is gone. You'll have plenty of time," Darby concluded.

He gave the man a pat on the back and reassured him that he wasn't in any trouble. He reiterated that the garbage needed to go out, then he left.

Ronnie's face was plastered to the front window as he watched Darby leave. Darby gave the man a final wave and a smile as he backed out of the drive. "Poor stupid idiot, what a waste of my time," Darby exclaimed. He put the cruiser in gear and punched the accelerator.

He couldn't get away from Ronnie and his parent's dilapidated old shack fast enough.

CHAPTER
FIVE

Scott Sharp was lying on his plastic mat tossing and turning. He couldn't get comfortable no matter how hard he tried. He had never slept on such a hard, lumpy surface in his life, even when he camped. It didn't help that the plastic mattress he was lying on smelled like decades worth of body fluids and vomit. He had to breathe through his mouth to keep from gagging.

He had just started to doze a bit when he heard a key in the door. His eyes opened, and he sat up just as Sheriff Darby swung the door open and turned the main overhead lights on in the room. Scott squinted against the brightness and shaded his eyes with his hand.

"Hello, Mr. Sharp!" Darby seemed to be in a fairly good mood. "I've brought you your supper, just like I said I would."

Scott looked at the wall clock that hung next to the bulletin board. Good thing he hadn't counted on the lawman being punctual. He was fairly convinced that Darby wouldn't come back until morning.

Darby noticed him checking the time. "I know," he said. "I'm a bit later than I said I'd be, but I had some official business, and by the time I was finished, old Dickie had closed the café. I had to bother him at home to get you a meal."

He approached the bars and slid a Styrofoam box through the six-inch slot at its center. Then he slid a paper cup with a lid for Scott to take. Scott stood up eagerly and took the items from Darby. His stomach was growling furiously as soon as he laid eyes on the items. Thanks to the altercation, he only managed to get down one french fry at the café.

Scott took the food and sat on the bed to dig in. "I know it isn't hot, but like I said, Dickie had to throw it together." Darby walked to his desk and sat down then put his feet up and stared at Scott as he observed the meal.

Inside the Styrofoam box was a bologna and cheese sandwich on dry white bread. There was also a small snack-sized bag of potato chips and a banana. The cup held lukewarm milk.

"It's fine, Sheriff," Scott replied and meant it. It was no Reuben, but it would certainly suffice under the circumstances. He tore into the sandwich as if he'd been brought a gourmet meal.

"So, I been thinkin' about your little uproar with Ronnie at Dickie's today," said Darby, breaking the silence. "I'm just wondering why you think it's okay to visit a place and pick a fight with the locals like that."

Scott looked up at the sheriff and searched his face as he chewed the bite of sandwich in his mouth. Was this guy serious? How bad of a detective was this man? By his expression, Scott gathered that he truly believed he got it right, or he was out to protect his own people no matter what the price.

He swallowed the bite in his mouth and said, "Sheriff, I didn't raise a hand to that Ronnie guy. Again, it should be obvious by my appearance that I was the one who got hit."

Sheriff Darby sat up and put his feet on the floor, chuckling with amusement. "Well, it sure may look that way, but not a one person was willing to back up your version of events. Now, what's a cop supposed to think?"

Scott stared at him and bit his tongue. He was getting nowhere fast with this one, so he focused his attention back on his food. He decided to stop talking or trying to explain anything to the Sheriff from this point on. It was an obvious setup, at least in his humble opinion. He hadn't even been allowed to make a phone call.

"So, are you going to let me have my call?"

Darby stood up and put his hands in his pockets as

he began to pace. He looked like he was thinking about it but was hesitant. "I'll tell you what. You eat that food fast enough, and I'll let you get a call in, but make it snappy. I got things of my own to do, you know?"

Worried he would change his mind, Scott wolfed the sandwich and chips down, demolishing it in record time. He saved his banana but finished the milk in two gulps. "I'm done. Can I make that call now?"

Darby approached the bars and started flipping through the keys on his big hoop. "Now, don't be trying any damn funny business, boy, you got that?" Scott nodded and smiled politely as he stood at the bars waiting for Darby to let him out.

Soon, he was standing at the phone with the receiver to his ear. The problem was, he didn't know who to call. Kelly had been his only family. He pushed his own blood relatives out of his life for a variety of reasons. Since she died, and he hit the road, he hadn't really spoken to any of their mutual friends or her side of the family either. He isolated himself and became a loner. His misery wanted no company.

Suddenly, he thought about Brian Weaver. He and Brian were best friends through high school, and their relationship was solid until Kelly's diagnosis. It was awkward and rude to call him after all this time, but he had to let someone know what was happening. He just hoped the guy had the same number.

He punched the numbers on the dial pad. It would

be long distance from here, but the sheriff didn't say anything after dialing a one, so he continued. The phone rang after hitting the last button.

"'Hello?" Scott recognized Brian's voice right away and was flooded with relief.

"Brian, it's Scotty," he began.

The other end of the line was silent. At first, Scott thought Brian may have hung up on him. He wouldn't have blamed him. He hadn't been a very good friend.

Suddenly Brian spoke, his voice surprised. "Scotty? How are you, man?"

Scott exhaled. "I've been all right, Brian. I know I haven't called, but after Kelly passed..."

"No, dude. No worries," his friend said. "So what's up?"

Scott cleared his throat and nervously shifted his weight from one foot to the other. "Brian, I've been traveling, as you probably know. My train stopped in this town, and I got myself in something of a bind. I'm in jail."

Silence again on the other end. Finally, Brian said, "What can I do to help, man? Do you need bail money or something?"

"No, no. I don't have a bond set. The town is pretty small, so I won't even see a judge for about ten days. I just wanted to let someone know where I was." Scott paused and glanced at Darby, who was busy chewing his toothpick and picking at his fingernails. "You know, just so I'm not winging it out here."

Brian must have heard something in his voice. "Are you okay, Scotty? What's going on? What did you do?"

"Well, I don't have an attorney, at least not yet," he replied, "so I really can't go into it in detail, but it's nothing drastic. I just wanted someone to know where I am, and that I'm alive." He shook his head and closed his eyes. He wondered if anyone cared if he was alive.

"So where are you then, dude?"

He opened his eyes once again to see Darby's eyes fastened on him. "A town called Burdensville."

"Where the heck is that?" Brian asked with a bewildered voice.

Darby stood. "You're gonna have to wrap it up, son."

He replied quickly. "Look, I gotta go. My time's up. I just wanted you to know what's going on."

"Well," Brian said sheepishly, "You call me if you need anything. Don't hesitate."

Scott smiled into the phone. "I won't. Thanks."

With that, he disconnected the call and looked at Darby. "Thanks, Sheriff."

Darby motioned for him to head back into his cell, which he did. As he was locking him back up, he questioned Scott, "So, it sounds like you lost your girl or something."

Scott sat on the bed and stared at his hands. "My wife," he said quietly.

Darby didn't respond right away, just took that detail in for a second. Finally, he said, "That's a tough break, son. A tough break." He stepped back from the cell, then continued. "I'll be back in the morning with some breakfast, and I'll make sure you get a shower in too."

Scott nodded as he struggled to keep the tears back. He was angry and frustrated by the lack of control he had over this forsaken situation. It was similar to the lack of control he had over his wife's illness. "Thanks."

Darby left and locked the door behind him. He thought about Scott as he struggled to get into his cruiser. The guy hit a rough patch, that was for sure. He lost his wife and took to the road to sort things out. Darby knew exactly how the guy felt. He had lost his own wife a while back, and now he found himself empathizing with his prisoner. Shame, he had to go to lengths like this when it came to Ronnie. At this point, he'd let the guy go if he could, but the paperwork had already been sent to the city courts.

Scott Sharp was just going to have to ride this one out.

"I swear, Meri if you keep messing with me while I'm driving, I won't let up when it's your turn," said Ted Bascom. "It's all fun and games, isn't it?"

Meri's laugh was like a melody, and Ted found

himself smiling through his frustration. He was so glad to have met her. With her strawberry blonde hair, button nose, and petite body she was the cutest thing he had ever seen! It was amazing that she agreed to travel with him to see their favorite band. They were playing in the city that weekend, and Ted intended to show her a good time.

Ted was in love.

"Aw, c'mon Teddy," Meri giggled. "Man up, will you?"

It was eleven at night, and they were traveling the last stretch to the city in the Mercury Tracer his parents had given him for his seventeenth birthday. Ted didn't want to stop anywhere else except for gas in Burdensville. They both agreed they would just drive straight through and save their money. They would have plenty of time to rest when they arrived.

"Hey, hand me a couple of those chips, will you?" he asked, holding his hand out expectantly. Meri put a stack of chips in his palm and began to tinker with the radio.

"There's nothing but country music in these parts, it seems," she said, her nose wrinkled in disgust. "I can't wait to hear some real tuneage."

She flipped the radio off, and they continued to drive in silence. Meri laid her head back against the rest and closed her eyes. It would be her turn to drive soon enough. She wanted to get a little shut-eye.

Suddenly the car began to slow down, and Meri opened her eyes to see what was going on. An old beater car was parked on the shoulder of the highway up ahead with its hood open. A man was standing in the middle of the road waving his arms back and forth.

"Damn," Ted said. "He's lucky I picked him up in my headlights. I could've killed the dumb bastard!"

Meri continued to watch the guy. "Maybe we should see if we can help. Maybe he needs a ride or something."

"I was thinking the same thing," Ted replied, and he continued to slow the car until they were able to pull right up alongside the man.

Ted rolled his window down. "Do you need some help, mister?"

The man nodded vigorously. His hair was thin and dirty, and his outdated glasses were smudged so badly that Ted could see the smudges in the dark.

"Ayuh," he replied. "I have a split at the end of my radiator hose. I just need to get the clamp off and trim the hose down, but I'm having' a hell of a time with the damn clamp."

"Well," Ted replied, "If you have the tools, I can see what I can do."

The guy continued to bob his head up and down. "That'd be great."

Ted put the car in reverse and pulled back behind the dinosaur the man was driving. He left his headlights on and turned to Meri. "You stay here. This shouldn't take too long, okay?" He smiled at her and leaned over to plant a quick kiss on her pouty little lips.

"You can't get rid of me that easy," she replied flirtatiously.

Ted got out of the car and approached the man, who was now standing on the passenger side of the car looking under the hood. He had a wrench in one hand and a hammer in the other. "See," he said, "If you look down here with the flashlight, you can see the split. The nut that needs to come off is right there." He motioned with the wrench, then handed it to Tim. "Flashlight's right there."

Ted took the wrench in one hand and the flashlight in the other and bent down to try and see the split. He aimed the light on the hose and turned his head back and forth. He didn't see a thing.

"I gotta tell you, mister, this hose looks fine to me," he said as he continued to look up the length of the hose.

The man cleared his throat nervously. "You don't say?"

Ted turned to look at him. Suddenly, pain exploded throughout his head, and he collapsed over the car and slid to the ground. He struggled to understand what was happening, and it was hard to see through the stars in his eyes. The guy was drawing back with the hammer like he wanted to hit him. Is that what just happened? Did this guy just hit me? Fear for himself was second only to what may happen to Meri.

The hammer came down again, and the last sound he heard was Meri screaming.

Meri sat in the car, panic-stricken with her hands over her mouth as she screamed. She watched the man drop the hammer to the ground and turn toward her. Oh, shit, she thought. He's coming over here! She thought quickly about her options.

She fumbled with the door handle but finally got it open. She was out of the car and running back up the road in the direction they had come. Meri was a runner in high school, but now she felt like her legs were bound in molasses. She continued to run and scream, "Help! Somebody help me!"

She could hear the man running behind her, and he seemed to be getting closer. She couldn't believe this was happening but tried to think logically. She took a quick left into a field in an effort to lose him but stumbled over a large rock. Meri hit the ground hard, and the wind was knocked out of her lungs. She rolled over and tried to catch her breath.

Suddenly the man was there, standing over her and smiling. He was shining a flashlight up into his own face, and Meri could see a strand of greasy hair falling across his forehead. She was beyond horrified.

Now he shone the light directly into her eyes. She squinted as she gasped. "Now what did you go and do that for?" he asked. "It would have been so much easier on both of us if you had just stayed put."

He dropped to his knees beside her and watched her as she gasped. She started to whimper and cry, and the man began to mimic her sobs. "Oh, boo hoo hoo! Boo hoo!"

Soon he tired of that game, and the smile fled from his face. It was as if he flipped a switch. He drew back his arm and brought the flashlight down hard on her face. Meri felt the bones in her nose and cheek break, and blood filled her mouth and nose. She couldn't see or breathe.

He hit her again and again, only stopping after he realized she didn't even look like a human woman anymore. No, she was bloody and mangled, completely unrecognizable.

He placed the flashlight about two feet from her lifeless body, making sure to illuminate her as much as possible. He stood and unbuttoned his filthy jeans, letting them drop to the ground at his feet. He lay on top of her and smiled at her bloody face.

"See, pretty lady?" he asked her. "We were meant to be together."

The only sounds in the dark night were his grunts and groans as he used her to relieve himself.

CHAPTER
SIX

Diane Jensen sat on one of the benches in front of the Burdensville K-12 with her best friend, Amy. "Did I tell you I was accepted to the nursing school? I just got my letter yesterday!"

Amy shook her head. "You didn't call me or anything. I see how I rate. Anyway, congratulations! I love you, and I know you're going to be the best nurse ever."

Diane wanted to study nursing for as long as she could remember. The thought of caring for people who needed her made her feel fulfilled and rewarded. She had volunteered at the retirement home on Buckley for the last two summers, and the nurses there told her she was a natural. She didn't think she would be accepted, but when she got the letter, she was beside herself. Plus, she couldn't wait to get the heck out of Burdensville. She would never meet her future husband in this podunk town.

Diane glanced down at her gold wristwatch. It had been her mother's, and it was her most cherished possession. "The bell is gonna ring in five minutes," she said as she stood up. "We'd better get going."

As they rose, a beat-up old car came clunking up the street. When it got to the school, the driver slowed and ogled the two teens. "Hey, hey, you pretty girls!"

"Ugh!" Diane said as she turned her back on the man in the car. It was smelly Ronnie Smith, the town clown. He was always gawking at her, and it not only made her uncomfortable, but it also made her sick. He always smelled bad, and his breath reeked of rotten teeth and alcohol. "Come on, Amy. That guy makes me nervous."

Diane Jensen and Amy hustled into the building, ready for their first class.

"So, Denise, have you heard anything about the young man from yesterday?"

It was Madelyn Harris, one of the oldest residents of Burdensville. She sat at the counter of Dickie's with her sister Margaret; they were twins in their eighties. They lived together in the largest home in town, and they tried to soak up as much of the town gossip as they could at any given opportunity.

Both sisters were in their yard, working in their garden the day before when the stranger walked by toward the café. They practically heard about the confrontation with Ronnie Smith before it was over. It was vital to keep up with the comings and goings. How else could you look out for your friends and neighbors?

Denise smiled at the ladies as she filled their coffee cups. They tickled her, the way they leaned toward her as if they were discussing something top secret, and the way they spoke in hushed tones while they looked back and forth to see who was paying them mind.

"I haven't, to be honest," she replied as she reached for a small container of half and half and set it down before them. "All I can tell you is that Dickie told me this morning that we'll be making his meals. He came back after we closed last night to whip something up for him."

Margaret shook her head, a look of disdain on her face. "I can't believe Sheriff Darby is holding him." She took a sip of her coffee and continued. "He should've taken crazy Ronnie in. He should've taken that nut case in years ago."

"I'll never understand it," Madelyn chimed in. "So many issues, so many incidents. Ronnie falls in crap and comes out smelling like a rose every time."

"I'd say he smells plenty like crap," Margaret added with a chuckle.

"Oh, Lawwwrd! True indeed." Madelyn replied with a laugh.

Denise smiled at the ironic analogy and the twins' comical exchange. "I should've said something," she muttered. "I feel terrible. It seems like anyone who approaches Darby about Ronnie ends up on his shit list. I feel like a bad person for not doing what was right."

"Ayuh," Margaret agreed. "I think, we all feel the same way. None of us understand it at all. It makes no sense. But don't you go feeling bad, honey. You have Diane to worry about."

"Well, all I can say is that Darby had a younger brother back when he was but a tyke," Madelyn said in a low voice, as she looked around the café. "The boy died, and as far as anyone in town knew, the Darbys never even had a service for him."

"Really?" asked Denise. "You know, I heard the same story in passing years ago, but I didn't think there was any truth to it. Why wouldn't they have a service?"

Madelyn replied, "The rumor is that the baby and the mother died at the hands of the father, but he never did a second of time."

Margaret nodded. "Really! Sister and I have always believed that the sheriff took Ronnie under his wing to make up for the loss, haven't we, sister?"

"Yes, we have," Madelyn replied. The two old women lifted their coffee cups to their lips in unison.

Denise stared at them and let that tidbit swirl around in her mind. Lost a brother? "How come no one ever talks about that?"

Margaret put her cup on her saucer. "The Darbys made it clear they didn't want to discuss it, and so no one ever does."

"He started hanging out at the Smiths' house down on Dire Street shortly after the loss. They would give him nickels to run errands. Mrs. Smith had Ronnie, and he wasn't easy. Took a lot of care," Madelyn elaborated. "The town just assumed that Darby dealt with the grief by forming a relationship with Ronnie."

Denise left the two women to their conversation and began to fill salt and pepper shakers, but she was busy digesting what she just learned. How had she lived here her whole life and never heard about Darby having a dead brother? Regardless, the Harris twins were probably right. If Darby started helping Ronnie's mom, he likely formed an attachment to the boy in the process.

The bell on the door jingled, and Denise and the twins all turned to see who was coming in. Speak of the devil. It was Sheriff Darby, looking rested and fresh. He had a broad smile on his face, making him appear happy.

"How are we doing this morning, girls?" He took a seat at one of the tables in the middle of the room. He never sat in the booths due to his stature, and the twins were at the counter, so he settled for the next best thing.

Margaret gave him a big plastic smile as if they weren't just gossiping about him. "Just wonderful, Sheriff. Just grand."

"Good, good," he replied. He turned to Denise and gave her a big smile as well. "And how are you, young'un? Have you rid yourself of yesterday's events?"

"Nothing, a good night's sleep, couldn't fix," Denise replied. "What can I get you today, Sheriff?"

He looked thoughtfully toward the ceiling. "Hmm. Let's see, shall we? I'm gonna need a couple of breakfasts to go. Make 'em fried eggs, taters, bacon, and white toast, will you? Oh, and milk for my prisoner. I'll have a coffee to go."

Denise scribbled on her pad as fast as he spoke, then turned the order over to Dickie in the kitchen using the carousel. She poured a black coffee into a to-go cup and secured a lid on top, then brought it over to the sheriff. He smiled, nodded at her, and took a sip. She sat down across the table from him.

"How is the stranger, anyway?"

Darby lowered the cup and searched her face trying to read it. "He's good, I expect. He'll see the Judge next week, and if he behaves, I'll request the charges be dropped." He took another drink of coffee. "I just want him to get the message that these smaller towns don't take kindly to strangers interfering and making trouble, you see."

Denise looked over her shoulder at the twins, who were sharing a newspaper and reading in silence. She turned back to the sheriff and leaned forward conspiratorially. "I gotta agree, Sheriff Darby. None of us here in Burdensville want trouble from outsiders."

Darby smiled big. Her words eased his conscience. "Ayuh," he replied. "We townsfolk have to look out for each other. We have to take care of our own."

Denise smiled back. "Yes. Yes, we do."

She stood and fetched the coffee pot, then refilled the twins' cups as well as Darby's to-go cup. As she stood at his table pouring, the bell began to jingle again. She looked up to see two state troopers enter.

"Just the person we're looking for, Sheriff Darby," said the older of the two. He marched up to the table and slapped the sheriff on the back. "We're gonna have to disrupt your mornin', I'm afraid."

Darby looked alarmed. "What's going on, boys?"

The younger cop spoke up. "Two bodies found, just out of town on the highway. A young man and a young woman. Skulls split open, bloody messes. The girl was raped. It's your jurisdiction. We'll need you to help with the investigation, but I think our boys will be taking the lead."

Darby only missed a small beat. He stood with his coffee in hand. "Well, heck. Let's hit the road, I suppose."

Dickie rang his bell to signify that the sheriff's order was up. Denise checked and then turned back to the sheriff. "What about the food, Sheriff?"

"Dammit, the food!" he replied. "I gotta get that prisoner fed. Listen, Denise, you mind takin' it to him? You can leave mine on my desk. I'll eat it later."

She nodded, trying hard not to look as happy as she was to deliver it. She couldn't believe she would get a chance to talk to the stranger. "Absolutely. I'll need the keys though."

He began going through the keys on his ring. He found the one he was looking for and handed it to her. "Listen, if he says anything out of the ordinary or suspicious to you, I want a full report. Can I trust you to do that?"

"Sure thing, Sheriff." She took the key and slipped it into her apron pocket then turned her attention back to the three lawmen. "It's awful about these murders. I sure hope you catch whoever is hurting all these people."

The young trooper smiled at her, flirting a bit. "Oh, don't you worry yourself, pretty lady. It's just a matter of time."

The men tipped their hats and walked back out the door. Denise made a beeline for the window and started packing the food in a plastic bag. "Dickie, Sheriff Darby had to go to a murder scene outside of town. Donna should be here any minute, then I need to run this food over to the jail."

Dickie looked concerned. "Do you want me to do it?"

Denise shook her head. "Don't be silly, Dickie. Who would cook? The breakfast rush is right around the corner. It'll only take me fifteen or twenty minutes."

"Well," he replied, sounding doubtful, "If you think you'll be all right, that's fine. Just be careful."

She finished packing up the food and warmed the twins' coffee. As scheduled, Donna opened the door to start her shift. "Mornin', Donna."

"Mornin', Denise. Ready for the day?"

"I was born ready," she said. "Look, I have to run this food down to the jail for the out-of-town prisoner. Sheriff Darby went to investigate a couple more murders outside of town. I'll be back in a flash."

Donna's mouth dropped open, and her eyes grew wide. "Two more murders? Good Lord! Wait, you have to tell me all about them!"

Denise zipped her jacket and grabbed the bags of food. "The twins will tell you. I'm positive they heard just as much as I did. She smiled and winked at the older ladies, who returned her smile and waved her away.

"Come on over, Donna Mae," Margaret said. "We have the scoop."

Denise left the three women to discuss the new crime drama and left in a hurry. As she walked to the jail, she thought about the news. Two bodies, likely murdered, right outside of town. She wished she could be more surprised, but this was becoming far too common. Anyone could go to the train station and look at the missing person's board. They could see how many people hadn't been found, and that was nothing compared to the number that had. It was disturbing as hell.

There was a slight chill in the morning air, and Denise enjoyed the way it felt when she breathed it in. She had a bit of pep in her step. She couldn't think of any reason to feel so good, but she did.

It took her all of five minutes to reach the jail. She set the bags down on the step and took the key from her apron. The lock opened easily, so she grabbed the bags and stepped into the dim, musty room. Scant light was coming from the few windows. She looked at the wall near the door and located the light switch. The light flooded the room, abruptly waking the man who had been sleeping.

Scott sat up on the edge of his bed and rubbed his eyes. It took a moment to register who it was, but once it did, he was very pleasantly surprised. What was she doing here? He jumped up and grabbed onto the bars, pressing his face against them.

"Good morning," he said.

Denise nodded. "Good morning." She walked over to his cell slowly. "The sheriff had business, and he asked me to... to bring your meal."

"Thank you," he said.

She placed the Styrofoam containers on the judge's

desk and removed her jacket. Scott watched her closely, but she seemed to look everywhere but at him. She owed him a look in the eye after deterring that maniac away from her at the café. He ended up in jail protecting her. Maybe she was embarrassed or ashamed that she hadn't spoken up in his defense.

Denise picked up the containers and made her way over to Scott's cell. She continued to avoid eye contact as she put the containers on a folding chair near his cell. "There's a pack of plastic utensils and a napkin inside the box," she said. She offered him a slight smile and backed away, looking around the room as if she had never been inside the place before.

Scott took the Styrofoam box and cup and maneuvered them between the bars carefully, then sat down on the bed to eat. "So," he began, "How are you feeling since all that craziness at the café?"

Denise paced around, looking everywhere but at him. "Oh, I'm fine," she replied lightly. "Ronnie Smith can be a bit strange, but everyone in Burdensville is used to his erratic behavior." She chuckled a little and continued walking around the room.

Scott took a bite of his fried eggs, which had begun to get cold. He didn't care; he was ravenous, and the food tasted pretty good. He chewed while he thought then looked back up at Denise.

"Well, being a stranger to this town, I certainly wouldn't know that. But you sure looked worried to me at the time." He watched her, looking for a response or explanation. She could make all the excuses she wanted, but Denise was frightened at the time, whether she was used to Ronnie's behavior or not.

Finally, her eyes flickered in his direction. "Well, Ronnie has some issues which is why he acts the way he does at times," she replied. "I guess, it doesn't matter how long you've known him. When he's been drinking, one can never tell."

Scott nodded at her, even though she didn't see him. "I'm sure," he said. "I'd say that dude is unstable. He made me more than uncomfortable. I just don't understand why the sheriff made a judgement to bring *me* to jail, especially now that you're telling me his behavior is typical for the guy."

Denise finally turned and faced Scott. "How's the food?" She desperately wanted to change the subject.

"It's actually surprisingly good," he replied with a smile. "After only bologna for supper, I suppose, anything would work."

Denise approached the cell and sat down in the folding chair. "Do you mind?"

Scott shook his head and smiled as he chewed. He finally swallowed and said, "Please, stay as long as you like." He took a drink of milk and looked at her again. "So, what did you say Sheriff Darby had to do?"

The question made her fidgety, and she began picking at a non-existent hangnail. It was challenging to discuss the local murders with someone who wasn't from Burdensville because no one had any answers. She supposed it was the least she could do, though.

"There were a couple of people found murdered just out of town, and the state patrol needed his assistance. It's technically his jurisdiction," she replied simply. Her eyes began to wander around the room again. Scott could see she was uncomfortable talking about it, even nervous.

He put his plastic fork down and wiped his mouth with his napkin. "Wow, that has to really shake up a small town like this."

Denise took a deep breath and closed her eyes. She didn't want to lie to this guy. After all, he was here sitting in a jail cell on her account. The least she could do was be honest.

She looked directly at him. "It does, but it isn't the first time. Sadly, these aren't the first murders in or around Burdensville."

Scott felt his eyebrows raise. "Not the first? I don't mean to sound shocked, but multiple homicides? That's a problem found in bigger cities. Wouldn't you agree? You don't seem very rattled by this... this trend."

To Scott's surprise, Denise laughed. "Not rattled? I guess that's appropriate." She turned her attention back to her hangnail. "The truth is there've been more murders than you could shake a stick at. And Sheriff Darby doesn't seem to have any leads, at least none that he wants to share with the public."

Disclosing that information, she stood up and retrieved her jacket from the judge's desk. She stopped with her back to Scott, thinking. He waited patiently for more details or for any theories she may have. "Look," she began. "I'm sorry about the crap that happened at Dickie's."

Scott stood up and walked to the cell door. He shook his head. "No, no," he said. "It is what it is, and from the way it sounds, you definitely have your reasons."

Denise smiled half-heartedly. "I guess, but that doesn't make it okay."

He shrugged and smiled back, not wanting to scare her off by pummeling her with questions. "No worries."

She walked to the door, pulling the keys out of her apron as she did. On her way out the door, she stopped and looked back at him. "Maybe we'll see you again before you head out of town."

"I'd like that," Scott replied.

Denise smiled once again. "Me too. I'll leave the lights on for you, okay?" He nodded, and she shut and locked the door behind her.

Scott stood at the bars of his cell for several moments, analyzing Denise and the things she revealed about the town. She certainly was a pretty one. The thought made him smile, even blush a little. Then he thought about the murders and the eerie fact that there were so many. It made him knit his brow. It all seemed to verify what he'd been thinking since he got here: something was very strange about Burdensville.

Diane finished her calculus assignment and closed her book with a bang. She was glad to be finished with homework. A quick glance at the clock told her that her sister would be home from work soon. The day had passed quickly, and she was tired. She had her mind set on a hot shower and a snack before she turned in.

She gathered her towel and toiletries and hopped in the shower. As she bathed, her mind drifted to Ronnie Smith. His catcalling that morning was creepy. Rumors about Ronnie made the rounds her entire life, and Denise always warned her to steer clear of him. That proved to be easier said than done, though. In a town this size, you were bound to run into nearly everyone on a regular basis.

He made her more than nervous. In fact, he put a bad taste in her mouth that she couldn't describe. She was downright terrified of him. Besides his immature advances, he had never done anything to deserve this degree of judgment, but as Denise said, it was important to follow your gut instincts. Well, when it came to Ronnie Smith, her gut told her to stay far away from him.

Diane dried off and slipped into her pajamas. She sat on the edge of her bed eating a couple of chips with a glass of cold milk. When she was finished, she climbed under the sheets and turned out the light. She was asleep in minutes, and Ronnie Smith was the furthest thing from her mind.

CHAPTER
SEVEN

Ronnie sat in the dust and dirt on the floor, his knees drawn up and his head against the wall. Next to him, on the floor, was a flashlight. He rolled it back and forth with his hand and watched the stream of light bounce around across the room. The light made him feel grounded and safe, especially when there was nothing but darkness, both inside and all around him.

His mind went to the girl in the field. He knew that she and her boyfriend had probably been found by now. When he finished with her, he went straight home and locked himself inside with all the lights off. A few weeks ago, he had covered all the windows with dirty towels and blankets, which added to the darkness. Funny, but the darkness, for all of its emptiness, made him feel better. It made him feel safer.

Things had gotten out of control lately; even he knew that. If they ever found out what he was doing, they wouldn't let him be free anymore. But the true magnitude of his actions and the consequences didn't truly sink into his brain. He was concerned only about relieving the pressure when it came. He had no more and no less motivation than that.

The recent murders were nothing, only the tip of the iceberg. The truth was that he had been doing this for a very long time. In the beginning, he would head toward the city, staying on rural roads. Getting their attention was easy. All he had to do was pretend to break down, and someone would inevitably stop. If it were a man by himself, he would just tell him that he had help coming, but if it was a girl...

After a while, it was difficult for him to travel so far. He began to suffer bouts of panic with each mile he put between himself and Burdensville. He knew what would happen if he were ever caught far from home, so he began to hunt victims closer. Now he feared that strategy wasn't such a great idea. The last five were just too damn close to home. He could feel the walls closing in on him and began to cry. He was afraid of what they would do to him if he was caught, but he wasn't able to stop. He tried a couple of times, but the urges took ahold of him. They took over him, and he had no control. It was especially bad after he drank. That's when the words in his head became loud, and the only thing that shut them up was killing. He felt no remorse, though. A person had to do what he had to do in this life. And this is what he had to do.

As Ronnie sat despairing, the root of his evil came to mind. His mother. When he was twelve, she turned on him terribly. Sure, he had been naughty, but he thought a mother's love was unconditional. He learned that it was not, and it killed him deep inside.

After his little brother came along, she started treating him differently. She just stopped loving him, and he hated her for it in return. When he killed the girls, he would pretend they were his mother, and that they wanted his love. Once he drained the life out of them, he could feel their love back, and it was satisfying, but only for a while.

It was as if his own mind would eat him alive. He had to relieve the nagging pain in his groin, the one that would make him pace in the darkness and filth until he did something or found someone to make it stop. Until he did, he was nothing but a tortured soul. It would pull at him and nag at him until he got rid of it.

When he was a boy, he would take pets from the townsfolk. He would do to the pets what he now did to the girls. Back then, it would take care of the pain, but it didn't last. Eventually, he got caught. Sheriff Darby, his good friend, had taken care of things, but he had to stop with the pets. By then, he had evolved, and he didn't even realize it.

He would leave and find what he needed: sexual release. But that was never enough either. He always had to see it or feel it... the life force as it left their bodies. The look in their eyes when they slipped away. Until he experienced those things, he couldn't stop.

He would appease the nagging pressure and feel utter relief, but it always came back, no matter how often he tried to make it stop. His mind would always beg for it again, and he had no way to control it. He simply acted in the only way he knew how.

Still sitting on the dirty floor, he picked up the flashlight and held it under his chin, so it shone on the entirety of his face. He made a few snorting noises, which caused him to laugh. Suddenly, he realized he was laughing out loud, and his smile turned into a frown. He dropped the flashlight back on the floor, and it hit the discolored tile with a metallic thud. He fished around in his front right hip pocket and brought out a small penknife. He straightened his legs and laid the flashlight on top of them, so the stream of light was facing him. Opening the penknife and holding it in his left hand, he slowly began carving into the soft skin on the underside of his forearm.

The pain made him gasp for breath but, as always, it faded too soon. The man shook his head in frustration as a small trickle of blood ran down his wrist. Not good enough.

This time, he held the penknife straight up and down

and placed the point of the blade against his skin. He began to hum as he turned it in a circle, as though he were screwing in a screw with it. It bore deeper into his flesh; blood spurted as he broke the skin. The sight brought him intense satisfaction.

He continued to bore into his arm with the knife, humming as he did, his teeth biting into his lower lip as he endured the exquisite pain he was feeling. Nothing he ever did made him feel so much relief. Not the murders, not the forced sex, nothing.

Soon he hit the point of release. His mouth opened and he let out a long sigh as the pain tingled, searing into his flesh. A broad smile crossed his face as a single tear ran down his cheek. His hum suddenly broke into a low song.

DENISE JENSEN GENTLY PLACED THE PLATE OF liver and onions before her customer. "Here you go, Mr. Marshall: liver and onions, green beans, and fried potatoes. Can I get you anything else?"

Mr. Marshall looked his plate over, a smile of anticipation on his lips. "No, dear, I think this is just about perfect. Would you mind warming up my coffee though, ayuh."

"Sure thing," she replied as she patted his shoulder. She started toward the counter just as the phone rang.

Donna answered it, so Denise grabbed the carafe of coffee off the warmer and turned back to Mr. Marshall.

"Dickie's, this is Donna, how can I help you?" Donna's pleasant sing-song voice made Denise smile as she poured Mr. Marshall's coffee into his cup.

Donna was speaking again. "Sure thing, Sheriff Darby. She's right here. Just a moment, okay?"

Denise turned around to see Donna covering the receiver with the palm of her hand. "Denise, it's Darby. He wants to speak with you." She raised her eyebrows out of curiosity, and Denise shrugged her shoulders. She put the carafe back on the warmer and took the receiver from Donna's hand.

"This is Denise, Sheriff. How can I help you?" She plastered a smile on her face in hopes that it would make her sound pleasant. But her stomach turned as soon as she heard that Darby wanted her. What could he possibly want now?

Darby cleared his throat. "Hey, Denise. How did things go with that prisoner this morning?"

"Oh!" she breathed a sigh of relief. Of course, he would want to know if things went smoothly. "Everything was fine, just fine. As a matter of fact, he was very polite. Sheriff, I really don't think…"

He cut her off. "Good, good. I was calling because it looks like I'm gonna be out here at this crime scene for quite a while. Would you be willing to take lunch to Mr. Sharp for me? Have Dickie put it on my official tab, and

I'll reimburse you later on. I might need you for supper as well if you're free."

Denise felt her heart go pitter-patter at the thought of getting to talk to Scott Sharp again. He was quite good-looking, not to mention friendly and respectful, despite the circumstances. Plus, she hadn't spent time talking to a man in years. "Sure, Sheriff Darby. No problem. I'll take care of it for you."

"Thanks, Denise," he replied. "Like I said, I'll probably need you tonight too. I sure appreciate it, and I won't make a habit of it."

"Sheriff," Denise said, "I think you should worry about catching whoever is committing these murders. That's way more important. Taking your prisoner a bite or two to eat is a small price to pay for your service, wouldn't you agree?"

Sheriff Darby chuckled but not in his usual way. Denise sensed a nervous laugh. "Sure, Denise. Sure, and thanks again." He disconnected the call without another word.

Denise looked down at the receiver in her hand and shook her head. He sure was an oddball, Sheriff Darby, but then again, he always had been. Probably just under a lot of pressure over the murders.

She hung up the phone and turned to the kitchen window toward Dickie. "Hey, Dickie," she said. "That was Darby. He wants me to take lunch and supper to the inmate at the jail. He said to put it on the official tab, okay?"

"Sure thing," Dickie replied. "Fill out an order and send it back, and I'll put a rush on it."

She fished her pad out of her apron. She didn't even need to think about it. She jotted down a Reuben, and fries, just like he had ordered before he went to jail. She would also take him an iced tea with a couple of packets of sugar. Maybe it would be a pleasant surprise for him to get what he ordered when he first arrived.

She placed the order on Dickie's carousel and asked Donna to cover her tables before checking on them one last time. By the time she was finished, the order was in a styrofoam container, ready to go. She bagged it up and headed out, a smile on her face. She was surprised at how much she was looking forward to seeing Scott Sharp once again.

DIANE SAT IN SECOND PERIOD SPANISH, HER book open in front of her, but she wasn't paying attention to it. She was tired and being tired made it hard to concentrate. She dreamt of her mother last night, and it made her sleep worthless.

She dreamt of her parents often, but most of the time it was bittersweet. In her good dreams, they were all a family again: Mom, Dad, Denise, and she. They would be at the lake, swimming and laughing together. She would wake with tears on her cheeks and an ache in her heart. It wasn't fair. How she missed them both, but particularly her mother.

The dream last night was different though. In the dream, her mother locked Diane in a big wooden box. She brought her food and water, and while Diane ate, she received a stern motherly lecture.

"You must stay away from the animal," she said to Diane, over and over again. "The animal will be the death of you, and I can't protect you." Diane pleaded with her mother to tell her what she was talking about, but she didn't reply. Instead, she began to hum a light, airy tune. It was infuriating. Her mother locked her back in the box and told her she would see her soon. Diane cried and screamed after her mother, but the woman disappeared into thin air.

She woke up covered in sweat. She had been crying in her sleep, and her hands were trembling. She hopped out of bed and grabbed a cool washcloth and a glass of water. Soon she was calm, but she was afraid to go back to sleep. Something about the dream filled her with fear and a sense of doom, and she just couldn't deal with it.

She sat in Spanish and tried to pay attention, but the dream was still terribly fresh in her mind. She raised her hand, and Mr. Mendes responded to her.

"Yes, Miss Jensen?"

"May I be excused to go to the restroom?"

The teacher smiled and nodded, then turned his attention back to the papers on his desk. Diane left the room and made her way to the girls' room. She was going to throw up, and she didn't want to do it in the hall.

Denise ran the last stretch to the bathroom, barely making it to the toilet before vomiting up her breakfast. She sat on the floor until the nausea subsided, then she flushed and walked over to one of the sinks. She filled her mouth with water and swished it around to wash away the taste of puke. She wished she had a mint or mouthwash.

She looked at herself closely in the mirror. Her eyes were red and her face puffy. Had she been crying again? She didn't know, but she looked terrible.

It was time to go back to class. She only had about fifteen minutes left to finish her in-class assignment. Good thing she was a straight-A student. She made her way back to class, sat at her desk, and forced herself to focus.

SHERIFF ROBERT DARBY CLOSED HIS FLIP PHONE and looked down at it for a long moment. He trusted Denise to take the food over to the prisoner. He didn't think it would cause any problems. She knew—heck, the whole town knew—that Ronnie Smith had problems. But the fact was that he was lifelong townsfolk. He belonged among them, even if he did cause trouble every now and then. In towns like Burdensville, people took care of each other. He kept reminding himself of that.

Even though he firmly believed in Denise, and the rest of the townsfolk, the stress of it all gave him cause for concern. It was constantly in the back of his mind. He wished the burden didn't fall completely on his shoulders. That he had someone he could trust, but with the people surrounding him right now, he just wasn't free to make the right phone call. He would have to just be patient and wait.

A huge mess had been made out here on the highway. Darby slid his cell into its case on his belt, then plucked a toothpick out of his hatband. He planted it firmly in the corner of his mouth and strode back to the group of cops and investigators milling around. Crime scene tape and evidence markers surrounded the Mercury Tracer on the side of the highway.

Darby knew they would be out here awhile with forensics. He was basically there to answer questions at this point, not do any hard investigating. The state police got involved right away, so he was there to provide details about the town and asked about suspicious activity or happenings. There had been far too many recent murders in and around Burdensville in too short a period.

He knew things were getting too close to home and he wasn't sure what his next step should be. All he wanted was for the folks of Burdensville to be safe, and that meant everybody. But during the questioning, the state troopers and their investigators dropped not-so-subtle hints that Darby hadn't been doing his job. They wanted to know why he didn't ask for help after such serious crimes. They basically accused him of being responsible for the ongoing murders and disappearances. That some of these lives wouldn't have been lost if he had just run it by the proper authorities. They were using words like 'negligence' and 'faulty,' and it made Darby very, very nervous.

It really didn't matter in the grand scheme of things. To Darby, some people were more important than others. He had made promises, and he intended to keep them. But right now, as he stared down at the smashed skull of the young man on the road, he wondered if he hadn't taken his sense of obligation too damn far.

He approached the other officers with a grim smile on his face. It would be important to walk this tightrope slowly and attentively. He simply had no other choice.

But he was getting to the point of throwing up his hands. He'd done just about all he could do without losing complete control of the situation. He knew he couldn't just give up, though. There was far too much at risk, and what could be lost would be very costly indeed, at least to him.

CHAPTER
EIGHT

Scott was lying on the bunk in his cell staring at the ceiling. It was so damn hot in there! He knew the weather outside wasn't the cause; the room and the cells were poorly ventilated and stuffy. He felt as though he could suffocate. He even thought about shedding the jail uniform and airing out in his underwear to cool off. But he remembered that the sheriff would be bringing his lunch soon, so he chose to sweat it out.

His mind went to the waitress, Denise. What a beautiful name for a gorgeous girl! Funny, he'd heard that name a thousand times in his life, but it never quite had the same ring as it does now. He smiled as he thought about seeing her come through the door that morning. She sure was a welcome sight, especially after enduring time with Sheriff Darby who seemed to be a lying, scheming excuse of a cop. Perhaps a dirty cop.

He wished he hadn't found this trouble. He wished he'd been able to simply order his lunch and talk to his waitress for a while like a civilized human being. Someone like Denise could potentially get his mind off Kelly. Maybe he could move on with his life. The thought of his deceased wife made his heart ache and stomach flip. He had to sit up on the edge of his cot to shake off the memories and flashbacks of watching her suffer.

Gone were thoughts of Denise the waitress. He let himself remember Kelly, her smile and laugh dancing around in his mind.

She underwent radical surgery and chemotherapy, but her prognosis was grim. The day came when he and his wife had to face the facts: Kelly was going to die.

Scott made sure she was comfortable at home, and he employed a well-reputed hospice service to come in and care for her so he could continue working. Each day, when he returned home, his wife would be sicker than when he left. She was withering away before his very eyes. With guilt, he found himself wishing she would pass so she wouldn't have to live like this.

He remembered one of their last conversations. It had been a good day for Kelly. She had gotten out of bed, and the hospice worker pushed her outside in the wheelchair so she could get some air. Scott joined her there. At first, they simply sat in silence, holding hands.

Finally, she had turned to him, and in a weak voice she said, "Scott, you have to let me go."

He looked at her, confused. "What do you mean?"

"I feel like I can't go. I feel like if I do, you'll fall apart. You're keeping me here, Scott."

It was like a punch to the gut. He realized that she had been toughing it out for him.

They cried together that day, but Scott still hadn't come to terms. He wasn't ready to let her go. About five days later, while he was at work, it occurred to him. She wanted to make sure that he would be okay, that he would keep on keeping on. Throughout her illness, he acted like he would die when she died.

Scott went home that night, and as he and Kelly went about their nightly routine getting ready for bed, he said to her, "Kelly, I'm going to be okay. I'm going to go on. I don't know how, but I promise I will."

She hugged him and kissed him. Then she thanked him.

When Scott Sharp woke the next morning, his Kelly was gone. Regardless of what he said, life would never be the same. Part of him fully expected to die when she did. It was an odd feeling surviving... a very painful and surreal feeling.

He squeezed his eyes shut in an effort to stop the tears, but they seeped out anyway. Here he was, in a hick town jail cell, mourning. All he could think about was his late wife. She wouldn't want him to live this way. She would want him to move on and find happiness. How could he, though? He wished he could have traded places with her. Wished he died instead of her.

Scott heard keys in the door. He stood up and quickly wiped the tears from his eyes. The clock read twelve-fifteen, probably his lunch arriving. He wondered about the person or people who had been killed, the ones the sheriff took off to investigate that morning. Maybe he had a break in the case already. Scott hoped so; no town needed the stress of having a murderer on the loose, especially a town the size of Burdensville.

The door swung open, and Scott's smile grew. It was Denise bearing Styrofoam boxes. She closed the door behind her and turned to him, and as soon as she saw his grin, she returned it, adding a cute little blush to it as well. Was it just him or did she look happy to see him?

"Hi," she began shyly. "Sheriff Darby is still at the crime scene, so he asked me to bring your lunch."

Scott's fingers curled around the bars of the cell, but his eyes were fastened on the woman before him. "I have no complaints," he replied. He was hardly aware that his thoughts of Kelly had diminished.

She approached him with the boxes and cup, this time passing the judge's desk without stopping to put a jacket down. Scott realized she wasn't wearing one. The day must've warmed up quite a bit. "Are the temperatures outside better than this morning?" he asked, then cringed. Do you really want to talk about the weather? He did a mental head slap.

"Oh, yeah," Denise said with a nod. "The mornings always seem to have a chill around these parts. Where are you from?"

"Coos Bay," he replied lightly. "We see a lot of rain and little snow, and it doesn't get too hot there."

"You're on the ocean, too," Denise replied. "We have to drive if we want to see it, but I never have."

Scott raised his eyebrows. "You've never seen the ocean?"

She shook her head, embarrassed. "Only in picture books." Scott made a mental note of that. He didn't know it was possible to live one's life without seeing the ocean.

Denise's smile grew, and she crinkled her nose just a bit. Scott thought she had the cutest little nose, and he found himself wishing he could plant a little kiss right on the tip of it. She was adorable, and he was growing more attracted to her by the minute.

She slid his food containers through the opening in the cell door, and Scott took them all too willingly. "What did the Good Sheriff order for me today? Bread? Water?"

The waitress belted out a laugh and found herself wishing she had brought a faux box filled with those items as a joke. She sat down in the folding chair and crossed her arms over her chest. "He actually let me decide. I thought today's special would appeal to you: liver and onions." This was the second-best way to tease him.

Scott looked up at her, struggling to hide his disappointment. He hated liver, and he always had.

But it didn't matter at this point, not from where he was sitting. He would force himself to eat it if it meant getting on Denise's good side. *Ugh.*

He took the box, trying not to show how squeamish he was really feeling. She caught the grimace, even though he tried to suppress his repulsion. It entertained her, and she had to struggle to keep from laughing out loud. Oh, yes, this little liver and onions prank would be a good way to loosen things up between them. It tickled her that she pulled the wool over his eyes.

He sat down and flipped the top of the box back. No liver, but a Reuben sandwich and fries. He smiled and looked back at Denise. "Well done," he said. "I'm impressed. You got me."

"Well, I figured you didn't get to enjoy your order before, so the least I could do was bring you what you wanted."

Scott picked up the sandwich and took a wolf-sized bite. It was delicious! He chewed with his eyes closed so he could savor the taste. Denise's eyes scanned his face amused. Even in jail, with mussed up hair and a jail uniform, he was quite the looker. She felt the blood rush to her cheeks and had to turn away.

When Scott opened his eyes, even they were smiling at her. "Thank you," he said sincerely. "I think, if the sheriff had gotten the food, it would've been liver for sure. After all, you said it's the special of the day."

"No problem."

The two were silent while Scott enjoyed a few more bites of his sandwich and then tore into his fries. Finally, he set the food down on the bed and looked up at Denise. "What's with this Ronnie guy, Denise?"

She expected him to ask her questions regarding the situation at the café that landed him in jail. She contemplated what to say on the short walk over, if he did. She decided she would simply tell him the truth, nothing more and nothing less.

"Ronnie is like, well, the town idiot, so to speak," Denise replied. "I think everyone in town sort of feels like he is their responsibility, especially Darby. It's a little complicated, I know."

Scott gave a short nod as he considered her response. "Seems like he might be the town drunk as well."

"Well," she said, "he does have a problem with the drink which clearly ramps up his bad behavior. He's really harmless, though. At least, I'd like to think so. He's never hurt me or mine."

Scott's heart sunk by the statement. "Are you married?"

"Oh, gosh no!" she replied. "Can you imagine the

type of man I would have to marry having lived in Burdensville my whole life?"

Scott studied her face, noticing that her eyes avoided his as she replied. "You didn't seem to think he was harmless the other day." He changed the subject back to Ronnie Smith.

Denise shifted nervously on the folding chair and began to pick at the hem of her work apron. "Well, that's only because he had been drinking. You never know what's going to happen if someone is soused, you know what I mean?"

"Yeah, I guess." He took another bite of his sandwich and turned her words over in his mind. "Does he hassle a lot of people around here?"

Denise shrugged. "I wouldn't say hassle; he just doesn't have any social skills. He's a lot like a kid. Sheriff Darby looks out for him, you know, takes him under his wing."

"That explains a lot," he replied.

She nodded back at him. "That's why none of us said anything. We knew it was pointless. He's just trying to keep Ronnie safe."

Scott felt a sense of relief for the first time since coming to this forsaken town. If what Denise was saying was true, there was a good chance he would be getting out as soon as he saw the Judge. The sheriff wouldn't want to prolong things. He would want Scott to leave town as soon as possible, and there was no better way to ensure this than to pop his butt in jail for a few days. He'd be more than ready to split when the time came.

He finished his sandwich, polished off his fries, then tipped back his iced tea, without adding sugar. He gulped the whole glass down without coming up for air. It was delicious.

"Thanks again," he said. "I can't tell you how much this really hit the spot."

She stood and approached the opening in the cell door to fetch his garbage. "I was hoping it would. Here, let me get rid of that for you, okay?"

He packed his cup and plastic utensils into the larger container and slid them through to her. Their hands brushed, and they both paused in place, making the sensation last as long as they could. Denise pulled away first and turned in an effort to conceal the pink color that was rushing to her cheeks.

"So, do you have to get back to work right away?" Scott gripped the bars again, looking at the waitress hopeful that she didn't.

She disposed of the waste and headed back to the chair. "I can stay a few more minutes if you like. I'm sure this place is even worse alone."

Scott sat on his cot, looking back at her through the bars. He was thrilled to have more time with her. "So, you have lived here your entire life, huh? Do you have kids? I mean, you said 'you and yours' earlier, so I was just curious."

Denise nodded. "Yep. Probably for the rest of it as well, and no, I have no kids, but I have raised my kid sister."

"What? Don't you want to break free? See the big world? You could take her with you!"

She shook her head and looked down at her hands. She was starting to pick at her apron again. "Nah. My parents were killed in a car accident when I was sixteen. I've been raising my younger sister ever since and making sure she's safe is my top priority. Traveling the world wouldn't allow me to do that." She looked up at Scott, her face glowing with pride. "She'll be leaving next year to study nursing. I couldn't be more proud. She'll be the one to put Burdensville behind her, and I wouldn't have it any other way."

The devotion this woman felt toward her younger sibling was almost tangible to Scott. Her entire face lit up when she spoke of the girl, and he could tell that she wanted to keep talking about her. It was his pleasure to keep the conversation going. "What's her name?"

"Diane," she said, looking up at him with sparkling eyes. "I tell you, she's as smart as a whip! She'll be studying at the Central Medical Center." Now she looked around the sheriff's office with disdain. "I can't wait for her to leave this crap hole behind."

Scott raised his eyebrows but didn't say anything. It was clear, Denise had true contempt for Burdensville.

"But if it's good enough for you here, isn't it good enough for Diane?"

She looked him in the eyes and shook her head vigorously. "I'm here for the duration, and I've accepted that. But I will not accept it for her. I won't have her carrying plates to locals for Dickie, and if she stays, that's what will happen." Denise cleared her throat and glanced around. "Don't get me wrong. I love Dickie, he's like a father to me. I just want more for Diane."

He could tell by her tone that she was finished talking about her sister for the time being. She even stood up looking like she was headed for the door. "Hey," he said, trying to keep her company for as long as he possibly could, "what's up with the murders? Any word?"

He had her attention once again. She sat back down in the chair, this time on the edge of it. She leaned forward, almost conspiratorially, looking over her shoulder at the empty room behind her. "When Sheriff Darby called to ask me to bring your meals, he said he would be a while. He even asked me to bring your supper. That reminds me," she said as she fished out her pad and a pen from her apron, "Did you have any special requests for your evening meal, master?"

Scott threw his head back and gave a hearty laugh. He couldn't remember the last time he laughed so hard, and it felt wonderful. He looked at her through twinkling eyes and winked. "What's on the menu?"

Denise had been working at Dickie's for so long that

the entire menu rolled easily off her tongue, impressing Scott even more. Not only was this girl beautiful, but she was also smart and quick-witted as well. The way they met was quite unconventional to say the least, but he was never one to throw in the towel easily.

He wanted to make things easy for her, so as she rattled off the food that was available. He made a quick choice and held up his hand to stop her from continuing. "How about I just go with the chicken fried steak and mashed potatoes?"

She grinned. "That's my personal favorite. Was the iced tea okay, or do you want something else?"

"The iced tea was perfect."

She tucked her pad back into her apron without writing anything on it. "Will you remember that?" he asked incredulously.

"You have no idea," she said, giving him a wink of her own. She already planned on surprising him with a slice of cheesecake.

After a moment of flirting with their eyes and smiles, Denise stood up. "I really should be going now," she said. "You're pretty good company, Scott Sharp."

"So are you, Denise... Denise...?"

"Jensen," she finished for him. "I'll be off when I come back. Do you play rummy?"

His heart skipped a beat. "I absolutely do."

"Well," she continued, another blush filling her soft

white cheeks. "Then you should resign yourself to losing a game or two this evening."

He rolled with laughter yet again, and by the time he got control of himself, she had the door open and was standing in the gap, waiting patiently. "Listen," she began, "if I don't personally bring your supper, it means that Darby finished up his business for the day." She looked at the ground and pushed an imaginary bit of debris with her toe. "I just wanted you to know I've really enjoyed your company."

With that she shut the door, locking it securely from the other side.

Scott plopped down on his cot and put his hands behind his head. He found himself thinking about the dreamy small-town waitress and her cute little nose. He found himself smiling at her jokes and teasing.

He hoped that Sheriff Darby would not be back before the evening meal.

CHAPTER NINE

Dickie's Café was in the middle of a great big rush, and Dickie felt like he was operating on total autopilot. Even after all his years cooking at the café, he still enjoyed the feeling immensely. It enabled him to shut out all the problems and everyday cares and go full steam ahead. And Dickie had plenty of problems and cares.

To begin with, his wife was suffering terribly with chronic obstructive pulmonary disease. He nagged her and nagged her for years to give up those damn cigarettes for good, but she kept going. For the last ten years, even after she started struggling to get a good breath of air, she kept puffing away. He was sure she did it just to spite him. But none of that mattered now. The COPD was irreversible, and he was left to work his butt off to deal with the repercussions. He loved her like a madman, and he would continue if it meant keeping her with him on this forsaken mudball a while longer. And then there was the bank. He was hassled about late payments on his second mortgage, which he had taken out to help with Doris' medical bills. He made sure to pay something every single month, just like clockwork, but he couldn't come close to paying off the balance, and sometimes he went just a little past due. It just kept piling up and piling up.

The only thing in Dickie's life that was operating above the water was the café, and he wasn't about to start slacking in that department. The café was everything to him. The so-and-so at the bank knew that Doris wasn't going to be around much longer, yet they shamelessly tormented him incessantly. How could that approach work if he just didn't have the money? The café was the only thing that kept him from going into foreclosure, and working seven days a week was the only thing that kept him sane.

Today, the place was packed, more than usual. The press had barnstormed Burdensville once again with their questions and curiosities. He hated them butting their turned up noses into town business, but he supposed that was only natural. Not every tiny town on the map had a full-blown serial killer running around. But Dickie wasn't going to complain about the press, either. Their money was just as green as the next guy's.

He flipped a burger onto a toasted bun and grabbed a

basketful of french fries from the deep fryer and dumped them on the plate. He put the plate in the window for Donna to pick up, along with the other three that waited for her. As he did, he glanced out the small window: chaos, complete chaos. Dickie smiled.

DENISE REAPPEARED AND HUNG THREE MORE orders on the carousel. "Dickie, two of these are for customers seated, but the third is for Darby's prisoner. Just get to it when you're ready."

A look of frustration washed over his face as he grabbed the three tickets. "Denise, we're damn slammed in here, darlin'! That guy's gonna have to wait 'til folks start to clear out. I'll put the order right here," he said as he used a magnet to tack it onto the outside of a metal canister on a shelf. "I won't miss it. You know me." With that, he turned his attention to the other two tickets and went back to work.

Denise grabbed a carafe of coffee and set about warming up cups around the place. When it got this busy, she and Donna took tables individually, but they carried the entire weight of the rush together. Then, at the end of the night, they would sit down and split the tips accordingly. These were their most lucrative nights, but they tended to wear the girls out like no other. Donna was a good ten years older than Denise, but by the end of the night, Denise felt like she was forty. She could only imagine what Donna felt like by the time she made it home.

The bell at the door jingled, and three more people entered the busy restaurant. They looked like tourists, which Burdensville was getting used to with each new murder. It's funny how seemingly normal people couldn't wait to get pictures of crime scenes or even try to steal shots of dead bodies.

She smiled and made her way to the door. "Hi, folks. You're lucky. We have one table left over there," she greeted them, pointing to a corner. "If you want to have a seat either Donna or I will be with you in just a few moments."

The three newcomers made their way to the table, and Denise continued with the coffee on a more expeditious basis. She glanced at the clock as she poured. Thank goodness; they would close in only two more hours...

RONNIE WANTED TO GO OUT. IN FACT, HE wanted to go out badly. He knew there was someone out there, someone just waiting for him to find them and... well, make them feel right at home.

But he knew that there were several police in town right now, so many investigators. He knew it was him they wanted to talk to, even if they didn't know it. He curled his fist into a ball as he peeked out the window through a dirty and torn black sheet he hung over it. It was dark now. Maybe he could go without being noticed.

No. Even he knew that would never work. He would have to wait for all the excitement to die down. Then he would be able to find whoever was next.

He never knew who they were until he saw them coming, then he recognized them right away. He could tell by the look in their eyes as soon as his met theirs. They couldn't wait for him to show them what he could do. He could see the smiles in their eyes and the anticipation.

He just couldn't understand why they always had to change their minds right before he was ready to show them exactly what he could do. They would go from friendly and flirty to scared and screaming. The running was frustrating, but the funny thing was it kind of got him ready for... the show.

He stepped away from the window and looked down at his hand. He had been making a hard fist and didn't even realize it. His fingernails had carved deep grooves into his palm, and now it was covered in blood. He held his hand up to his nose and closed his eyes, inhaling deeply. His eyes flew open in frustration, and he stuck out his tongue. Then he ran his tongue slowly, languorously even, up the length of his dirty palm, lapping up the blood and dirt that covered it. It tasted heavenly, and he closed his eyes in ecstasy, savoring every second of the metallic flavor as it seemed to caress the inside of his mouth.

Oh, he could hardly wait for all these strangers to leave. It was time for them to go! Hadn't they been here long enough already? He needed to taste some blood that wasn't his own.

He made another fist with the same hand and swung it hard, punching the wall next to the window. The old plaster and drywall crumbled immediately, making him feel powerful and in charge. It calmed and soothed him.

He took a deep breath and squared off his shoulders. Yes, he could wait another day or two if he had to, but he sure hoped all those cops, Darby included, would hurry the hell up. But yes, he would wait.

He stepped backward in the dark until his back came into contact with the wall. He looked down and saw his flashlight on the floor at his feet, right where he had left it when he moved from the kitchen to the living room. The bulb was beginning to weaken and was flickering as it struggled to stay on. He picked it up and took it back to the kitchen. He opened a drawer filled with packages of tiny flashlight bulbs and batteries. He changed the batteries first which did the trick. He smiled and went back to the living room, where he sat down on the floor at his post. From there he could see the headlights of the cars that passed his way, and it would indicate that they were wrapping things up at the murder scene.

He put the lit flashlight on the floor next to him and began to roll it back and forth between his fingers as he fixed his gaze on the tattered black sheet. Beads of sweat formed on his forehead, which he absentmindedly wiped away with his other hand. It was so hot in the room all the time. It made him crazy.

But with each passing minute, he was closer to the next one, and that was all he wanted.

As much as he wanted to get out of the house, something inside of him told him to stay put, no matter what. He found himself wishing he had some kind of company to keep his mind off the nagging. As he sat thinking, his head grew heavy, and it wasn't long before he nodded off to sleep.

RONALD'S MOTHER WAS SITTING AT THE TABLE having her coffee. He came in from outside because he was hungry, and it was very near lunch.

His mother looked at him, surprise and anger all over her face. "What have you been doing, Ronald?"

"Nothin' ma," he replied. "I was just playing in the yard."

"You're bloody and filthy. Where did the blood come from, Dirty Boy?"

Ronnie felt his heart begin to pound, and he was beginning to wonder if what was happening wasn't real.

"It's a dream, it's a dream," he was saying over and over, but he couldn't wake himself up.

He looked down to see what his mother was talking about, and he took in a sharp breath. It was true; he had blood all over him. Where had it come from? He hadn't hurt any pets. He was all of five years old in the dream.

Now, he began to stutter as he turned his hands over and saw the shiny red blood. It had begun to congeal in spots, and he could even see chunks of skin in it. "I-I-I don't know, Mother."

He looked up at her, and her face began to change. Her cheekbones sharpened under her skin, and two horns broke through the flesh of her forehead. She cackled at him loudly.

"Dirty boys need a bath!" She walked to the kitchen sink and pulled out the sink cleanser and a chunk of steel wool.

"No! No! I didn't do anything!"

She laughed at him again as she grabbed the whistling teapot from the stove top. "Only hot water will do!"

He crumbled to the floor and put his hands over his head to protect himself. His mother was still laughing, and Ronnie could even hear her footsteps as she drew closer and closer to his cowering body.

"Filthy skin on a bad, bad filthy boy!"

Ronnie screamed.

He jerked awake violently just as his mother poured the scalding water onto the flesh of his arms. He struggled to come back to reality as he screamed over and over again. Finally, he realized it had been a dream after all, and he broke down in tears.

"Damn, I wish I had a drink," he said into the nothing of his dirty, grimy house. The walls were the only thing that listened to him. Everyone else wanted him to hurt, and it had been that way as long as he could remember.

CHAPTER
TEN

"Oh my, I think my feet are gonna fall plumb off," Donna said to Denise as she rubbed the arch of her left foot. Her shoes sat on the floor next to the booth. Denise could smell the sweaty odor, but she didn't dare say anything.

They cleaned up the dining room and prepared all the necessary side work for the next day, then they sat together and split their tips. It was an extraordinarily good night. Between the two of them, they made a hundred and fifty bucks apiece, which was way more than usual. Denise found herself smiling as she tucked the money into her coin purse and dropped it into her apron.

The two of them teased Dickie about hiring more help for them, but they really didn't want it. Sure, Diane could use a bit of extra cash during the summer, but she got by just fine with what she earned helping the locals with yard work and errands. Besides, they didn't typically have enough business for three waitresses, and they both really needed every cent they earned. Donna's kids were grown, and they both hit the road long ago.

Denise stood up as Donna put her shoes back on and gathered her tips. She approached the counter just as Dickie put two Styrofoam boxes in the window. Scott's supper was ready.

"Here you go, girlie," he said to her with a smile. "I'm sure your boyfriend is dying for a bite, so you better go on now, and get it over to him."

Denise gave Dickie a sarcastic grin. "Funny. But you might not be so far off, mister."

"Are you serious?" Dickie looked alarmed. "You don't need to be foolin' around with no strange men, Denise. You don't know anything about the man, do you?"

Denise shrugged as she poured a cup of iced tea and capped it, then grabbed a plastic bag for the meal boxes. She also grabbed one of the two decks of cards from behind the counter that Dickie kept on hand for his regular local customers. "I might know a thing or two about him already, but I'm hoping to learn more!"

She opened the cooler and grabbed a slice of New York cheesecake she had boxed up earlier. Dickie came through the swinging door that led to the kitchen and leaned his back against the counter. He looked so tired,

Denise thought. His hands and arms were covered with burns, and he had dark circles under his eyes. "How's Doris these days, anyway Dickie?"

He shrugged and looked away. "'Bout the same, you know." He scratched behind his ear then met her gaze again. "And don't be changing the subject. I don't think it's safe for you to be fraternizing with strangers."

Denise offered him a smile to calm him, then she patted him on the shoulder. "Well, he ain't really no stranger now, is he? Besides, we've been talking a bit, and he did try to help me. No one tried to help him though!"

Donna's sing-song voice came across the room. "I'm outta here, you two. I feel like my feet have done fell off. I'm ready to go home and finish reading *Passing Through*. Have a good one."

Dickie turned to her and scrunched his face. "Why are you gonna read that garbage when you got the real deal goin' on right here at home?"

Donna stuck out her tongue and waved goodbye to them both, letting the door swing shut behind her.

"Look, Dickie," Denise continued as he turned back to her. "You don't have anything to worry about when it comes to me, okay? That guy ain't interested in hanging out here in Hicksville, and I'm not looking to leave." She rubbed his shoulder reassuringly then turned to pack all the boxes in the bags. She tied a secure knot at the top and checked her apron pocket for the keys to the jail, then grabbed her things to go.

"Call me when you get home, girlie," he said to her with a wink. "I just wanna make sure you're okay."

She smiled and stood on her tiptoes to kiss his cheek. "I will, and I love you, Dickie. Thank you for all you do, okay?"

He nodded and followed her to the door, which he locked as soon as she went out. He reached up and flipped off the dining room light just as the phone pealed with its loud ringing. Dickie crossed the room and grabbed the receiver from its cradle on the wall.

"Dickie's."

Sheriff Darby's voice came over the line. "Hey, Dick. How's tricks?"

It was a greeting he used in good cheer, but his voice sounded anything but. The sheriff sounded exhausted and frustrated. Dickie's squinted his eyes as he spoke cautiously, trying to read the cop's mood.

"Oh, all's well, I s'pose," he replied. "We got slammed in here today, for sure. The press and tourists 'bout ate me outta business."

"Ayuh, I expected," Darby replied. "Are the girls still there?"

Dickie leaned back against the counter, a common resting place for both him and the girls. "Nope. Donna's gone, and Denise just left to take your boy his supper. Sorry, we got it out late; we were just too busy."

"No problem," Darby reassured him. "That's what I wanted to talk to you about anyway."

Now Dickie's antennas went up. They always did when the sheriff wanted to talk to him. Every topic he wanted to discuss made him worry, though he didn't always know why. "What's up, Bobby?"

Darby took a deep, audible breath on the other end of the phone. "I guess I been worrying about that inmate. You don't think it's... dangerous to be letting Denise take him food, do you?"

Dickie was quiet for a moment. He scratched his chin as he thought. He'd been living in Burdensville way too long, and he felt like there wasn't much left to know. He toyed with the idea of selling everything and moving with Doris to the city, but he knew deep in his heart he was trapped here, partially because of his roots and partially because... well, he was trapped.

"Look, Bobby, it wasn't a good idea for you to take the guy in, to begin with," Dickie replied. "If you really aimed to avoid unwanted attention, you should've packed up Ronnie, but you and your hard-headed sense of misplaced obligation, you know?"

Darby cleared his throat. "Dickie, I didn't ask for your opinion about my personal life. I have reasons for the way I do things, and I keep everyone's best interest in mind all the time." He was getting agitated, but so was Dickie with the entire confusing situation. "Just answer the question, please. I'm tired, and I just wanna know what you think."

"I trust Denise with my own life, and you can trust

her with yours as well," Dickie said, not hiding his own frustration. "You should've thought about that more clearly before you recruited her to deliver food. I didn't like putting her in that position to begin with."

"Well," Darby said, tension leaving his tone. "That's all I needed, buddy. I have to travel to the state police station in the morning with some paperwork concerning recent incidents, you know, photos and the like. The next day, I promised to do some yard work for Ronnie. His lawn is overgrown, to say the least. If you feel okay about Denise, well, I'd appreciate her help for the next day or two. If you're uncomfortable, well..."

Dickie shook his head to himself. Damn Darby. "I'd do it myself if I could. But we're too busy with all the newcomers in town. Bunch of busybodies. She'll do it, but if I were you, I'd offer her a reward when you can. She's handling your damn dirty work and doesn't even know it."

"Fine," Darby continued. He'd think about it. "Thanks for all your help, and I'll give you a ring tomorrow."

The phone went dead, and Dickie stared at the receiver before hanging it up. He let out a sigh and went into the kitchen to shut things down and turn off the lights. Darby had a way of using people, and Dickie knew it. It bothered him to no end, but what could he do?

He locked up the café and started the short walk home. He would make it a point to go by the jail and peek in the window to check on Denise and the prisoner before going home to Doris. He hoped his wife remembered to take her medicine. It seemed like lately, her mind was going out the door right along with her ability to breathe.

Dickie trudged along up the narrow sidewalk, his back aching and his feet throbbing.

CHAPTER
ELEVEN

"So, you were really married before?" Denise was sitting in the folding chair outside of Scott's cell, while he sat on his cot tearing into his chicken fried steak. She was eager to take him on in a game of rummy, but he needed to eat first. The poor man was starving by the time she got there. She had the cards ready to go when he was finished.

He wiped his mouth with his napkin, then swallowed. "Yes, briefly." His voice had a bit of a drag to it, and Denise could sense his grief.

"What happened?" she asked. "I mean, you don't have to tell me if you don't want to, obviously." She laughed nervously and began her habit of picking at her apron.

Scott shook his head and took a drink of his tea. "I don't mind," he replied. "I mean, just last week I may not have wanted to talk about it, but you have a way of making me comfortable."

Denise looked up at him and smiled, the blood rising to her cheeks. She sat on her hands and waited for him to divulge whatever details he was willing to share. Scott sat back and crossed his hands over his chest. He took a deep breath.

"Breast cancer," he said. "It ran in her family. We were married for only two years, but we were together longer."

Denise sucked in a breath, a typical reaction to learning of something so tragic. But she composed herself. From personal experience, she was sure he was tired of pity and awkward condolences. When people asked about her parents, which didn't happen so often anymore, it could be overwhelming.

"I'm so sorry, Scott."

He shook his head and began to stir his mashed potatoes around with his plastic fork. "Don't be. I'm finally starting to come to terms with it. That's the reason I started traveling, you know. I had to work my way through the pain somehow. I guess I thought I could run away from the anguish, but I soon realized the pain travels from town to town with you."

Denise nodded her head in agreement. "Has it helped at all?"

"Well," he continued, "I thought I would lose my mind missing her after she first passed. There was definitely a big empty hole in every aspect of my life, and there was nothing to fill it. When she died, my sense of home died with her, so I just up and left."

Denise nodded once again, being able to relate. "I know the feeling you're talking about. If it weren't for my sister, I think, I would have felt the exact same way, but she gave me a reason to... live. A reason to stay. She was home."

"The truth is that, up until now, the running hasn't helped a bit," he explained. "In fact, it seemed to make it worse."

Scott smiled and took another bite of his food. It was actually very exhilarating to talk to someone, anyone, about Kelly. Especially feeling like someone got it. What a relief to know that, no matter how he had felt since she passed, someone on Earth really could relate.

He put his fork down. "Denise, I know you know why the sheriff acted the way he did, and I also know you are holding back. I shared, now it's your turn. Please tell me what's going on with him and Ronnie?"

Denise stood and began to pace nervously. She looked around as if someone were hiding in the shadows listening to what they were saying. When she seemed satisfied that they were alone, she got close to the bars of the cell. "Sheriff Darby has always sort of taken Ronnie under his wing, like I said."

"Yeah, but why?" He stood across from her, his hands curling around the bars.

Denise shrugged and let her eyes flitter here and there. "I don't know, really. It's been like that for as long as I can remember. I know both Ronnie and the sheriff lost parents. Maybe that's why he feels so obligated. You know, maybe it fills a void."

Scott understood the concept of a void but wasn't buying this excuse. "So, he arrests strangers?"

She laughed lightly. "No, silly," she said. "Actually, that's the first time he's ever done anything like that, as far as I know. I think everyone was a bit surprised, but we all know how he feels about Ronnie. So no one wanted to get in between that whole thing. And, certainly, no one wanted to piss him off anymore, you know?"

Scott stared at her for a minute, then said, "No, I don't know."

"In your situation, and knowing Darby like I do, I feel fairly confident saying that he took his side versus a stranger. He probably got extra defensive because you don't understand him the way we all do. I'm sure that's all it was."

Scott started to pace around his cell, his food forgotten. He needed to tread lightly here. It was not his place to presume and judge too harshly. He didn't want to offend her, and she was right after all. That's precisely what he had done. Now was a good time to change the subject.

"Do you think you'll be bringing me my breakfast?"

Denise smiled at him and blushed once again. "I

don't know. We still hadn't heard from Darby when I left the café. Why?"

"Well," Scott replied. "Don't go out of your way, especially if Darby is bringing it, but if you do, would you mind bringing me the paper? I sure would like something to read."

Denise flashed him a big grin and turned around. She walked toward a small row of padded chairs next to the main entrance. On top of the first one sat a pile of rolled up newspapers. She grabbed them all and came back to him. "I'll still bring you tomorrow's edition if I come, but these should tide you over until then."

It was Scott's turn to smile, and he flashed her one of his best. "You're amazing!"

She giggled like a schoolgirl and shook her head. "I'll even leave the lights on, the ones back near you. That way you'll actually have enough light to read, okay?"

She shoved the papers through the bars one at a time. There were six in all, which probably meant the sheriff hadn't been reading them. Or perhaps he brought them from home and read them in the morning with his coffee, Scott thought. That made more sense.

"Well," she said. "I should be going, I guess. If Diane's still up, she may be worried. Maybe I'll see you tomorrow?"

Scott threw the papers onto his bunk and grabbed onto the bars again, putting his face between two of them as far as it would go. "I really hope so," he said. "Hey, what about our game?"

Scott's stall tactic was successful. The two spent the next half hour playing rummy. They both laughed more than they could remember, and they found each other's company mutually enjoyable. Denise finally looked at her watch as she stood.

"It's getting pretty late. I'm pretty tired."

"Me too," he said as she shifted her weight from one foot to the other and crossed her arms over her chest. She looked him in the eye, then shyly looked away. It tickled him how nervous she became around him. He wondered what it would be like to kiss her something good.

Suddenly, Denise leaned forward and kissed him square on the lips. It wasn't quite what he was fantasizing about, but it sent a jolt of electricity down his pants, nonetheless. She pulled away and waved her hand at him, then abruptly turned to leave. No words were spoken, and she shut the door and locked it behind her.

Scott stared at the door, perplexed. Slowly a smile came over his face, and he got a dreamy look in his eye. She hurried out so quickly she forgot to shut off the lights at the front. He sat down on the foot of his cot and kicked his feet back and forth like a teenager. She was certainly something special.

Pushing his thoughts aside for a moment, he stood up and gathered the food he hadn't eaten and neatly placed it in one box. That's when he found the cheesecake. He was touched. She tried to surprise him, and it worked. He used his fingers to eat it, dropping graham cracker crumbs down his front as he wolfed it down. Then he gulped the rest of his tea and put the remainder of his food aside to snack on later.

He sat cross-legged on the bed and sorted the papers by date. They went back five days, as well as the current day's edition. He started with the oldest, taking the rubber band off and snapping it across the room. It was no *New York Times*. There were only four pages altogether. It wouldn't take him long to read it.

The majority of the paper consisted of local updates about sports and activities at the high school as well as information about local clubs and committees. There was also a feature story about a stack of quilts that a pair of twins from town made and donated to a cancer hospice center in the City.

State sports, weather, and county obituaries were on the following pages. He was almost through when he caught a short piece on the very last page with two small paragraphs.

**Young Woman Found Murdered
Outside of Burdensville.**

The details were slim. A woman's body was found in a ditch about two miles outside of town. She had been raped, and her larynx had been crushed. A 2001 Beetle with a flat was found deserted, and while they had traced it to an owner, the article didn't specify if it belonged to the murdered woman or not. Her identity wouldn't be released until notification of kin.

The last paragraph mentioned, very briefly, that the murder was the latest in a string, and the killer had not yet been captured. The paper went on to warn residents to avoid travel on roads just outside of Burdensville until the 'offender' was captured. It ended there.

Scott's interest was piqued, and he opened the next paper eagerly. He was disappointed, though. None of the following three papers contained any kind of continuance or update regarding the murder. He assumed that the State Police hadn't gotten involved in that investigation.

Finally, he grabbed the last one with no high hopes about what he would find. He was surprised to see the front page headline blaring.

State Police Investigate
Latest Burdensville Murders

Two people were found dead outside of Burdensville. State Police say the line must be drawn on negligent and faulty investigative tactics.

State Police have intervened in the investigation of two killings which were just discovered outside Burdensville. The homicides are only the latest in a string of unsolved massacres which have taken place on the outskirts of town. Initially, Sheriff Robert Darby of Burdensville was leading the investigations, but according to Mary Kay Monroe, spokeswoman for the State Police and Bureau of Investigation, state officials have stepped in due to what they are calling 'gross negligence' on the part of Sheriff Darby.

At the current time, there are a total of five murders which have taken place just outside of town. The first body was discovered two months ago at the abandoned Wilson farm by three local junior high school students. The body was that of Katie Castleman, 19, of Handom. Castleman was a student at the State College, and according to family, had been on her way to visit friends in Rumming. It was reported to this paper that Castleman had been driving a 2000 Taurus, but the vehicle was never recovered.

The second victim was murdered and discovered one month ago. She was identified as Jane Feister, 21, of Greenville. Feister's body was discovered along Highway 16 by a passing motorist. She was partially clothed and severely beaten. Feister's family reported that the woman had been driving a 1990 Prelude, but as in the first case, a vehicle was never found.

Victim number three was Carly Reed, 23, of Fester.

Ms. Reed had been traveling to an interview for a teaching position, but reportedly never made it. Her body was found by Burdensville locals, who wish to remain anonymous. Her vehicle, a 2001 Beetle, was also discovered approximately eight miles away from where her body was found.

The most recent victims, which State Police are currently investigating, after interjecting in Sheriff Darby's investigation, were Timothy Bascom, 18, and Meredith Downs, 17, of Rumming. The two teens were reportedly on their way to a rock and roll concert in the City. Bascom was discovered with fatal head trauma alongside Highway 16. Miss Downs was discovered in a nearby field. The vehicle they were driving was parked on the highway about fifty feet from Bascom's body.

All the victims, except for Bascom, had been sexually assaulted and severely beaten. The women all showed signs of their throats crushed. No other details regarding the victims have been reported at the current time.

Sheriff Darby is being interviewed by State Police as to why he didn't request assistance at any point. There are also accusations that an abundance of evidence may have either been ignored or overlooked during his crime scene investigations.

We will report any further updates on the case as they are received.

. . .

Scott looked up from the paper, his heart beating fast. He couldn't believe what he had just read. A town the size of Burdensville that had fallen victim to such extreme violence should've been swarming with State Police from the start. Perhaps even the FBI. It's obvious by the signature, they definitely have a serial killer on their hands. How did Darby manage to sweep these atrocities under the rug the way he had? Someone was helping him. Someone was covering for him somehow. Or maybe many were.

Scott flipped through the few remaining pages of the paper, paying special attention to the box ads that took up most of the page space. There was an announcement for the Burdensville K-12 school about a fundraiser they were having. There was also an ad for a dentist. Finally, in the lower right-hand corner of the last page, he found what he had been seeking, and his eyes lit up.

It was an ad for the Burdensville Medical Center. It was smaller than the rest of the ads on the page, and he almost missed it. The head doctor, and from the looks of it, the only doctor at the center, was Dr. Ivan Smith. He ran the center as a family practice. It specified that Dr. Smith gave referrals for major care as needed and was a lifelong resident of Burdensville. "Dr. Smith is your friend in medicine!" the ad boldly stated, and next to the catchy phrase was a yellow smiley face.

Scott stood up and began to pace in the small confines of his cell. Sweat was pooling around his armpits, and he was aware of the odor emanating from them. He wanted to get out of this cell, and badly. If these murders had taken place without the knowledge or investigative assistance from the State Police, then someone had removed and transported the bodies... to where? It sure didn't seem like a local undertaker. Someone also had to contact the next of kin and performed an autopsy, or at least prepared the body for transport to another coroner.

Had it been Ivan Smith?

He plopped down on his cot and put his head in his hands. Certainly, the police were going to check into this. Surely, they were going to figure out how the murders slipped through the cracks. Indeed, they were already asking all the right questions. They were probably getting ready to blow the whole thing wide open. This would gain national attention. Meanwhile, here he sat like a criminal himself. It was a ludicrous scenario.

He cleared the papers from his bed and lay down. He could hardly wait for the paper the next morning. He hoped like hell that Denise would be the one to bring his breakfast. From the sound of it, Darby was going to have his hands full trying to clear his name, so Denise was exactly who Scott expected to see.

CHAPTER
TWELVE

Darby steered his patrol car down Highway 16, the radio off and his finger tapping the steering wheel nervously. He would be home in about twenty minutes, but the first stop he was going to make was not his home. No, he needed to deal with the mess that had been made, and a great big damn mess it was, too.

Sure, the State Police had told him to go ahead and get back to Burdensville. After all, he was the only cop in town. They wanted him back bright and early in the morning, though. They were far from finished with their probing and fishing, and his stomach roiled nervously at the thought.

He needed to talk to Ivan, but, most of all, he needed to have words with Ronnie... some very, very serious words.

He found himself fretting over the mess that plagued he and the town. But not for the victims themselves. No, he fretted for what he considered to be his failure. He had failed Ronnie.

As he drove, Darby flashed back to where it all started. Back to when he truly got off course by his sense of obligation to the man the town knew as Ronnie Smith.

BOBBY'S MOTHER HAD BEEN GROWING. AT least, that's how he saw it. Her belly was getting bigger and bigger. Bobby thought she was beautiful, but his daddy hated it. He called her 'fat pig,' and sometimes when he drank the soda pop in the white and red can, he would even hit her just for getting fatter.

He would hit her in the belly or the face. She hardly made a sound, but tears would come out of her eyes. She would go about her business taking care of Bobby and Daddy, but sometimes after she was hit, it would be even harder for her to move around in her condition.

One day, right after Mommy put some spaghetti in front of him, his daddy came home early from work. When he saw that all Mommy made was canned pasta, he became enraged. "This is why you're such a fat pig, you pig!" He hit her in the belly with his fist, and Mommy had fallen on the floor.

She had blood coming out of her. It was on the hem and the back of her dress, and she started to holler and cry. She was saying 'It hurts!', and it looked like she couldn't breathe. Bobby left his bowl of spaghetti at the table and crouched in the corner of the kitchen, shaking. Daddy paced around while blood continued to seep out of his mother. "What do you want me to do? I suppose you want me to call Doc, but I ain't doin' it!" His father looked worried, pacing around trying to figure out what to do. "Doc has his own problems, you know. His missus just lost a kid herself, and I ain't goin' ta jail on account of you!"

The pain continued to get worse for his mom, he could tell, and finally, she had splayed her legs out and started to act like she had to poop. Bobby covered his eyes, and when he opened them, his daddy was on the floor between his mom's legs. "Bobby, go get me a towel or a sheet or somethin'!" Bobby jumped up and ripped his own blanket off his bed and ran it to his dad. When he got there, his daddy was holding a slippery little person covered in blood. It was crying and screaming, but his mommy was lying there still. She wasn't crying, but she was sure bleeding all over.

"Mommy needs a Band-aid, Daddy," Bobby said, but his daddy didn't listen. He was too busy wrapping the baby up in the blanket. Bobby bent over his mommy. Her eyes were partially open, and she was white and sweaty. "Do you need some Band-aids, Mommy?"

Mommy smiled a little bit, but not very much. "Mommy's goin' away now," she said. She was only whispering, and Bobby had to get really close to her face to hear her. "Where you goin', Mommy?" She didn't answer his question, though. She just kept on whispering. "No matter what, you take care of him, okay? You take care of that baby..."

Those were the last words Bobby's mommy ever said to him, and they never left him, never gave him any relief.

Darby shook his head aggressively, shaking the memories from it, and along with them, the pain. He slowed the car as it approached the gravel road he was looking for. It was dark, but he knew Burdensville and all of its outskirts like the back of his hand. Sure enough, the darkened road appeared in his headlights, and Darby swung a left.

He was only a few miles from Ronnie's now, the home that had been his when he was a boy. Even in the darkness, he could recognize every tree and fencepost. It made his mind wander once again...

Mommy did go away that day. She went to Heaven, and Bobby never saw her again.

Daddy called Doc Smith, and he came over to the house. "I don't know what I'ma gonna do, Doc. Ain't no one gonna believe I didn't cause this... no one."

Doc Smith covered his mommy with a sheet and sat at the table with Daddy. Bobby was supposed to be in his bed, but he hid around the corner in the hallway and watched and listened to the men. For a long time, Doc sat with his head in his hands while Daddy held a bottle in the baby's mouth, I can't do this! I can't handle a little baby. Finally, Doc looked up and said, "I have a solution, and it's the only one I can think of." They talked about Doc Smith taking the new baby to his house to live. His own had just been stillborn, and he hadn't told anyone per his wife's request. They could take the child as their own, and his wife would help tend to the baby. He would make up the right papers that said Bobby's mommy died having the new baby, and the baby died as well.

Bobby didn't understand everything they were saying, but it sounded like they were formulating lies. Bobby got a spanking if he told lies, and he didn't understand why it was okay for grown-ups to tell them.

The doctor took the baby, and then his daddy started for the hallway. Bobby ran to his room like lightning, but his dad knew he'd been sneaking. "I ain't gonna beat you boy. I've screwed up enough for one day." His daddy looked worn out and covered in blood. "Now, I heard what your momma told you. That boy is goin' to live with Doc and his wife. They'll be his ma and pa. But you,

you will always be his brother. Your ma was right; you need to take care of him, no matter what. You got it?" Bobby nodded, and without another word, his daddy left the room.

About a half-mile up, Darby saw the single light that stood high over the old house where all those things had taken place. It was Ronnie's house now; his brother Ronnie. It was broken down and overgrown. He suddenly remembered that he needed to mow the yard that coming weekend. Overall, the house was a safe place for the messed-up man to live. It was better than being homeless, as surely, he would otherwise have been.

He finally reached the drive and took another left. He pulled up the dirt drive slowly, his eyes peeled in the darkness as he tried to see any movement or lights in the windows. All was still, and very, very quiet.

He turned off the ignition and heaved his large body from the driver's seat. Then he reached into the passenger side and retrieved his big, heavy flashlight. Darby turned it on and aimed it at the front of the house. That's when he saw one of the window coverings flutter. Yep, Ronnie was inside, and he was awake. He was likely waiting for Darby to come and give him the talking he knew he was in for.

The sheriff made his way around to the back door

which led to the kitchen. It was slightly ajar when he reached it, so Ronnie must've opened it for him, expectedly, before hiding in the house. He entered, then turned around and secured the door behind him.

"Ronnie, you need to come on out here now, ayuh," Darby hollered. He could be anywhere in the house, and Darby wasn't about to engage in a game of hide and seek like he had done so many times before. "Now I ain't playin', Ronnie. If I gotta come to look for you, we're gonna have us a bit of a brawl."

He saw the man's shadow slowly creep around the corner of the living room and come into the kitchen. Darby shined his light at the shadow, and there Ronnie stood. He held his own unlit flashlight with an iron grip in his hands. He was dirty, and there was a shy smile on his lips.

"How you doin', Bobby?"

Darby shifted his weight from one foot to the other and focused on maintaining a stern look. "Not so damn good, Ronnie. Not good."

"Whassa matter?"

Darby felt fury. Ronnie knew exactly what was the matter. He was so much like a damn kid, and sometimes it was just too much of a burden for the single small-town sheriff to bear.

"We've talked about this before," he began, "And I've told you what could happen if you kept up your crap, hurting these girls, killin', and rapin' but you didn't wanna listen, and now the crap's fixin' to hit the fan, boy."

Ronnie started to tremble, but he took a step toward Darby anyway. The stench of alcohol hit the sheriff in the face like a brick wall, and in the stream coming from the flashlight, he could see blood running down Ronnie's arm.

"You been hurtin' yourself, again?" he asked.

Ronnie looked down and didn't answer.

"Well, I'm just gonna lay it out. They're fixin' to have my job, and my ass, over the covering I been doing for you," he said. "They're on to us now but good, and I don't even know if I can do anything about it."

Ronnie looked up at him, his eyes frightened. "You'll fix it, Bobby. You always fix it. I didn't mean any harm. Them girls, they liked it. They liked me!"

Darby took three steps forward and slapped the man hard across the face. Ronnie staggered as his hand went to his cheek. "No! No, they didn't like it! You've been killing! You sick pain in my ass! You're takin' their lives!"

Ronnie began to cry, and Darby felt a lurch of nausea. "Look, Ronnie, I'm sorry I hit you." He reached up and took the man in his arms and pulled him in. He held him and let him cry it out. Oh, ma, he thought as he rubbed Ronnie's back. "I can't do this. I don't think I can take care of him anymore."

After the man's sobs subsided, Darby stood him at arm's length and shone his flashlight on his chest just enough to get a look at his face. He pulled a handkerchief out of his brown trousers and handed it over. "Blow your nose," he said gruffly, and Ronnie obeyed.

"Now, I need you to listen to me close, and I need you to do what I tell you, no matter what."

Ronnie nodded as he wiped at his nose and sniffled.

"No drinking, Ronnie. That's the most important thing," Darby said, shaking a finger at the man. "None of this evil started until you started sucking on that damn bottle day in and day out. No drinking."

Ronnie looked panicked and stricken, but nodded. "Next, I want you to stay here. No leaving, no going to town, not for anything. Where're the keys to your car?"

Ronnie took a step back. "No, Bobby. Don't take Old Mabel. Not my car."

"What are you gonna need it for if you're doing what I tell you to do?" He was starting to raise his voice again. He needed Ronnie to understand that he had to do everything he was telling him to do. There could be no deviation whatsoever.

Ronnie squared off his shoulders a bit and shoved the hanky in his front pocket. "What if there's an emergency, and you're not around, huh? I ain't got no phone, and there ain't no neighbors nearby. What then, huh?"

Darby considered his words. He was right. He didn't have any way to get ahold of anyone if something happened. That's why he gave him the car in the first place. "Okay. But there ain't gonna be no drinking, and no driving unless you just gotta, understand?"

Ronnie nodded again, a huge look of relief on his face. Darby continued, "I'm gonna be dealing with the State for the next day or two. This weekend, I'm gonna come and help you with the yard and such. Do you have enough food to get you by for a day or two?"

Ronnie thought about it. "I have some chips and a few cans of spaghetti, and I got my can opener! I've got some soda in the can."

"Okay," Darby replied, satisfied. "That'll do you for a couple of days. I'm hoping to be gone only tomorrow, but at this point, I still don't know what's gonna happen. That's why it's so important for you to lay low. We don't want anyone to suspect that you done these things."

"Do they now?" Ronnie's voice was low, and he sounded worried.

Darby shook his head. "Naw, I don't think so. But if they start asking questions around town, I can't guarantee that no one will talk about you and me, and about the way you act. That's why you gotta lay low, so you'll pass from their minds, you see."

Ronnie let out a loud sigh. "Okay. I'll do what you say."

Darby gave another nod, one that said they were through talking. He patted Ronnie on the shoulder. "So I'm gonna go now. Are you gonna be okay here?"

"Ayuh," Ronnie replied. "Wouldn't wanna be anywhere else."

Darby left and aimed his car up the gravel road toward town. As he drove, he gave the gravity of the situation deeper thought. This was serious business and he suddenly felt like it was suffocating him.

HE SPENT HIS LIFE LOOKING OUT FOR THAT KID. It was obvious from the start that something just wasn't right with Ronnie Smith. He didn't learn like other kids in school, and right after first grade, Doc Smith took him out of public education. Mrs. Smith started teaching him from home instead. Bobby would visit about three days a week and play with him, but Ronnie never had any idea the boy was his own brother, his own flesh and blood.

"You don't ever tell no one about it, you hear me boy?" His father had drilled it into him from the start. He was to remain in Ronnie's life, be there for him and have his back, but no one was to know they were kin. This was to protect his dad from what he did to his mother and protect Doc Smith from what he did to cover the whole thing up. "Someday, I'm gonna be gone and so are the Smiths. The only one Ronnie is gonna have is you, so I expect you to mind that carefully."

Robert Darby had done just that.

After a couple of years, Doc and Mrs. Smith had

another child, another boy. They called him Ivan as well, and Ivan was the apple of his parents' eyes. He excelled in all he did. He was at the top of his class. He participated in, and ran, all the sports he could. He was good-looking, and he wanted to be a doctor, just like his father. It wasn't long after his birth that Ronnie started to fade into the background of the perfect family photo. He was the idiot, the embarrassment. Ivan was favored, and it showed.

Robert saw it too, and he despised the Smiths for it, but there was nothing he could do. As the boys all grew into their teen years, things got increasingly worse for Ronnie. He would wander around town on his yellow bike with the banana seat, and the neighbors would give him change and candy. Everyone knew that Ronnie Smith was the boy his parents didn't want.

Robert started to hang out down at the police station. The old sheriff, Mac Ludwig, became his mentor. Robert's father had taken ill and was put in a home with alcoholic dementia at a pretty young age. He died of liver cancer, and he left Robert the house, but Robert stayed with Sheriff Ludwig, who eventually got him into the police academy. He was being groomed to take over as the sheriff of Burdensville.

Ivan Smith went off to college and studied medicine. He would take over his father's family practice at Burdensville Clinic, now known as Burdensville Medical Center. Ronnie stayed in Burdensville—lonely, unloved, and confused. He rode his bike around town and entertained himself the best he could.

While Robert was away at the Academy, Ronnie had a spot of trouble. Ludwig was called by some of the locals to help them deal with their pets and livestock that were found brutally killed. At first, Ludwig thought it was teenaged toughs terrorizing the townsfolk from one of the bigger cities. Perhaps kids just trying to get their kicks, but one day, right before graduation, Robert got a call from Ludwig.

"Ronnie was caught slicing up one of the old twins' cats. He was inflicting the same atrocities that were done to all the other animals in town."

Bobby asked him, "Are you gonna lock him up?"

Ludwig replied, "Naw, I just can't do it. Mrs. Smith's had a stroke, and Doc ain't too well himself. We promised the folks it would stop, but we just don't know what to do with him."

Robert had gone to bed that night with the weight of the world on his shoulders. He cried with his face in his pillow, begging his deceased mother to forgive him for leaving Ronnie and going off to the Academy. That's when he thought about the house.

It hadn't been cared for in a while, but he could take early graduation and go home and clean the place up. He had all his credits, after all, and would be interning with Ludwig. Then Ronnie could have the house and he'd be living on the outskirts of

Burdensville, where he wouldn't hurt the animals or scare the townsfolk.

It was the perfect solution...

Darby pulled into town behind the wheel of his cruiser. Finally! He was so damned tired and hungry that he could hardly stand it, and he wanted a hot shower.

The town was peaceful and picturesque. Not a soul stirred, and Darby felt a rush of love and sentimentality for Burdensville that he hadn't felt in a very long time. He had to figure things out, had to fix the situation. He had no idea what to do about Ronnie, but there had to be a solution.

He was thrilled to finally be home. The first thing he did was heat up a microwave dinner. Then he turned on the small TV in the kitchen to watch the news. Happy not to see himself or Ronnie in any breaking news headlines, he took a steaming shower and made his way to bed.

He was glad to be home, but even in his exhausted state, sleep evaded him. He was in real trouble here, and he knew it. Best case scenario was being forced to resign. The worst, he was going to do some time. His life had become an unstoppable nightmare.

CHAPTER
THIRTEEN

Scott woke early in his jail cell, while the sun was still hiding from the sky. He had read and reread the papers Denise gave him the evening before. Scott found that he had more questions building up in his mind than a passing-through stranger should. He could hardly wait for her to arrive because some of them she could answer.

He washed as best he could in the small stainless-steel sink. He could smell himself, and when he thought about their brief kiss the night before, he feared she had as well. If she did, she didn't lead on, so all he could do was hope that she was none the wiser.

By sunrise, he was very antsy. He tried to entertain himself by playing Solitaire with the cards Denise left for him. He thought about doing a crossword, but he didn't even have a pencil to use. He supposed that was against the rules in jail. The cards would have to do. He did some push-ups and sit-ups. He made his bed and straightened his cell. Finally, at seven, he lay back down on his cot and tried to ground himself until his food came.

It was all he could do to not stare at the knob of the jail door.

Denise Jensen was a surprise. Scott had convinced himself that he would never be interested in another woman, yet here he was in a small-town jail cell, and he couldn't get the little waitress off his mind. His brain wanted to play tricks on him and tell him he was horrible, that he was betraying his precious Kelly, but his heart knew better. Trying to buck up and move on was the very best thing for him, and Kelly would want that for him too.

Denise was cute, funny, smart, and independent. He found himself wanting to know everything about her. He also found himself wishing he could take care of her and protect her, and he hadn't felt that way in a very long time. When Kelly died, part of his sense of manhood died with her. If he couldn't protect her, what good was he? Was he even a man at all?

Deep down, Scott knew he was being hard on himself. He knew he was being unfair. But he was afraid if he wasn't hard on himself, he may forget, and then it could happen again. He wouldn't be able to cope if something like that happened a second time. No, he wanted to run and hide. But the way he felt about Denise wasn't going to allow him to do that anymore. He couldn't imagine leaving the forsaken town of Burdensville if it meant leaving this fun-loving waitress behind. She was a great catch, and he knew he couldn't let her go if he got lucky enough to reel her in.

He lay back down on his cot, trying to force himself to be patient, but it didn't work too well. Before long, he was going through the personal entertainment cycle again: cards, exercise, pace, lie down. It was driving him nuts having to wait like this.

She would be here soon, and he would survive until then.

"Denise, I wonder if you could come in a bit early today," Dickie was saying into the phone. "Sheriff Darby already left for his business, and he needs us to take care of that guy down at the jail."

Denise was still in her pajamas and robe. Diane was in the shower getting ready for school. Even with the morning being so crammed, she found herself more than excited at the thought of seeing Scott Sharp once again. The kiss made her want more. Scott looked like a movie star compared to the men around town, especially with that chiseled chin and all. Yeah, she was excited to see him again.

"Absolutely, Dickie," she replied. "Diane will be out

of the bathroom in a bit, then I'll shower and be right down to the café. Will, that do?"

Dickie looked at the clock on his kitchen wall. It was six-thirty. Darby had called him at six. The café didn't technically open until eight, but he had already taken care of Doris and made sure she had eaten and taken her medicine. She was watching TV, so that timetable would work out just fine for him.

"Sounds good, honey. So I'll see you down there by seven-thirty?" he asked.

Denise smiled into the phone. Dickie sounded anxious. "How about seven-fifteen, at the latest."

"Aw, girl, I love you like one of my own." He hung up the phone and went into kiss Doris. "I'll be home tonight, not sure what time with all the rigmarole. The neighbor will be here to bring you your lunch and your midday remedies, okay lover?"

Doris nodded, and he bent over and kissed her warmly. Then he put on his jacket and went out into the cool of the day. The sun was up, and the birds were singing. It would be a good day, even if they were as slammed as yesterday.

By the time he opened the café, got the grill heated up, and the coffee going, Denise walked in, flushed with good health and a grin. "How'd you sleep?"

"As good as possible, ayuh," he said, returning her grin. He cracked a couple of eggs on the griddle and laid out a package of bacon. "I'll have breakfast ready for

Darby's inmate shortly. Go ahead and get the extras bagged up for him. I don't know what today's gonna be like, so I want you to get back as soon as possible."

Denise poured a cup of milk and one of coffee, then lidded them both. Dickie had Scott's breakfast made quickly and put it in the window. "Here you go," he said to her as she opened up a plastic bag to put the food in. "I'll see you shortly."

Dickie turned back to the kitchen, and Denise bagged the food and headed out the door, bag on her arm and a cup in both hands. The morning was a little cool, but the sun was shining brightly. She put her face up to the sun and inhaled deeply. It was going to be a beautiful day.

IN LESS THAN FIVE MINUTES, SHE WAS AT THE jail. She sort of expected the sheriff to be there to check on his inmate before he left to deal with the State Police. But there were no cars in front of the building. She put the cups down on the railing of the front porch and dug the keys out of her pocket. Soon, she was inside smiling at Scott, who was wide awake and standing at the bars.

"Good morning," she said cheerfully. "How did you sleep?"

Scott smiled, happy to see her. "Not so good, to be

honest. You're a sight for sore eyes, though. I was beginning to think you would never come."

"Well, here I am," she replied. "And here is your breakfast. I'll just grab the morning paper too."

Denise gave him the food and beverages, then went back to the door to fetch the morning paper from the front porch. "What kept you from sleeping?" she asked him over her shoulder.

"I read the papers you gave me last night," he began. "Do you read them?"

Denise came back to his cell with the rolled up newspaper and handed it to him through the bars. "No, I really don't. I don't watch much television, either. I guess you read something that got your attention."

Scott nodded at her. "It seems the State Police are investigating Darby for negligence concerning the murders that have happened around here."

Denise's jaw dropped, and she raised her eyebrows. "Really? That's why he has to go to headquarters, huh?"

"Looks that way," he said. He took the lid off his coffee and took a swig, then set it down and took the rubber band from the paper she handed him.

"The whole town is talking about it, but I have a hard time believing he'd get in much trouble," she continued. "He's only trying to look after Ronnie." She said it so many times, she was beginning to sound like a broken record. But it was the truth.

Scott took another drink of his coffee. "There's something that bothers me."

"What's that?"

"Well," Scott said, "The papers listed all the recent murder victims by name, even age. And now Darby is being questioned for possibly covering them up. How did he do that so well? I mean, he would've needed help to deal with the corpses. You know what I mean?"

Denise nodded, a faraway look in her eyes. "My theory is that a doctor helped him. Who else would have the ability?"

"Maybe Dr. Ivan Smith?" Scott asked.

Denise met his gaze. "Dr. Smith is good friends with Darby. He would be the only one I can think of that would do such a thing."

Scott unrolled the paper and laid it flat on his cot. The headline blared out at him.

Investigators Believe Murderer is Local. State Police Continue to Question Burdensville Sheriff.

Police will continue their line of questioning concerning the recent murders in the Burdensville area, and Sheriff Robert Darby is in the hot seat. While investigators have not revealed why Darby is suspected of wrongdoing, they have indicated that it's their belief that the murders were committed by someone local to Burdensville or the surrounding area.

Darby is expected to undergo questioning throughout the day today, perhaps into tomorrow. The press has been unable to get a statement from the sheriff himself, who stated that he has no comment pending the closure of the investigation.

A spokesperson for the police stated that they will also begin questioning area locals on an extended basis. These interviews may begin as early as Monday morning, post the Sherriff's official statements.

If anyone has any knowledge or information regarding the murder cases, they are encouraged to contact the State Police.

THE ARTICLE WAS BRIEF, BUT EVEN AS SCOTT read it aloud to Denise, he had a feeling that things were about to crash down on Burdensville. He looked up at her to try and get a read, but her stare was blank. He didn't want to upset her, but he had a feeling she was thinking the same thing, or maybe she already knew something that he didn't. After all, Burdensville was her life-long home.

"Denise," he began slowly, "I know I'm not from here, nor do I personally know a soul who lives here, but I have my own suspicions."

Denise shot up from her chair. "I really can't stay.

Dickie thinks we're gonna have another rush again. I'll bring your lunch, but it might be a little late."

"I know you know what I'm thinking," Scott persisted.

Now, she looked him right in the eye.

"So, what do you think?"

"I think, there's more to Ronnie Smith than meets the eye," he said. "He's more than a poor slob to be pitied and protected. And I think, you know that. I mean, how couldn't you. He threatened to kill you."

"Look," she began, "I've lived here my entire life. I have my younger sister going off to college, and I have a peaceful existence. I'm not a cop, and I don't want to second-guess someone I've known since I was born."

Scott approached the bars of the cell, weighing his words carefully so he wouldn't piss her off or offend her. "If the police are coming to Burdensville to interview the locals, they're going to ask much more pointed questions than I am. Don't you think it's vital that you answer them honestly, or do you want people to continue dying?"

Ouch! Denise glared at him, but he could see she was thinking things through. How he wished he could read her mind. "I have to go right now," she said abruptly. "I'll share my thoughts with you later, probably when I bring your supper."

Scott nodded but kept his mouth closed. Enough said for now. Denise turned around and left the jail, locking the door behind her. He knew he had upset her, but if she had the same suspicions as he did, she needed to share them with police. Holding back would end tragically in that community. More people would die, and that's exactly what needed to stop.

He grabbed the bag of food and the cup of milk and began unpacking it. He was very hungry, and his stomach was growling loudly, but the food was the furthest thing from his mind. His thoughts were on Sheriff Darby and the way he responded to the scene when they first met in the café. He was thinking how messed up it was that Darby went so far as to lock him up instead of the true offender.

It seemed to Scott that Darby was willing to go to any lengths to protect Ronnie Smith. It made him think that Ronnie was guilty of much more than drunken, mouthy debauchery.

Scott was willing to bet that the murderer was Ronnie, but he couldn't rule out Sheriff Darby either. Was the local cop capable of committing these heinous crimes himself? Was Ronnie covering for him and getting away with bad behavior in return? Or was the sheriff protecting Ronnie for reasons he couldn't possibly understand? None of it was adding up. Scott's curiosity was piqued, but there was nothing he could do except sit in his jail cell and read newspapers.

Ronnie Smith had taken down the black sheet on the front window first thing that morning. He hadn't had a drink in a couple of days, and for the first time in a long time, he wanted to see and feel the sun.

Bobby told him he needed to stay inside and out of sight. He told him no driving. He told him he couldn't drink. Ronnie had gotten angry and frustrated by all the orders and demands, but he had agreed. Now, as he sat in the sun thinking about everything, he found himself craving a beer or a shot more than ever.

His head had never been right, and drinking was the only thing that dulled the sting of his torturous mind. His brain just didn't work right, though Ronnie wasn't fully aware of it. He had the mentality of an eleven or twelve-year-old, but he was trapped in the body of a thirty-two-year-old man.

He had always used alcohol to deal with it, and yes, the more he drank, the more he lost his inhibitions. That's when the beast inside of him got stronger, and it would demand that he find satisfaction. So that's what he did.

When he was just a boy, the demands in his subconscious mind had started, and he took it out on the animals. Yes, he would hurt them, but only for a little bit. Then he would show them mercy by crushing their throats. He would stomp on their necks to end their suffering fast. That's as far as he took it in the beginning.

But when he got to be a teenager, he took things a

step further. It wasn't enough to hurt the local cats and small dogs. Now, he had another hunger growing inside of him that needed to be satisfied. And it was not a hungering he understood. It was a physical drive, a need for physical release. That's when he started having sex with the larger animals he killed. That's how Ronnie was able to make the demands in his head stop for many years.

The fact was that all the girls started to look very, very appealing to him. They smelled good and looked pretty, and thoughts of having sex with them drove him crazy. But none of them wanted to talk to him, much less touch him or let him touch them willingly. It pissed him off. Ronnie decided he was going to take what he wanted, whether they liked it or not.

The mixture of sex and murder with a human female victim was unlike anything he had ever experienced. They all really loved him, he knew. Just like that last girl, the one he had in the field. So what if she had been with another boy? Ronnie knew she really wanted to be with him, not that kid. He had done her a favor by caving in the boy's skull.

He thought about the way she sounded, the fear in her screams. He thought about her scent, and it started to nag at his brain. He moved his hand to his crotch and began to rub himself through the heavy denim that covered him. While he did, he thought about how that girl felt on the inside and the terrified look in her eyes. It didn't take long for Ronnie to climax in his jeans.

As soon as he was done, the feelings came. He felt shame. He felt dirty. And he felt self-hate. It reminded him of mother Smith.

IT WAS THE DAY AFTER HIS TWELFTH BIRTHDAY party, which had been the best one of his life. He had gotten several items of clothing and a new bike, and he was beside himself with eager joy. His mother told him he could take the bike out and ride it today, but she had gone shopping and forgot to get the new bike out of Father's shed. It was locked up, and Ronnie didn't think he could wait.

He suddenly got a brilliant idea. He would go get the key to the shed out of his father's desk drawer. He would get his bike out and then lock the shed and return the key. Mother said he could ride it so she wouldn't be angry. If anything, she would be happy that he was able to do it all by himself.

He went to the den and opened the top drawer in Father's desk, where the key was always kept. He pulled the drawer out pretty far, almost pulling it completely from the desk itself. His eyes were on the key, which was nestled in the very front compartment. He steadied the drawer to keep from spilling the contents, and that's when he saw it.

There was a magazine in the back of the drawer, a magazine with shiny paper pages. On the front was the most beautiful lady he had ever seen. His eyes were immediately glued to it, and the key to the shed was forgotten.

Ronnie took the magazine carefully from the drawer. The woman on the front hardly had any clothes on, and she was so attractive that Ronnie was holding his breath. He began to flip through the pages.

A long page in the middle suddenly folded out, and there she was ... the same girl. But in this picture, she was completely naked. Her body looked so soft. He could see everything, even her most secret place. He stared at the photo and let himself plop down into his father's desk chair.

He felt his penis growing harder, and he reached down to adjust it, but as soon as his hand got there, it sprang up larger than ever. He continued to look at the naked woman as he ran his hand over his crotch, slowly at first, then faster and faster. All of a sudden Ronnie was overwhelmed with pleasure that ran from the top of his head to the bottom of his feet. He closed his eyes and continued to stroke himself frantically.

"Ronnie, what are you doing?" His eyes flew open to see his mother standing at the door, her mouth and eyes wide. "That's dirty, Ronald! Dirty!"

She ran to him, grabbed him by his hair, and started dragging him across the room. The magazine had fallen from his hand to the floor, forgotten. He was only aware of the pain of his hair being pulled.

"Mother, I'm sorry!" He was yelling it over and over. Soon, she had him in the bathroom, and she turned the shower on full blast. She kept his hair in a firm grip to control him. Ronnie could see the steam rising from the hot water.

"Get in now, Dirty Boy!" The water was too hot, and he knew it. He tried to resist, but mother began to beat him about the head with her other hand, and she forced him into the water. It scalded his skin, and he screamed for mercy.

She got under the sink and pulled out the brush she used to scrub the floor. She threw it at him hard, the wooden handle knocking him in the head. Then she got the bathtub cleanser and dumped it all over him.

"Clean yourself! You're filthy and disgusting!" He was so confused and scared that he froze. By then, his mother had grabbed the brush. She scrubbed him all over so hard that his beet-red skin became raw.

He had continued to cry, and she had continued to scrub him and hit him until she drew blood.

Ronnie would never forget what a nasty, dirty boy he was, but the booze helped him put it out of his mind.

Ronnie stood up abruptly, shaking his head violently to rid himself of the memory. He was dirty and disgusting. He needed to wash. He began to tear through the house trying to find the cleanser, but there wasn't any.

That's when he remembered seeing a can of the blue-green powder in the basement. Yes! That's where it was! It was on the very top shelf in the basement. He used it in the basement shower to clean himself after he killed that first girl. He ran through the garbage and debris to the basement door. He flung it open and took the steps down two at a time, his flashlight bobbing erratically.

He shined the light on the top shelf. There it was... the bathroom cleanser that stung and burned. He directed the stream of light around the basement until he saw the metal pail. He grabbed it and turned it upside down before the shelves. He wasn't tall enough to reach without it.

He stepped up and shone the light on the cleanser. He grabbed it up eagerly, relief flooding his body. He would feel better in no time.

There, on the very back of the top shelf, was a bottle of whiskey, and it was three-quarters full.

Ronnie dropped the powdered cleanser to the floor, forgetting it completely. At first, he stared at the whiskey, but soon his mind started to nag. Bobby told him no drinking. That's what Bobby said.

'But Bobby's not here now, is he?' the voice nagged. 'He won't come 'til this weekend when he comes to do the yard.'

That's all it took. Ronnie grabbed the bottle and took the cap off, then he took a long, hard pull off the bottle. Then another, then another. He stepped down off the pail, a warm feeling coming over him. He didn't remember hiding the bottle, but right then he was so glad he had.

Where had the flashlight gone? He squinted his eyes in the dim light that came through the small windows. It wasn't on the floor. He gently put the bottle down, smiling at it and caressing it, then stepped back on the pail. The flashlight was on the shelf, right where he left it when he found the whiskey.

The voice was quiet, but he knew it would be back. It always came back. He pushed the thought out of his mind and got down off the pail, grabbed his bottle, and ran up the stairs of the basement.

Ronnie sat down in his place among the filth on the floor. He cracked the bottle once again and took another drink. It warmed him and made him feel loved, and that's all he cared about right then.

He just wanted to feel loved.

CHAPTER
FOURTEEN

Darby sat on the cold, hard chair at the State Police headquarters. His stomach burned with anxiety, and he was antsy as hell. It took all his strength to keep from fidgeting around. He didn't want to look as nervous as he felt.

He watched the cops and workers who were milling around, taking care of their business. He found he was jealous of all of them. They were oblivious to the weight he was carrying around on his shoulders, and he wished he too was none the wiser. The fact was that he was in trouble, and he knew it. He put himself in this position, though he didn't feel he had a choice. He was keeping his promise to his mother.

Gone was his job; maybe not today, but soon enough. He had no idea how to handle the upcoming questions. Should he continue to sidestep and lie to save

Ronnie's hide? Even if he did, it wouldn't work. They might not know anything about him yet, but once they start interviewing the townsfolk, they'll be aware soon enough.

As far as murder goes, suspecting Ronnie was a no-brainer. The red flags would be flying.

He was becoming more and more convinced that it was time to talk. He couldn't continue to do this anymore. Not only was it tearing him apart, but it was also enabling Ronnie, and people were dying as a result. His duty in life was not just to protect his brother, but the citizens of his town. He was failing them.

Yes, he thought it might be time to show his hand.

As if on cue, the door across from him opened and a man in a suit and tie, with a badge on his belt, nodded at him. "Sheriff Robert Darby?"

Darby stood and nodded curtly. "Yes, sir."

"Follow me, please," he said.

The two men walked through the door, and Darby let it shut behind him. His mind was scattered, and he was a nervous wreck, but he knew what he had to do. His decision to spill the beans gave him great relief. It was the right thing now, and he knew it. If nothing else, maybe they could get Ronnie the help he needed.

It suddenly occurred to him that he may have misinterpreted his mother's wishes. She told him to take care of his little brother all those years ago, but she didn't mean to cover his rear, so he had no consequences.

The door they had walked through offered a long corridor on the other side, with doors up and down both walls. The two men walked silently down the hall to the last door on the left. Here it is, he thought to himself. It's time.

They walked inside the room. There was a table at one end, and two men in suits were seated there with laptops open and pens and paper ready to go. A third chair sat empty next to them with the same items on the table before it. A tape recorder sat ready and waiting along with an empty metal chair, obviously meant for him.

"Sheriff, I'm Investigator Frye," said the man who had brought him back. He motioned to the first man at the table. "This is Investigators Garris and Stein. The three of us will be conducting this interview. Have a seat, please."

Darby sat in the cold metal chair, a serious look on his face. He focused his attention on the men and waited for them to speak. They were all tapping away at their keyboards at first, then the man named Garris spoke.

"Are you ready to begin the interview, Sheriff?"

Darby nodded. "I am."

Stein reached out and pressed record on the tape player. "This is the official State Police interview with Sheriff Robert Darby of Burdensville. Present are Investigator Miles Garris, Investigator James Stein, and

Investigator Ken Frye of the State Police. Also present is Sheriff Robert Darby."

Darby cleared his throat and waited expectantly.

Frye began. "Sheriff Darby, the line of questions we will be asking are about the recent slew of murders committed in and around Burdensville. Your full cooperation is expected, as we are focused on putting a stop to these killings."

Darby nodded.

"The machine can't record a nod, Sheriff," Frye said sarcastically.

"I understand," Darby replied.

Stein took the ball. "Sheriff Darby, is it true that there have been a total of five murders in the Burdensville area in the last two months?"

"Yes sir, it is," Darby said.

"To date, you have not apprehended the killer, nor have you conducted a thorough investigation into any of the deaths?"

He cleared his throat again. "No sir, I have not."

The men exchanged glances before Stein continued. "Can you explain this, and why you failed to reach out to any other official agencies for assistance?"

Darby sat quietly for a moment. He looked each man in the eye, individually. Finally, he took a deep breath and sat back. He was ready.

Darby began to speak.

As expected, Dickie's Café was slammed the next day. As a matter of fact, it was worse than the day before. Denise had taken Scott his lunch around an hour before and returned to work as quickly as possible. The two didn't have time to talk, but she reassured him that she would be back later that night with his supper, and they would have a discussion then.

The customers at every table wanted the scoop about Burdensville, but Denise skillfully sidestepped their questions. Three groups of reporters, all from news networks, came to the café. Their curiosity made it hard for either her or Donna to be productive. It bordered on harassment.

Thankfully, business began to dwindle down by three in the afternoon. Denise was able to take a quick meal break, and she finally had time to think. Scott wanted to talk about the murders, and his questions from early that morning had resonated. He was right. She suspected Ronnie Smith. Unless the killer was from out of town, there was no one else she could think of. Ronnie fit the bill, plain and simple. And she had heard information over the years that would back up her theory.

Numerous times, she heard gossip that Ronnie went about killing the townsfolk's pets. She had even heard that he was doing despicable things with their little bodies. She chalked it up to just that: gossip. It was too appalling to think someone, even Ronnie, would do something like that in her hometown.

Then she thought about the day Scott came to Burdensville and the circumstances that landed him in jail. She'd never be able to forget the things Ronnie said to her, and the look in his drunken eyes when he said them. She had been afraid of him, believing that he was fully capable of hurting her. She had been more frightened of Darby, but now she found that fear had fled.

She wanted to see the killer caught and punished. She wanted all of this to be over so she could move on with her life. If the State Police came and did interrogations, she would tell them anything they wanted to know as best as she could. Scott was right, she needed to cooperate.

Denise finished her light lunch of egg salad and cold milk, then she went back to work. She wanted to get this day behind her so she could talk to Scott. Then she wanted to go home and lock the doors and spend time with her sister. Soon Diane would be going away, and Denise was both ecstatic for her but also a little achy knowing she wouldn't be there to come home to every day.

"Sheriff Darby, are you willing to give a legal statement verifying everything you just told us?" Garris asked. He had just finished telling them everything, and he felt like he had gotten rid of a hundred pounds of extra weight.

He nodded. "Of course. I do have only one request."

Stein replied, "What would that be?"

"I want to be the one to arrest Ronnie and bring him in," Darby said. "He's done some terrible things, but he's still like a kid. I think I should be the one."

The investigators all looked at each other, and finally, Frye said, "I think we can arrange that, considering your cooperation. You're still the Sheriff of Burdensville, at least for now."

Darby nodded with relief. Yes, it was only right that he be the one. After all, his negligence had let this thing get out of control.

CHAPTER
FIFTEEN

Ronnie saw double. He looked at the whiskey bottle on the floor before him and saw that there were only about two shots left. He was furious, but he was going to have to go to town for more.

The voice in his head began to taunt him. You're not supposed to drive. You're stuck here, and soon you'll be out of booze. The only way you can get more is to climb in your trusty car and go into town.

No, Ronnie thought. Bobby told him no. He shook his head back and forth, trying to clear it, but the voice was just too damn loud.

He grabbed the bottle and held it up to his lips. He guzzled what was left inside then threw the glass bottle against the wall, where it shattered to pieces.

His rage shifted, and he suddenly burst into

hysterical laughter. He laughed so hard that he fell from a sitting position. Ronnie went with it, then he struggled to sit himself back up. He looked for the bottle; where the hell was it? He made up his mind, he was going to climb into Old Mabel and run to the general mercantile. He needed more whiskey.

Ronnie stood and made his way out the back door, leaving it hanging open behind him. He staggered a bit, then righted himself and felt in the pocket of his filthy jeans for the key. Once he had it, he started to laugh again. That stupid Bobby should have taken his keys if he didn't want him to drive.

He walked to the back of the dilapidated building where Old Mabel was parked. He managed to get himself behind the wheel, start the car, and then he floored it. It didn't go quite as he planned.

Old Mable crashed through the wall of the building like it was made of paper. Ronnie didn't stop to observe the damage. He didn't give a damn about that building, or about anything except his next bottle. He continued to speed out of his dirt driveway, then he took a sloppy left onto the gravel road leading to town.

He would be at the general mercantile shortly, and he thought it best to get two bottles instead of one.

Diane Jensen stood on the steps of the Burdensville K-12 talking to her best friend, Mandy. "So, why don't you come with us tonight to the bonfire? We're not gonna stay out too late, Di. Tomorrow's a school day."

Diane shook her head but offered her friend a genuine smile. "Naw, I can't, and you know it. I have too much homework, and I'm supposed to hang out with Denise tonight. She's getting all sentimental that I'm leaving for college in the fall, so I have to go home."

Mandy shrugged. "Well, girl, if anything changes give me a call. We can jump in Connor's truck and come to get you."

"Fine," she replied. "I'll see you tomorrow, okay?"

The two girls parted ways, and Diane began to walk home. The school was on the very edge of town, and the walk took her about fifteen minutes if she went straight home. Today, she had to stop at the general mercantile and pick up a pack of black pens. Her last one had given up on her during the last period.

She walked in a leisurely manner until she reached the store. Parked outside was that old beater car that belonged to that weirdo, Ronnie Smith. The way he gawked at her always made her nervous. It was like whatever was going on his dirty mind about her made him look like he was going to drool. He was not only weird, but he also smelled foul and was dirty and disgusting. She wondered if he ever washed his clothes or took a bath.

She pulled on the heavy door, and the bell rang. Mildred Castner, the store's owner, was at the single register.

"Hey, Diane, what can I get for you today?" Mildred was a large woman with a beautiful face and a spirit to match. Just hearing her voice made Diane smile.

"Just some pens today. I'll grab them." She walked down the aisle to the school and office supplies. Her pens were right there, and she grabbed two packs instead of one.

"Hey, you," she heard the voice from behind. "Pretty girl.... you're a pretty one." *Oh, no!*

Diane spun around, the hair on the back of her neck standing up. Ronnie Smith stood there smiling. She smelled him before she saw him. His clothes were covered in filth, and he looked like he hadn't bathed in months. The smell of booze came off him in waves.

"Hi, Ronnie," she said timidly. "Good to see you. I gotta be getting on now." She turned around and headed to Mildred and the register.

But Ronnie barged past her, then laughed at himself. "Ima wanna go first," he told her. "Ima in a hurry."

Diane let out a sigh of relief. Good, go ahead, she thought. The last thing she wanted was for this guy to harass her or follow her home. She watched as he lurched toward Mildred and steadied himself on the counter. The woman jerked backward as she got a nose full of him.

"Gimme two bottles of that there mash," Ronnie breathed. He was digging through his pockets for money.

Mildred had a concerned look on her face. "You seem pretty good already, Ronnie, ayuh."

The man withdrew a wad of bills from his pocket and slammed them on the counter. Either he hadn't heard her, or he didn't care what she had to say. "Two of 'em now," he repeated.

Mildred looked torn. She was like everyone else in town. They all knew Ronnie could make trouble for them, and he wasn't worth it. She exchanged looks with Diane then turned around and grabbed two pints of whiskey from the shelf behind the counter. She punched the numbers into the register. "Sixteen eighty-five, Ronnie."

The man shoved the bills across the countertop and held his hands out eagerly. "Don't you want a bag, Ron?"

"Nah. Don't need no bag," he said. He took the bottles and turned around to face Diane. "You wanna come with me an' have a l'il sippy?"

Diane scrunched her nose up with distaste, and Ronnie noticed. "No thanks, Ronnie," she answered, forcing a smile. "I have homework due tomorrow for school, and I have to get it done."

Ronnie's eyes clouded over, and he whirled around.

With that he was gone, leaving the bell tinkling behind him.

Diane approached the counter and gave Mildred a smile as she laid her packages of pens down. "That guy really gives me the creeps."

"I know, right?" Mildred replied. "Most say he's harmless, but I remember otherwise. Did you know that when he was a kid, he was going around killing people's pets? It's also said he would do, you know, sexual things with them."

Diane gave Mildred a look of disgust. "I've heard rumors, too, so I just try to dodge him if I can."

"That's your best bet," the store owner replied. "That'll be three dollars and forty-two cents, sweetie. How's your sister lately?"

Diane paid the woman and picked up the pens. "She's good. She's been super busy down at the café, what with the murders and all."

"Yeah, nothing draws a crowd quite like horrible crime." Mildred shut the door to the till and handed the girl a dollar fifty-eight in change for a five. "Well, good luck with your schoolwork, doll. We'll see you later."

Diane walked out into the sun and started for home. She saw a couple of classmates on the other side of the street and gave them a wave then continued on. She loved her afternoon walks home, especially in spring. The wind would blow through her long hair, and the sun kissed her skin. Her life was good.

She made it home in no time and rooted around for the key to the front door. It took her a minute to find it at the bottom of her bag. Once she got it in her hand, she slid the key in the lock and opened the door.

The house was still. Perfect, really, for the work she had to do. She tossed her bag onto the couch and shut the door behind her. She would grab a quick snack and get down to business.

Suddenly, she smelled him, and she knew he was behind her before he grabbed her. Her reflexes were poor, though, even dealing with Ronnie in his drunken state. His arm came around, and he put her in a tight headlock, then ran his nasty tongue up the side of her face. "You should've just had one l'il sippy with me. Jus' one."

Diane began to fight in earnest, but his arm just tightened around her neck, and he fought her back. He was so strong, and he was flinging her around as if she were a five-pound bag of potatoes. A lamp crashed to the floor off an end table near the door, along with a couple of other knick-knacks. They both fell over the couch, and he was able to grip her even harder.

"Don't fight, Pretty," he breathed. "Just be still. Be still."

She could no longer take in any air, and she was getting dizzy from the lack of oxygen. Ronnie could tell she was getting weaker, and he tightened his arm around her even more. She was beginning to see stars, and she could feel his other hand fumbling with the button on her jeans.

Diane Jensen jerked in his arms and then lost consciousness. Ronnie continued to squeeze her throat as he violated her with his fingers. He didn't let up until he was sure the girl was dead. He laid her body clumsily on the floor and brushed her hair out of her face. "Pretty one you are," he mumbled as he tore her clothes from her body.

By the time Ronnie finished his heinous act, he had sobered up quite a bit. He pulled his filthy jeans up and looked around the room. The reality of what he had just done hit him like a ton of bricks. He had just killed one of the townsfolk. In a panic he went out the same way he came in, through a back window. He had parked his car a couple of blocks away, and the girls had a privacy fence around their backyard. He would be able to get away easily, but there was no way he could ever go home.

SHERIFF DARBY SIGNED HIS STATEMENT TO THE State Police with flair. He felt nothing but relief about coming clean. It didn't even matter if he lost his job; he would relocate and start over.

Garris took the statement from him and sat back in his chair. The other two officers were in the same relaxed position. They were all eyeing him up, but it was Garris showing the most concern.

"Are you going to be all right?" he asked Darby.

Darby took a deep breath and let it out, nodding at the man as he did so. "Yep. I'll be fine. It's all for the best this way, for everyone."

The three cops nodded in agreement but didn't directly respond to him. Finally, Stein broke the silence. "So, Darby you head back to Burdensville and pick him up. Bring him directly to the main County jail. We'll contact them and let them know to expect you before the night is over." He looked Darby over carefully once more. "If they don't have the prisoner by midnight, we're gonna have to issue a warrant for your arrest as well, Darby."

"I understand," he said in a low voice. He put his hat on his head and stood to his feet. "It has to be done, and I need to be the one to do it."

The three investigators stood and shook his hand. "Are you sure you don't want an escort from another officer?" Frye asked.

"Nah," Darby replied. "If it's just me, it will go a lot smoother. If anyone else comes, well, I'm afraid of how he might react. I don't want anyone else to get hurt."

The men nodded, and they all left the room. Frye escorted Darby out to his patrol car. "We'll be waiting to hear from the jail. You've made the right decision." He patted Darby on the shoulder. "You're doing the right thing."

"I know it. I know." With that, he unlocked the cruiser and heaved his large frame behind the wheel. "You'll get word soon," he guaranteed, and then drove away.

CHAPTER
SIXTEEN

The café was dead after another packed day. Denise, Donna, and Dickie weren't in as high of spirits as they had been the evening before, but they were all relieved that the day was finally over. The girls sat in their regular booths, separating tips and balancing the register while Dickie prepared Scott Sharp's supper for Denise to take to him.

"Wonder what happened with Sheriff Darby today," Donna said. "I'm pretty sure we're gonna be getting a new cop in town."

Denise folded her stack of bills together and put them in her coin purse. "Yeah, I have the same feeling. But if Darby was negligent, then it's something that needs to be done."

"I know," Donna replied. "But it sure is gonna be strange not having him as our sheriff."

Dickie put Styrofoam boxes in the window, and Denise stood up. "Guess it's time for me to get this over there to him. He's probably pretty hungry. I promised Diane that we would hang out tonight, and Scott wants to chat, so I gotta get moving."

She packed up his food and drink, put her jacket on, and shouted through the window, "I'm out of here, Dickie. See you in the morning?"

"I wouldn't have it any other way," the man replied. "Don't you stay down at the jailhouse too long, now. There's still a crazy man running around out there somewhere, and I can't afford to lose you."

Denise gave a hearty laugh. "Always thinking about the bottom line, aren't you."

"Yeah, well somebody has to."

She left the café and headed directly to the jail. The night was very still, eerie, and had a heavy feeling. Something was unsettling about it. The streetlights created shadows in and around the corners that played tricks with her mind. She was spooked, but she had no real reason to feel danger.

Still, she hurried to the jail and let herself in. Scott was sitting on his bunk when she entered, and he smiled at her when he saw her. "Look, Denise," he began. "I'm sorry for giving you pressure earlier this morning. I don't have any business pushing anyone."

Denise brought the food to him and then sat down in the folding chair. She took off her work shoes and began to rub her feet. "No worries," she replied. "You were right."

He sat down on the bed and started unpacking his food. He was surprised by the admittance. "I was?"

She nodded. "You were. All you did was say what everyone in town is already thinking. I believe we've all fallen into the habit of looking the other way when it comes to the sheriff and Ronnie."

She sighed and continued. "There has always been something... unhealthy about their relationship. In a town this size, you learn to go with it, whatever it is. I appreciate that you got me to see that none of that was normal."

Scott tore into his food, and they sat in silence for a while. It was a comfortable silence, though. Denise watched him as he ate, and a smile played on her lips as she did. "You sure are a cutie, you know that?" She blushed by her gumption, but she was too damn tired to care what he thought at that point.

He finished quickly and approached the bars. "Thanks for not holding a grudge," he said. "You mentioned spending some time with your sister tonight. I'm not gonna keep you, but I do want to thank you for all you've been doing for me."

Denise put her shoes back on. "No problem. You've actually made my life more interesting." She stood and walked closer to him. "I have to say, I'm going to miss you when you're gone."

She leaned forward and put her lips firmly to his. His mouth tasted sweet, so she began to explore his lips with her tongue. She wished she could put her arms around him and pull him to her, and he was thinking the same.

The kiss lasted, and it was wonderful. By the time she pulled away, she was breathless. She reached through the bars and tousled his hair. "I'll see you in the morning, Scott Sharp unless the Sheriff says otherwise. By the way, I will be talking to the cops if they come to town to interview."

He watched her walk to the door and clung to the bars as if it might help him get closer to her. She opened the door and turned around and winked at him. "Sure would be nice if we could spend some real time together."

"It's not like I'm kicked out of town," Scott replied. "At least, not yet." He winked back at her. "Oh, and hey. Will you shut the lights out tonight?"

Denise smiled and did as he wished, then shut the door and locked it. Her mind went to Diane. She planned for them to make homemade pizza together, and maybe watch a movie or play Scrabble.

She was looking forward to it, and began the walk home, humming and smiling to herself as she went.

Sheriff Darby's cruiser sliced through the darkness as he made his way back to Burdensville. He thought about his day with the state investigators, and he considered the elaborate statement he had given them. He had been so dishonest for so long that he had forgotten what it felt like to do the right thing. He had forgotten the reason he became a cop in the first place.

Once he resigned himself to be honest, the only thing he worried about was Dr. Ivan Smith. He had helped Darby brush the murders under the legal rug, and Darby felt a certain amount of guilt for snitching on him. But he knew the facts, and the facts were that they had both done wrong, and now the chips had to fall where they may. Both he and Smith had done deeds that had resulted in death and devastation, and they both deserved what they got.

He felt lighter and freer than he had in years. He even began to hum an old song as he drove through the dark, and it wasn't until he neared the turn that led to Ronnie's that he began to sober up. His nervous system was tapped, and he knew it was time for the tough love. He couldn't let a promise he made to his dead mother thirty-two years ago affect his decision to do the right thing.

Darby took the appropriate left onto the gravel road and put on his brights. His heart started beating faster, and his hands started to tremble, but his decision was steadfast. He wanted murdering Ronnie to pay the consequences. It had to be done.

He finally reached Ronnie's and made a left into the dirt drive. His bright lights flashed across the outbuilding to the right rear of the house, and for a second, his mind was unable to register what he was seeing. In fact, he was sure he was hallucinating.

"What on earth?" He stopped the cruiser and put it in reverse. He put it back in drive and put the headlights on the outbuilding. Oh, dang, he thought, his mouth hanging open.

The entire wall of the outbuilding was gone. In its place was a gaping hole, and splintered wood was everywhere. He stared in disbelief, trying to reason out what could have caused the massive damage. That's when he realized that Old Mabel was not inside the building, as she should be.

Darby slammed the cruiser into park and grabbed his flashlight. With adrenaline pumping, he climbed out effortlessly from the driver's door and shined the light on the outbuilding. He approached it with haste, his heart pounding as he neared.

"Oh, no," he said. "No, please no." By the time he reached the building, there was no denying it. The car was gone, and Ronnie had driven it right through the side of the building.

Now, Darby was in full panic mode. If Ronnie had gone to this extreme, he was drunk. Sober Ronnie would never have done something like this. Old Mabel was his pride and joy, even though it was a piece of junk. The sheriff turned toward the house. The lights were all off, and a quick shine of the flashlight told him that the back door was wide open.

"Ronnie!" Darby was jogging toward the house. "Ronnie, it's Bobby. Where are you, boy?"

He was met with silence, and the silence was deafening. It made him want to scream into the night. He went through the back door and shined his light around the filthy kitchen. He could smell Ronnie all over the place, and it made him gag.

"Ronnie?" Darby moved through the kitchen and into the living room, where he carefully exposed everything to the light. Right by the front window was a shattered whiskey bottle, and Darby was sure it hadn't been there when he left with his strict orders. "Dammit!"

Darby knew with sick surety that another body would soon be found.

This was all his fault, and he knew it. Ronnie should've been put out of his misery as soon as they realized what a sick bastard he really was. But Darby knew they were twenty years too late.

There was no time to spare dwelling. He had to get it together. Ronnie was out there somewhere. Instantly, he was sure Ronnie was going to resist arrest. Darby wanted an extra pair of handcuffs to secure his ankles, so he would head straight to the jail for extra cuffs. There he would also use the jail phone to call the State Police and get ahold of Judge Rupert Allen to request a warrant.

Darby fled from the house at a fast jog and got into the cruiser. He put his top lights on, whipped a donut, and then aimed the cruiser out of the drive, taking a left on the gravel toward town. He had to get moving, and he had to figure out where Ronnie might be right now.

RONNIE SMITH WASN'T AS DUMB AS EVERYONE believed; at least, he didn't think so. He got out of the Jensen house in broad daylight without being seen. He took Old Mabel out to the deserted farmhouse where he had killed the first girl, and he parked in the dilapidated barn. Now he was inside the house, which was nothing more than a skeleton. He had his trusty flashlight and two pints of whiskey. They wouldn't find him here.

But he got cold, so he decided to build a fire. He figured he would use the lighter from Old Mabel and built it at the rear of the house, away from the highway, it wouldn't be seen. He gathered some sticks from outside and managed to get a small fire going. Then he sat down to warm up. He cracked his first pint and took a nice, long drink. The amber liquid warmed him from the inside out, and after another long pull, he didn't care whether they found him or not.

He hadn't done anything wrong, after all. That

damn Jensen girl looked at him like he was garbage, and all he had done was ask her if she wanted a drink of his hootch. He took another pull from his bottle and leaned his back against the outside wall. He was feeling toasty now, so he closed his eyes and tried to recall every detail of the time he spent in the Jensen house with Diane. She had been the best one yet.

Ronnie smiled to himself and began to sing his favorite song.

CHAPTER
SEVENTEEN

Denise left the jail feeling really good about everything. She knew she could be honest with police without fear. Scott helped ease her concerns and build her confidence. She was also completely smitten with Scott. It seemed the stars were aligning, and this would be the perfect time to get to know a man. After all, Diane would be leaving in the fall, and she would be able to do things that she turned down to care for her little sister. Fun things, like traveling. Maybe see the ocean for the first time.

She was so proud of the young lady Diane had become. She smiled as she thought about the bright future she had in front of her. The world was her oyster. The smile was still on her face when she put the key to the front door of their little house. She was excited to spend an hour or two with the girl, even if it was a little late to watch a movie. It was a school night, after all.

As she turned the knob, it occurred to her that none of the lights were on in the house. Had Diane gone on to bed? Maybe she was exhausted after her homework. Oh, well, Denise thought, there was always tomorrow, and tomorrow was Friday.

She reached to her left to turn on the lamp that sat on the end table, but she groped fruitlessly in the dark. "Diane? I'm home!" she shouted.

The smell hit her first. It was a smell she knew all too well. It was a mix of sweat and booze and bodily filth. It was the smell of Ronnie Smith.

Startled, she began to feel along the wall for the overhead light switch. Her eyes fluttered rapidly as they tried to adjust to the brightness.

Then Denise saw her. At first, she thought her sister fell asleep on the living room floor, just to bother her. She hated that, and Diane knew it.

But something wasn't right. She was naked and without a pillow or blanket. Her eyes were wide open, and she stared lifelessly into nothingness.

"Diane?" she ran to the body and started to scream at the top of her lungs. "Diane! Wake up!" She grabbed the girl's bare shoulders and began to shake her hard, but Diane was lifeless.

Denise was in shock. Her first thought was to call the sheriff, so she ran to the phone and dialed the number. It rang and rang. She slammed the phone down in frustration and ran out the front door.

"Help! Somebody help me!" She continued to scream as she ran in the direction of the jail. She could use the radio system there to get ahold of the State Police. She could dig through the sheriff's desk to find the spare key to the cell, and she could let Scott out so he could help her wake, Diane.

Denise couldn't process what was happening and couldn't think straight. She was borderline hysterical and continued to scream as she ran. A few lights came on in nearby homes, but she didn't notice. She was out of breath by the time she reached the jail and struggling with the keys from her apron to unlock the door.

Right then, Sheriff Robert Darby pulled up in his cruiser, lights flashing.

"Denise!" he yelled. He immediately noticed her distress as she fought to find the right key. He got a horrible feeling seeing her crying and sobbing hysterically. Darby grabbed her. "What's going on? What's wrong, Denise."

She looked at him, eyes wide. "Diane! He's killed, Diane! We have to call an ambulance!"

"Who did, Denise? Who killed Diane?"

Denise whirled on him, her eyes mad. "My house stinks like Ronnie Smith!"

With that, she fainted dead away.

Darby caught her in his arms just in the nick of time.

As he stood holding her up, with jail keys in one hand, the gravity of her words hit him. Was she saying Ronnie was in her home? Was she saying Diane was dead, and that Ronnie was the reason?

He continued to hold her up with one arm, and with the other hand, he unlocked the jail door. Darby reached around the door frame and flipped on the overhead lights inside to see Scott standing up against the bars.

"What the hell is going on?" He heard the commotion outside but couldn't make out the words. The sheriff proceeded to haul Denise's small body into the building, where he sat her on a chair by the door. He turned to Scott as he caught his breath.

"I've done a terrible thing, and I need your help."

Scott was nearly out of his mind with concern. "What's going on, Sheriff, is she okay?" the terror of losing Denise emanated from Scott's voice.

The sheriff opened the door to let Scott out. "It's a long story, but the gist of it is that you shouldn't even be here. I have to call the State Police for assistance, then I need your help, Mr. Sharp."

Darby grabbed the phone from its cradle and proceeded to punch in a series of numbers. Scott ran to Denise's side who was slumped over in the chair. When he realized that she was out cold, he frantically looked around the room. He remembered a small refrigerator was situated behind the sheriff's desk. He made a dash for it and opened it to find cans of soda, a couple of containers of vanilla yogurt, and a single bottle of water that was half empty. Scott grabbed the bottle and ran back to care for Denise.

"This is Sheriff Robert Darby of Burdensville. I need to speak with the duty officer immediately, please. It's an emergency." Darby turned to see Scott pour water into his own cupped palms and splash it onto Denise's ashen face.

"Hello, Officer Keating. This is Sheriff Robert Darby of Burdensville. I have a report of a homicide, and the suspect is the same man I was going to bring directly to the main County jail by midnight. We don't know where he is, but we have a dead girl here in town."

Scott anxiously looked over his shoulder confused. A dead girl? Denise passed out from shock? Dread instantly filled his soul.

Darby continued. "Yes. I need backup. I'm going to start searching the area immediately. I know the subject well, and I have some thoughts about where he might be hiding." He paused for a moment, then continued. "Yes, I'll radio if I find anything. Thanks. See your men soon."

He hung up the phone and turned to Scott. "Denise told me her sister Diane Jensen is dead. I need you to come with me to find Ronnie Smith. I have no other officers."

Denise's eyes began to flutter open, and for a brief moment, she looked confused. "Where... what?"

Scott spoke to her soothingly. "Denise, I need you to lie down in my cell, and I need you to stay there."

The look on her face changed drastically as she recalled the scene she just witnessed. She jumped up but was unsteady on her feet, and Scott had to help her sit back down. "We have to get to Diane. She won't wake up."

"Denise, we're going there now," he replied. "I need you to stay here and hold down the fort because the State Police are on their way."

Darby dialed another number and paced as he waited for his party to pick up. "Ivan, it's Bobby," he said into the receiver. "I need you right away at the Jensen residence." He paused again. "I'll fill you in when you get there."

Scott had Denise in the cell, and she was sitting on the edge of his cot. "I want to come with you!" Tears were falling freely from her eyes as she recalled the look on her sister's face.

"Listen, Denise," he told her gently, "I need you to stay here. We're going to your house to take care of Diane now, but you have to stay here, okay?"

She nodded, a dazed look on her face, then she threw herself into Scott's pillow and began to sob. Scott turned to Darby. "Let's go."

The two men left the jail. Darby made sure to secure the building behind them. They jumped into the cruiser and Darby tossed the extra cuffs on the seat and sped off, heading for Denise's home. "We need to see exactly what she's talking about," Darby said. "But I'm pretty sure what we're going to find."

Scott was furious with the sheriff. "I guess, I just don't understand how a man of the law could sweep something this horrific under the rug for so long. What's wrong with you?"

Darby shot a glare in his direction, but Scott could see the guilt and shame in his eyes as well. "I don't expect you to understand, but there's a lot more to it than you realize. All I can do is deal with the here and now. And believe me, there are consequences to what I've done. I'm going to suffer plenty for my poor decisions, so mind your own business."

"Well, you've pretty much made it my business at this point," Scott retorted. The sheriff couldn't disagree with that.

They pulled up in front of Denise's small white bungalow. A man with a bag and a jacket was standing on the sidewalk. "Dr. Smith," Darby muttered as the two of them climbed quickly from the cruiser and approached the doctor.

"Thanks for getting here so fast, Ivan," Darby began. "I came back to town with the intent to arrest Ronnie. I'm supposed to deliver him over to the State, but instead of Ronnie, I found Denise Jensen. She's hysterical, says Diane is dead inside the house."

"Well, let's see what we have," Ivan Smith replied, disturbed.

The three men approached the house, and Darby opened the screen door. The overhead light in the living room was still on, and the door was wide open. "Police!" he shouted, hand on his gun. "We're coming inside!" He knew it was a long shot to find Ronnie there. If he had still been in the house when Denise got home, Darby doubted she would've stood a chance either.

The men entered the living room to find Diane in the same position Denise had discovered her. "Shit," Darby said, his eyes closed in disgust. Ivan Smith jumped into action and grabbed an afghan from the back of the sofa. He knelt next to the girl and closed her eyes, then covered her body.

Darby turned to Scott, whose eyes were flaring with rage and dismay. "I can't believe I let this go so far."

"She was just a baby. I can't believe it either." Scott shook his head. "We need to find Ronnie, and we need to do it now before anyone else has to pay this steep of a price."

Darby nodded and wiped his face with his shirtsleeve. "Ivan, Scott and I are going to go check a couple of places outside of town. I've already been to Ronnie's place. His car is gone, and I found a broken booze bottle that wasn't there before, so I know he's trashed. There are a few places I think he could have gone. You stay here and wait for the State Police."

The doctor gave him a nod, his face was grief-stricken. He knew that his role in covering Ronnie's murders had led to this, just as Darby's had. He was disgusted with the entire situation, and he was ready to throw in the towel. He didn't deserve a medical license.

Darby and Scott got into the cruiser and drove off. "So," Scott began, "what makes you think you're gonna be able to track him down? He could be in Timbuktu by now."

"Yep," Darby replied, "But what you don't understand is that I know Ronnie better than anyone. We'll go by his house one more time, but I don't expect to find him there. There are few places he could truly hide near home. There's a vein of the Allagash River just outside of town here. Ronnie fished there pretty regularly up until he was a teen, then he just stopped. I figure he'll either be there or at the old Wilson farm."

"Why would he hide somewhere that you'd be able to figure out?" Scott asked.

The sheriff turned to him, a resigned look on his face. "He has the mentality of a twelve-year-old. He's not able to reason rationally or effectively at all. Besides, there's no other place for him to go."

"Why did you let yourself get involved with this in the first place?" Scott questioned. "Why not leave it to his brother Ivan? Why didn't he get the man help a long time ago?"

Darby took a deep, ragged breath. "Doc Smith isn't his brother," Darby replied. "I am."

"What? What the heck are you talking about?"

Darby told Scott the abbreviated version if there was one. He told him the truth about the relationship he had with Ronnie. How he managed to become so twisted and distorted in the way he protected the man. He wrapped it up as they pulled into the dirt drive at Ronnie's house.

"Everything just snowballed, and I let it happen, but I'm gonna make it right now," he concluded.

Darby parked the cruiser but left it running. "You stay here. I'm just gonna give the house a quick run through once more. I don't expect he's here, so I'll only be a minute." He handed Scott the extra cuffs, "if he resist arrest we will use these on his ankles." He grabbed his flashlight and headed for the house.

Scott was in utter shock by what he'd just been told. He was struggling to comprehend the mess created by the sheriff and the doctor. Sure, he listened closely to Darby's story, but he felt no compassion for the lawman. He had allowed and covered up all those murders, and the result was more death and grief. He only hoped the sheriff meant what he said... that he was ready to make it right.

Poor Denise! He hadn't known her long, but what he knew for sure is that her sister Diane had been her whole life. He closed his eyes and shook his head. How did his travels bring him to a town and a situation like this?

Darby was back quickly. He jumped into the cruiser and put it in gear. "No dice; he ain't here." He backed out of the drive, and soon they were headed up the gravel road to Highway 16. "I'm going to take us to the Allagash. We'll be passing the Wilson place on the way, so we'll stop and check that too. The State Police should be arriving soon. They'll be getting in touch with me on the radio at any time, and that's when the real searching will start."

Darby was anxious to find Ronnie before anyone else got killed.

CHAPTER
EIGHTEEN

Scott took a breath. "Look, Darby," he began, "I'm not comfortable helping you look for this madman without some kind of protection. I mean, you have a gun, and all I have are my fists. I've never killed anyone, but your brother has, and I'm pretty sure he won't hesitate to try to kill me."

Darby winced visibly at Scott's loose 'madman' reference, but what could he say? The guy was right; Ronnie was out of his mind. "I'll let you use the rifle." He jerked his head back toward the gun that hung on the safety glass that separated the back seat from the front.

"Appreciate it, Sheriff," Scott replied. He was keeping his eyes to the windows, staring out into the darkness that hid everything they needed to see. He didn't want to miss any sign of life out here, because any sign was likely going to be Ronnie. They were far out in the sticks at this point, and who else would be out this time of night?

"Up here about half a mile on the right is the Wilson farm. The Allagash is another five miles past that, and we're gonna have to hike a bit to get to his old fishing spot," Darby said. "Just keep your eyes peeled."

Scott nodded vaguely. "I already am."

A house was barely visible to the right. Scott could see its shadowy skeleton. He strained his eyes as they got closer, and that's when he saw light flickering off an outbuilding at the rear of the place. "Slow down, Sheriff, I see a light."

"At the house?" The sheriff asked as he slowed the cruiser. "I don't see nothin'."

Scott began to point into the night. "Not bright light. Look," he thrust his pointer finger toward the house as he tried to show Darby. "It's flickering off that barn or garage or whatever it is. In the back, there!"

Darby saw it then. It was so faint that if he hadn't had Scott with him, he probably wouldn't have noticed it. "Ayuh," he replied as he pulled the cruiser to the shoulder of the road. "Someone's there alright. I don't know if you know it or not, but this is where Ronnie's first victim was found. I'm not surprised. It's gonna be him."

Darby left the cruiser running and turned to Scott. "This is gonna be hard for me. I just want you to know. He's my brother, and I love him, so it's gonna be hard."

"I understand," Scott replied, "But you need to get over it."

Darby nodded and took a deep breath. He turned around and took the gun from its rack on the safety glass. "You know how to shoot?"

"A little," Scott replied, as he took the rifle from Darby.

Prepared, they were ready to head up to the abandoned house where the light was flickering.

"Now, don't slam the car doors when we get out, got it?" Darby was already whispering, and they were still in the car.

"Got it," Scott said. "Listen, if it looks to me like you're losing your nerve, I'm gonna act, Sheriff. I can't get the image of Denise's sister out of my mind. This animal needs to be caught."

"Understood. Let's go," said Darby.

The two men got out of the cruiser and shut the car doors slowly and carefully. They held their guns, ready to use, and headed quietly up the hill to the empty house at the top. That's when Scott heard the singing.

"Stop." He whispered as he reached out and touched Darby's arm. "Do you hear that?"

"Hear what?"

Scott was straining to hear. "Listen."

They took a few more steps forward, then Darby heard it. Ronnie was singing, and it was obvious he was drunk. He slurred his words terribly as he sang them, and he couldn't keep his tune...

Darby and Scott looked at each other in the darkness. "He's around the house, in the back," Darby whispered. "You go around that way, and I'll go opposite. Now listen, I wanna try to take him alive. I wanna try to reason and talk to him, so when you get back there, try to not let him see you right away. He's liable to get upset after what happened between you two at the café, okay?"

"I'll stay out of it unless I have to get in it," Scott replied, then he took off to the right of the house and Darby went left.

The two men came around the rear at the same time. Scott stopped, poised frozen with the rifle. There sat Ronnie, at a small fire he had built. In the light of the fire, Scott could see that he had a pint of booze in his left hand, and he was swinging it back and forth to the screwed-up rhythm of the song he sang. Next to him, on the ground, was another pint bottle. It was empty, and the bottom was broken off.

He was good and drunk for sure.

Darby had his gun pointed at the man, and from where Scott was standing, he could see that the man's hand was shaking. "Ronnie," Darby said gently, "what are you doin' out here all alone?"

Ronnie stopped singing and jerked his head to look at Sheriff Darby.

"What you doin' here?" His voice was almost like that of a child.

Darby cleared his throat. "I come to take you home."

"What-cha got that gun for then?"

The sheriff took a small step toward the man who was his biological brother. "Ronnie, what did you do?"

Ronnie put the pint to his lips and took a draw off it. "I ain't doin' nothin'. Just having a fire, Bobby." He tried to get to his feet, but he was having a hard time standing. He fell back on his butt hard, then pushed himself up again. It was slow going, but he finally made it to his feet. Scott kept the rifle pointed at the killer but kept his mouth shut.

"Now Ronnie," Darby continued, "I know what you did today."

Ronnie gave a hearty drunken laugh. "Ha! You don' know nuthin'."

"Yes I do," said Darby, his voice taking on a slightly stern tone. "You saw Diane Jensen today, didn't you?"

Ronnie's face scrunched up as if he were struggling to find the mental file on Diane Jensen. Suddenly his eyes lit up. "Pretty, pretty girl."

"What did you do, Ronnie?" The sheriff's voice was controlled and calm.

Ronnie put the pint to his lips and drained the last of the whiskey from the glass bottle before lobbing it as hard as he could into the darkness. It hit the ground with a small 'thud' a short distance away. Then he turned his attention back to Darby. "I wanted to share with her, but she wouldn't share with me. I visited her house, I did."

"What did I tell you about drinking?" The sheriff was taking small steps toward the man, and so far Ronnie hadn't noticed. "See what happens when you drink? You killed that girl."

Now the man shook his head rapidly, his eyes closed. "No! She wanted me to visit; she wanted to be with me." By the time he opened his eyes again, Darby was only a few feet away from him.

"You have to come with me now," Darby said firmly.

He shook his head again. "I'm stayin' here now. I'm stayin' here."

Darby reached out to take him by the arm, but wasted Ronnie somehow expected it. In a flash, he swung his arm, and the next thing they knew he had knocked Darby's gun out of his hand and out of sight. Suddenly the two men were on the ground struggling.

Scott leapt into action. He hurried over to the fighting brothers, who were right next to the small fire Ronnie had made. Ronnie was on top of the sheriff, his arms flailing as he hit Darby in the head over and over again. Scott tried to aim his gun at Ronnie, but the men were flailing about so much that he knew if he shot Ronnie, he was going to shoot Darby as well.

Scott was beginning to panic. He didn't have a lot of experience with guns, and he vowed silently to himself that if he ever got out of this, he was going to learn more.

As he stood there wondering what to do, Ronnie reached out and grabbed the jagged broken pint bottle. Things were getting worse by the second. Ronnie had ahold of it by its short neck. He swung the glass at Darby's head, and Darby dodged him. He swung it again, and again.

The third swing found its target. The broken glass tore into Darby's neck and ripped it apart. Blood sprayed into the air, and in the firelight, Scott could see the stream splatter across Ronnie's face. He continued to swing, but Darby wasn't fighting anymore. His hands had gone up to his neck, his eyes wide with shock as blood pumped through his fingers.

"No!" Scott yelled, and for the first time, Ronnie realized that he and his brother weren't alone. He fell backward off the bleeding man in a panic, his arms and legs trying to gain traction to get away from Scott and the rifle.

Scott had the firearm trained on the man's head. Ronnie stared at him, open-mouthed. "It's you. You're that man from the café, ain'tcha?" His voice was trembling with fear, and suddenly he appeared very sober.

The gun shook in Scott's hands. "Yeah, I'm the one, and now you're coming with me. You should've listened to the sheriff."

The sheriff gave a gurgle, and Scott shifted his gaze in the man's direction, just in time to see him take his last breath. He looked back at Ronnie, sickened and furious.

"Now look what you've done, you maniac!" Scott stated in a matter of fact tone. "You just killed the only person that gave a crap about you!"

Ronnie stood, his movements clumsy and his legs shaky. He looked down at Darby then back at Scott. "I ain't goin' no place."

Scott thought about the pretty girl lying dead at Denise's house. He thought about all the murders he had read about in the paper. Rage built up inside of him as it all ran through his mind. "You're right, Ronnie," he said. "You're not going anywhere."

Scott pulled the trigger of the rifle, and the projectile tore through Ronnie's head, making it explode before Scott's eyes. Ronnie stared at Scott with contempt and confusion as he staggered to the right. Suddenly, his body crumpled under his own feet, and he fell on his face into the fire.

Scott dropped the rifle to the ground and knelt down by Darby's body. "Darby?" he said once, but even as he said it, he knew the man was gone.

He fetched Darby's flashlight from the ground where it had fallen when Ronnie took his first swing. He made his way around the house and down the hill to where the cruiser was parked. He could hear the police radio going crazy inside, so he opened the passenger door and sat in the front seat.

"Sheriff Darby, are you still local?" The voice coming from the radio was that of a female.

Scott picked up the mike and pressed the button on the side. "This is Scott Sharp. The sheriff has been killed. So has Ronnie Smith."

The woman's voice replied. "Tell me where you are, and we'll get units there right away."

"I'm at an abandoned farmhouse out on Highway 16, about five miles from Burdensville." He released the button and leaned his head back against the headrest. His heart was trying to return to its normal speed, but it was still beating out of his chest, and he was panting.

"Officers are in Burdensville. I'll give them your twenty," the woman replied. "Stay right where you are."

He pressed the button and said, "I ain't goin' no place."

When he realized he had just repeated Ronnie's last words, Scott laughed as though he had just told the funniest joke of his life.

CHAPTER NINETEEN

Scott had a cup of coffee in one hand and the morning paper in the other. He couldn't wait to dig in.

Burdensville Sheriff Killed During Attempted Apprehension. Recent Murders Solved.

Sheriff Robert Darby of Burdensville was killed while trying to apprehend the man suspected of six homicides that recently took place in and around the town. Ronald W. Smith aka Ronnie Smith of Burdensville is said to have raped and killed a number of people in recent months, including one local high school girl.

State Police had been conducting an investigation into Darby's involvement. According to police spokeswoman Mary Kay Monroe, the sheriff had just given police a thorough statement about Ronald Smith and the murders. Darby was ordered to locate the suspect and take him immediately into custody. Both the sheriff and the suspect were killed during the attempted arrest.

Acting Deputy Scott Sharp of Coos Bay, Oregon was with Darby during the incident. According to Sharp, Ronnie Smith killed Diane Jensen, 17, of Burdensville, then hid at an abandoned farm on the outskirts of town. The two men were searching for Ronnie Smith. After finding him, a physical confrontation ensued, during which the sheriff's throat was cut. Sharp was able to use a firearm from the police vehicle to kill Ronnie Smith in self-defense. Both Ronnie Smith and Darby were declared dead at the scene.

For those not familiar with the story, Ronnie Smith was suspected of the rapes and murders of Katie Castleman, Jane Feister, Carly Reed, Ted Bascom, Meredith Downs, and local student Diane Jensen.

The town physician Dr. Ivan Smith is under investigation in connection with the suspect. It is also reported that the state will provide a temporary replacement for Sherriff Darby since he was the only policeman in the town. Donations for the victims' families are being received by the State Police in lieu of flowers.

. . .

SCOTT CLOSED THE PAPER AND FOLDED IT IN half. He tossed it onto the chair next to him and took a big sip of his coffee, which Donna had just refilled. He was waiting to meet Denise. She was grief-stricken and took some much-needed time off. Scott barely left her side as she mourned the loss of her sister.

He heard the bell jingle on the café door and turned around. Denise was coming toward him. She looked a little better. Her hair was combed, and she had a little mascara on. Scott smiled when he saw her, and he stood up in greeting.

"You look like you're feeling better," he said.

Denise shrugged. "A little, I guess. I'm just relieved that it's all over."

"Me too." He sat next to her and put his arm around her. He gave her a gentle kiss and then turned back to his coffee.

Donna approached carrying a carafe of coffee. "Hey, honey. It's so good to see you getting out. How are you feeling, dear?"

Denise took a breath. "I think about as good as could be expected."

Donna put the carafe down and embraced her friend. "Are you planning to come back to work?"

Denise shook her head. "At least, not in the near future."

"Well," Donna continued, "you know Dickie will let you come back whenever you're ready."

Dickie popped his head through the window. "Hey!" he came through the kitchen's swinging doors, his arms outstretched. He took Denise in a bear hug. "How's my girl doin'?"

"I'm good. Well, I'm better anyway," she replied. "I think I'm gonna make it."

"Well, with this guy by your side, I think you stand more than half a chance." He released Denise and gave Scott a hearty pat on the back and a smile.

Denise grinned at Scott, her eyes filled with affection. "Isn't he amazing? I don't know what I'd do without him."

"Where are you staying, hon?"

Denise turned her attention back to Dickie. "Right now, we're staying at the Morning Dew Motel, but that's only for a bit. Scott has decided to attend the academy so he can police this rat hole of a town. We'll be moving into Sheriff Darby's old place. I can't even imagine trying to go back to my house."

Dickie offered her a sympathetic nod. "Well, I better get back in the kitchen, or all these people are gonna have my head." He gave the pair another firm slap on the back and disappeared through the swinging doors once again.

"All these people?" Donna and the pair turned around. The only other customers were the Harris sisters. "Dickie is gonna end up dying in that damn kitchen. Everyone's tickled about you going to the academy, Scott."

"Well, we all see a lot of potential in Burdensville," he replied. "I think, it's time someone started to act on it."

"Keep it up," Donna said, then she turned to Denise. "Now, you take care. We'll be seein' you around, okay?"

The two women hugged once more, and Donna went back to work. "Are you hungry?" Scott asked.

"Nah," she replied. "I had a bowl of soup before I came."

Scott stood. "Well, I'm finished with business in town for the day. Are you ready to head back to the motel?"

Denise rose from her seat as well. "I'm ready to go anywhere you want to go."

Scott leaned forward and kissed her on her cute little nose. "I love you, you know."

"Ditto," she said as she planted a kiss on him back.

Scott wrapped his arm over her shoulder, and together they walked out of Dickie's café to the new car they had just purchased. As they drove out toward Highway 16, they left the past behind them. It was time to head into the future.

EPILOGUE

Scott drove his cruiser up and down the narrow streets of Burdensville, making it a point to stop and visit with anyone who happened to be out and about. It was a warm, sunny day so there were quite a few. He loved to visit with the locals as often as he could.

He was looking forward to supper. Denise was making fried chicken and noodle salad, which had become his favorite. He planned to have a tall, cold glass of her iced tea with his meal.

More than four years had passed by so quickly. Denise did the honor of becoming his wife, and they had a handsome, smart little boy named Raymond. Raymond was four and in preschool. He loved to ride his bike and play with his little friends. He was the spitting image of his mother, which made Scott happy. His heart swelled every time he thought of them.

Denise was getting ready to have their second child any day. It was to be a boy, and they were going to name him Brian. She seemed to be nesting the last few days, so Scott suspected the child would come very, very soon.

He pulled the cruiser into the driveway of their home, which used to be Darby's. He shut the ignition off but sat for a moment, reflecting on his time with the old sheriff. Burdensville was turned upside down for a while after his death. Scott opened the door and climbed out of the car. He hated thinking about those days, but they were always with him, permanently seared in his mind. He was just glad the town had rebounded so well and took pride in the work he did to make it happen.

He slammed the car door shut, and that's when he heard the crying. Scott ran for the house as fast as he could. He flung open the front door to see his pregnant wife lying on the floor at the bottom of the stairs.

Denise was lying on the hard floor, heaving, and pushing. She was ghostly white. Raymond was seated next to her, a stricken look on his face.

He turned to Scott. "Mommy fell down the stairs, Daddy. She fell hard."

Scott could see the blood between her legs. "Raymond, call Dr. Eddings. You know how; his number is on the fridge."

The boy ran to obey his father while Scott positioned himself between her legs and worked her yoga pants down. "It's going to be okay, Neece. I'm here now."

She looked at him through half closed eyes. Her breathing was labored, and she looked very pale. She gave him a half-hearted smile and shook her head at him.

"You're going to be fine," he said once again. She was losing a lot of blood.

Raymond, "Did you call?"

"Yes, Daddy!" Raymond ran back into the room and knelt next to his mother. She began to push in earnest, but she didn't have the strength. It didn't matter. The baby was coming.

"Look, Daddy, the baby's head!" Raymond turned to his mother with excitement while Scott focused on delivering the child. "The baby's head, Mommy!"

She seemed to be drifting in and out of consciousness. But she smiled at Raymond while Scott worked, and soon the child was born. Scott ripped his uniform shirt off as best as he could with one hand and wrapped the new baby in it.

"Look, Neece," he said to his wife with tears in his eyes. "He's perfect."

Denise turned to Raymond once more. "Raymond," she said weakly, "No matter what happens you protect your brother."

Raymond understood, and he made the silent promise. He would make sure nothing ever happened to baby Brian. Scott heard a car door slam in front of the house. He looked lovingly back and forth between the infant and his wife. "Not so fast, love. You're not going anywhere."

ENTREATY

This book was made possible by reviews from readers like you. Reviews fuel my creativity. If you enjoyed this novel, I implore you to write a review and share your experience on the retailer's website. Please tell a friend or loved one, who may also like to give this heart pounding book a read! In return, I thank you from the bottom of my heart, and sincerely appreciate your time and effort.

Humbled, with gratitude,
R.W.K. Clark

About the Author

I am a father of two beautiful children, Jon and Kim. They are my motivating forces. They are the lighthouse in this vast ocean. In my life, they are the air that I breathe, the oasis in this desert of uncertainty. They are my greatest joy in life and my number one priority. I have a long list of hobbies, and I attribute that to my lust for life! I like to surround myself with positive people who share the same interests. Family values, the arts, outdoors, nature, and travel are tops on my list. I embrace attending cultural and artistic events because I believe dramatic self-expression is the window to the soul. I wear my heart on my sleeve, and I still believe in chivalry, and I always treat people the way I want to be treated.

www.rwkclark.com

Made in United States
North Haven, CT
14 January 2022